Preface books

A series of scholarly and critical studies of major writers intended for those needing modern and authoritative guidance through the characteristic difficulties of their work to reach an intelligent understanding and enjoyment of it.

General Editor: MAURICE HUSSEY

Available now:

A Preface to Wordsworth   BY JOHN PURKIS
A Preface to Donne   BY JAMES WINNY
A Preface to Milton   BY LOIS POTTER

William Wordsworth, 1818 by Benjamin Robert Haydon

A Preface to Wordsworth

John Purkis

CHARLES SCRIBNER'S SONS

New York

A 2.72 (1)

Printed in Great Britain by
Lowe & Brydone (Printers) Limited London
Library of Congress Catalog Card Number 79-38526
SBN 684-12849-7 (Trade cloth)
SBN 684-12892-6 (Trade paper, SL)

Lucy's book

JOHN PURKIS is a Senior Lecturer in English at the Cambridgeshire
College of Arts and Technology. He has specialized in the literature
of the nineteenth century, published an essay on William Morris and
is the editor of *A Selection from Arthur Hugh Clough* (Longmans
English Series, 1967)

Contents

List of Abbreviations

Poetical Works	*The Poetical Works of William Wordsworth*, edited by E. De Selincourt and H. Darbishire, 5 vols., (Oxford University Press, 1940–9 with subsequent revisions.)
Prelude (followed by 1805 or 1850)	*Wordsworth's Prelude*, edited by E. de Selincourt, 1926; revised by H. Darbishire, (Oxford

University Press, 1959). 1805 and 1850 refer to
earlier and later texts.

Immortality Ode	*Ode: Intimations of Immortality from Recollections of Early Childhood*
Notebooks	*The Notebooks of Samuel Taylor Coleridge*, edited by Kathleen Coburn, 2 double vols., (Routledge and Kegan Paul, 1957–62).
Journals	*Journals of Dorothy Wordsworth*, edited by E. de Selincourt, 2 vols., (Macmillan, 1941).
Moorman	Mary Moorman, *William Wordsworth: A Biography*, 2 vols., (Oxford University Press, 1957–1965).

List of Illustrations

Foreword

This study of Wordsworth is intended as a first book for the newcomer to the work of the poet. Advanced level students and others will find it a stimulating guide to the poetry itself and many intelligent ways through which still greater appreciation can be secured.

While it is the critic's task to draw attention to the specific verbal art and energy of every writer he discusses it should not be forgotten that there are other tasks that call upon him. Much literary study today is related at the same time to a variety of other artistic and cultural themes to be found in the society of the day. The critic therefore needs to turn our attention to the complex English and European world in which Romantic poetry arose. The present study leans most heavily upon the artistic, philosophical and religious elements in that culture but devotes considerable space to the economic world, showing that Wordsworth was unexpectedly sensitive towards it. This makes the poet a much more representative and significant figure than the reclusive Nature-worshipper and pantheist to which we are accustomed.

General Editor MAURICE HUSSEY

Introduction

The arrangement of this book is as follows: the first part provides historical information about William Wordsworth, though references to the poetry are continually breaking in. It seemed unnecessary to begin with a long biography; many good biographical and interpretative studies are available, and so much detail is known about Wordsworth that even an extended summary in continuous prose may seem inadequate; I have therefore contented myself with family trees and a chronological table, followed by three topics—education, politics and character—where critics disagree on which points need to be stressed. The second chapter, on economic history, is necessary to correct the popular impression that Wordsworth was completely divorced from the main developments of his age and spent most of his time observing flowers: he was not, in fact, a very accurate botanist. The third chapter, on philosophy, offers a survey of those philosophers who are known to have influenced him in his formative years; in dealing with the period between 1798 and 1805, when the most characteristically Wordsworthian answers to philosophical questions emerge, I have deliberately avoided the use of the word 'Pantheist': I have not found any record that Wordsworth used this word about himself, and, like 'Nature', the term has been so overworked that it has become almost meaningless. The first part of the book concludes with a discussion of Wordsworth's relationship with his closest friends, and with his reading public.

The second part consists of a selective survey of Wordsworth's verse, from his earliest school poems to the work of his final years. Ten examples are chosen for close analysis, and I have tried to pick poems which differ in date, style and kind, though there is an attempt to trace the history of the Lyrical Ballad. These are not offered as the ten best poems—or extracts from poems—that Wordsworth wrote but as a series of worked examples of critical method. I hope that many readers who do not know 'what to say about a poem' will be provoked, perhaps by diametric disagreement, into trying to write their own responses down. Finally, I must stress that this second section is only opinion; many of Wordsworth's poems, for example *The Idiot Boy* or *Resolution and Independence*, have survived outright condemnation by famous critical authorities, and the fact that these poems continue to irritate many people shows that they are still very much alive.

The third part is offered as a reference section, a little Wordsworth encyclopaedia. Long lists of persons and places can, I know, look like very dry bones indeed, but a full index, intelligently used, may be more helpful than acres of unsignposted prose. The indices are complementary to the text, and have enabled me to avoid excessive footnoting and the spelled-out descriptions which put off the reader who knows the elementary facts already. On the other hand, if Hartley Coleridge or Basil Montagu, for example, are unfamiliar names when they first appear in the text, a quick glance at the index will provide the necessary information. This part of the book is rounded off with a short bibliography and notes on the critical responses of different generations of readers.

As T. S. Eliot pointed out in *The Use of Poetry and the Use of Criticism*, it was Matthew Arnold's influential selections, made nearly a hundred years ago, which cut Wordsworth away from his age and the things in which he was interested. Since that time, Eliot says:

It has become a commonplace to observe that Wordsworth's true greatness as a poet is independent of his opinions, of his theory of diction or of his nature-philosophy, and that it is found in poems in which he has no ulterior motive whatever. . . . If we dismiss Wordsworth's interests and beliefs, just how much, I wonder, remains? To retain them, or to keep them in mind instead of deliberately extruding them in preparation for enjoying his poetry, is that not necessary to appreciate how great a poet Wordsworth really is?

It is because Wordsworth cared about politics and society, and because his 'interests' were the problems of his own age, because, in short, he was involved in the unending crusade against human suffering, that we are compelled to study his life and times before we can begin to understand his poetry as a whole. Of course individual poems by Wordsworth, like *The Complaint of a Forsaken Indian Woman*, will 'search our hearts', to quote Professor Donald Davie, without the need for an interpreter to stand between us and the truth which the poem conveys. It is in order to make more of Wordsworth's poetry just as accessible, that this *Preface* has been written.

Part One

Historical Background

Family trees

A—Ancestral and fraternal

Richard Wordsworth = Mary Robinson
(from Falthwaite, S. Yorkshire)

William Cookson = Dorothy Crackanthorpe
(linen-draper of Penrith) | (of Newbiggin Hall)

John Wordsworth = Anne Cookson
1741–1783   1748–1778
(law-agent)

Christopher Crackanthorpe
(drops name of Cookson, guardian)

Richard
(guardian)

WILLIAM
1770–1850

Dorothy
1771–1855

John
1772–1805
(sailor)

Christopher
1774–1846
(Master of Trinity College, Cambridge)

Richard
1768–1816
(lawyer)

B—Marital and paternal

John Hutchinson

WILLIAM = Mary Hutchinson
          1770–1859

Sara   Peggy   5 others

John
1803–1875

Dora
1804–1847

Thomas
1806–1812

Catherine
1808–1812

William
1810–1883

Annette Vallon
1766–1841

Caroline = Jean-Baptiste
b.1792   Baudouin

1 Biographical summaries

John Morley: I once said to Matthew Arnold that I'd rather have been Wordsworth than anybody (not exactly a modest ambition); and Arnold, who knew him well in the Grasmere country, said, 'Oh no, you would not; you would wish you were dining with me at the Athenaeum. He was too much of a peasant for you.'

Mr Gladstone: No; I never felt that: I always thought him a polite and amiable man.

JOHN MORLEY, *Life of Gladstone*

Chronological table

My life is in my writings.

WORDSWORTH

WORDSWORTH'S LIFE	EVENTS IN BRITISH AND EUROPEAN HISTORY.
1766 Marriage of Wordsworth's parents.	
1769	Birth of Napoleon Bonaparte. James Watt patents his steam engine.
1770 *7 April* William Wordsworth born at Cockermouth, Cumberland.	Birth of Beethoven. Birth of Robert Owen.
1772	Birth of S. T. Coleridge.
1775	Birth of Turner.
1776	War of American Independence (ends 1782).
1778 His mother dies. Wordsworth sent away to Hawkshead Grammar School, where he stays, apart from holidays, until 1787.	
1783 His father dies.	
1787 At St John's College, Cambridge until 1791.	
1789	French Revolution begins. Fall of Bastille.
1790 *Long vacation* Fourteen weeks tour in France and Switzerland with Robert Jones.	

1791	Leaves Cambridge with a pass degree. *November* Goes to Orleans to perfect his French.	
1792	In love with Annette Vallon, 25-year-old daughter of a surgeon of Blois.	*20 April* France declares war on Austria and Prussia. *August* Louis XVI imprisoned; later dethroned. *September* September Massacres in Paris. *20 September* Revolutionary army defeats Prussians at Valmy.
	Wordsworth in Paris on 29 October and soon leaves France. *15 December* Caroline, child of William and Annette, born at Orleans.	*29 October* Louvet the Girondin accuses Robespierre of despotism.
1793	Wordsworth in London. *February* Publishes *An Evening Walk*, and later *Descriptive Sketches*. *July* After staying in the Isle of Wight Wordsworth crosses Salisbury Plain (Stonehenge), then proceeds via Tintern Abbey to North Wales. *October* Secret visit to Paris. (Wordsworth told Carlyle he saw the execution of Gorsas.)	*21 January* Louis XVI executed. *February* England declares war on France. Jacobins in power in France. *September* Reign of Terror begins in France. *7 October* Gorsas the Girondin guillotined. *October-November* Girondin leaders executed.
1794	In Lake District. At end of year he nurses Raisley Calvert who dies in January 1795 leaving Wordsworth £900.	*28 July* Execution of Robespierre. Later the French begin wars of conquest.
1795	Meets William Godwin in London and is influenced by his ideas.	*22 August* Establishment of the Directory. Aggressive policy of foreign conquest to fill French treasury.

October William and Dorothy
at Racedown Lodge, Dorset,
until July 1797.

First meeting with
Coleridge.

1796   Napleon's Italian campaign.

1797 *June* Coleridge visits the
      Wordsworths, who then
      (*July*) rent Alfoxden House
      for a year to be near
      Coleridge.

1798   *August* Battle of the Nile.
                                                 French subjugation of
                                                 Switzerland.

      September Publication of
      Lyrical Ballads.
      16 September Wordsworths
      and Coleridge land at
      Hamburg; then separate,
      Wordsworths staying at
      Goslar from October to
      April 1799.

1799 On their return to England,
      Wordsworth and Dorothy
      settle at Dove Cottage,
      Grasmere, their home until   *November* Napoleon First
      1808.   Consul.

1800 Coleridge comes to
      Greta Hall, Keswick.

1801 *January* Second edition of
      Lyrical Ballads in 2 vols.

1802   *27 March* Treaty of Amiens;
                                                 temporary peace between
                                                 England and France.
      August William and Dorothy   *15 August* Napoleon Consul
      visit Calais for four weeks   for life.
      to see Annette and Caroline.

      4 October Wordsworth
      marries Mary Hutchinson;

	Dorothy continues to live with them at Dove Cottage. Third edition of *Lyrical Ballads*.	War between England and France resumed.
1803	Tours Scotland with Dorothy and Coleridge.	
1804	*2 April* Coleridge leaves for Malta.	*May* Napoleon becomes Emperor. *2 December* His coronation.
1805	*5 February* Wordsworth's brother John drowned in the *Earl of Abergavenny*, wrecked in Weymouth Bay. Fourth edition of *Lyrical Ballads*.	*21 October* Trafalgar.
1806	*August* Coleridge returns to England.	
1807	*Poems in Two Volumes* published.	
1808	Leaves Dove Cottage for Allan Bank, Grasmere, where he lives until 1811 (Coleridge also resident).	Convention of Cintra.
1809	*May* Publishes tract *On the Convention of Cintra*. *June* Coleridge begins to issue a magazine, *The Friend*, to which Wordsworth also contributes.	
1810	Quarrel with Coleridge.	
1811	Moves to the Rectory, Grasmere, until 1813.	
1812	Reconciliation with Coleridge. Death of his children Catherine and Thomas.	Napoleon invades Russia.

B

1813	Settles permanently at Rydal Mount, having been appointed Stamp-Distributor for Westmorland.	
1814	*The Excursion* published.	
1815	Publishes his collected *Poems* and *The White Doe of Rylstone*.	*18 June* Waterloo. End of Napoleonic Wars. Corn Laws passed.
1817	Meets John Keats at Haydon's house in London.	
1818	Publishes pamphlets on Tory side at elections.	
1819	Appointed J.P.	Peterloo.
1820	Visits Continent. New edition of *Poems* in 4 vols. and *Duddon Sonnets* published.	
1822	*Ecclesiastical Sketches* and separate edition of *A Description of the Scenery of the Lakes* (guidebook) published.	
1827		Death of Beethoven.
1829	Dorothy Wordsworth seriously ill.	
1831	Last meeting with Coleridge.	
1832	Wordsworth opposes Reform.	Reform Bill.
1834	Coleridge dies.	Poor Law Amendment Act.
1835	Mental deterioration of Dorothy.	
1838	Campaigns for authors' copyright. D.C.L. (Durham).	

1839	D.C.L. (Oxford).	Copyright Bill.
1842	Resigns office of Stamp-Distributor. *Poems, chiefly of Early and Late years* published. Receives pension from Civil List of £300 a year.	Chartist agitation.
1843	Appointed Poet Laureate.	
1844	Campaigns against extension of railway to Lake District.	
1847	Death of Dora, his daughter.	
1849	Final edition of collected *Poems*. Hartley Coleridge dies.	
1850	William Wordsworth dies, on 23 April, at Rydal Mount. *The Prelude* published.	
1851		Death of Turner.
1855	Dorothy Wordsworth dies.	
1859	Mary, his wife, dies.	

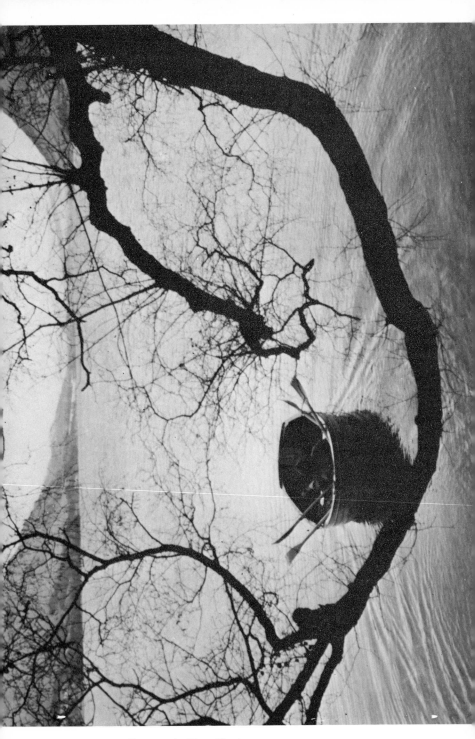

Boat on Ullswater, by Tom Sharpe

Education

I had a full twelve months' start of the freshmen of my year.
WORDSWORTH, of his first year at Cambridge

Let Nature be your Teacher.
WORDSWORTH, *The Tables Turned*

William Wordsworth was necessarily a highly intelligent man: he was a learned, clever, even a witty poet. This catalogue of adjectives needs to be frequently declaimed and asserted, even in the teeth of what most people will call 'the evidence'. The trouble is that the evidence is misleading: in the poetry of his maturity the pose of simplicity is assumed, and Wordsworth refers to book-learning as a poor substitute for Nature's revelations; Science and Art are 'barren leaves'—

> One impulse from a vernal wood
> May teach you more of man
> Of moral evil and of good,
> Than all the sages can.
> *The Tables Turned*

The Prelude, Wordsworth's long autobiographical poem, tells us that natural objects are most important in forming the mind of the child, and hardly any polite references are made to the curriculum at Hawkshead Grammar School and Cambridge University. As a result the impression has grown up that Wordsworth was rather a simple soul— an impression aided and abetted by the maid at Rydal Mount, who told visitors that her master's study was 'in the fields'.

In the late 1790s and early 1800s, when the poems mentioned above were written, Wordsworth was trying to justify and illustrate educational theories ultimately derived from books like Rousseau's *Émile* (see page 72). Children were to be brought up in accordance with Nature; when describing the progress of little Basil Montagu in 1796 Dorothy says:

You ask to be informed of our system respecting Basil. It is a very simple one, so simple that in this age of systems, you will hardly be likely to follow it. We teach him nothing at present. . . . He knows his letters, but we have not attempted any further step in the path of *book-learning*.

Moral impressions were to be associated with enduring things such as lakes and mountains, for so Wordsworth and Coleridge interpreted the philosopher Hartley's system of the association of ideas (see p. 77). In the poem *Frost at Midnight* Coleridge announced that his child Hartley was to be educated according to this theory, and Wordsworth, in writing about his own childhood, makes out a case that he was an example of the same process: *The Prelude* describes Wordsworth's formative years from this point of view, and though the facts may be correct, the *selection* and *emphasis* of the facts is open to question. We might say that Wordsworth has slanted his autobiography to fit a theory; in doing so he denied his own high academic attainment.

In fact he was one of the intellectual élite; none of his contemporaries ever thought that Wordsworth was ill-educated. The fury of the critics was directed at the intellectual poet who wrote *deliberately* like a simpleton in the *Lyrical Ballads* and the *Poems* of 1807. If Wordsworth had been a simple country boy, they could have patronized him; the Johnsonian style of the *Preface to Lyrical Ballads* showed that he could write like the gentlemanly reviewers if he wanted to, and nothing is more infuriating than one of our own sort who 'lets the side down'.

Wordsworth's earliest reading is remarkably similar to that of Charles Dickens; it consisted of folk-stories and eighteenth-century novelists, works of imagination rather than of fact. He refers to Robin Hood, Jack the Giant Killer, St George, and the Arabian Nights. His father's library was open to him and we are told that his 'father set him very early to learn portions of the works of the best English poets by heart, so that at a very early age he could repeat large portions of Shakespeare, Milton, and Spenser'. In his *Autobiographical Memoranda* Wordsworth remembers first of all his freedom to read at Hawkshead:

Of my earliest days at school I have little to say, but that they were very happy ones, chiefly because I was left at liberty, then and in the vacations, to read whatever books I liked. For example, I read all Fielding's works, Don Quixote, Gil Blas, and any part of Swift that I liked; Gulliver's Travels and the Tale of a Tub, being both much to my taste.

Hawkshead Grammar School was at the highest point of its reputation when Wordsworth arrived; boys were sent to it from all over the north-west of England and even from Scotland. From 1781 to 1786 the headmaster was William Taylor, who seems to have been responsible for directing Wordsworth's attention to poetry. In its curriculum the school concentrated on mathematics and science; there were courses in algebra, geometry and Newtonian physics. This was unusual in schools at this time, for the classical languages were pre-eminent. Wordsworth received a 'good grounding' in the classics, but the object of the intensive mathematical training was to prepare him for success at Cambridge University.

When Wordsworth arrived at St John's College, with which his school had strong connections, he found that he was already in advance of his fellow-students in the basic requirements for the first year's work. In mathematics he was clearly *one year ahead*, and was immediately awarded a Founder's scholarship and two small exhibitions—and this at St John's College which was noted at this time for its academic distinction. Obviously Wordsworth's performance in his studies at school must have been outstanding for him to have started off at Cambridge with such a lead, and it is hardly surprising that in the college examination in 1787 he was placed in the first class.

The road to academic distinction now lay open. His guardian uncles intended him for an academic career, and his brother Christopher, presumably of similar intelligence and attainment, later became Master of Trinity. The way was also clear to holy orders and advancement in the Church; this was never of much appeal to Wordsworth, who regarded compulsory chapel as an abomination. In fact he took neither course; in his own account—in *The Prelude*—he gives the impression of a drifter, 'detached from academic cares', and he tells us that he 'did not love . . . our scholastic studies'. He dropped to second class in the examinations of June 1788, and after that was unplaced. He chose not to read for a fellowship, and once it became clear that he was no longer in the race for academic honours he was not required to take all the examinations.

Some critics, arguing from the cases of Blake and Keats, have assumed that a 'Romantic' poet would obviously be hostile to the demands of a university dominated by the influence of Newton. In fact Wordsworth *liked* geometry; he describes the 'pleasure gathered from the elements of geometric science' (*Prelude* 1805 vi, 135–87), and in the famous dream in Book v of *The Prelude* the two things to be saved from the impending Deluge are 'Poetry and Geometric Truth'. Furthermore, the window of his college bedroom was cherished in his memory because it enabled him to see the Antechapel of Trinity College,

> where the statue stood
> Of Newton, with his prism and silent face,
> The marble index of a mind for ever
> Voyaging through strange seas of Thought, alone.
> *Prelude* 1850, iii, 60–3.

The simplest explanation lies in his *greater* ability, his superiority over his contemporaries, and his wider interests. Because he was so far ahead in his first year, he spent his time on other things. He says modestly that he 'got into rather an idle way', but Wordsworth's way of 'idling' offers little comfort to those who might consider him as a precedent for their own incapacity. He seems, on his own initiative, to have put himself through an extensive course of classics, modern languages and English literature, a combination of subjects that it was not then possible to offer at any university. Dorothy reported to a friend that 'he reads Italian, Spanish, French, Greek, Latin, and English, but never opens a mathematical book'.

If anything, he was more bookish and intellectual than many of his fellow-students who were pursuing with success the required courses of study. He was already determined to be a poet—between 1787 and 1789 he had composed *An Evening Walk*—and part of the aim of his 1790 long vacation walking-tour was to gather the material which was to form the basis of *Descriptive Sketches*. These, his two earliest publications, are aimed at an educated public, and are, if anything, too clever, and give too much evidence of extensive reading, being full of reminiscences of earlier poetry. Wordsworth had to *learn* to be simple.

The pass degree which Wordsworth received in 1791 was hardly fair evidence of his abilities. He had, in his own way, educated himself beyond the requirements of the university system. He continued to read voraciously throughout the 1790s, and there seems no reason to doubt Coleridge's belief that Wordsworth was eminently equipped to write philosophical poetry.

Political experience and change of attitude

> It is enough for complacency and hope that scattered and solitary minds are always labouring somewhere in the service of truth and virtue; and that by the sleep of the multitude the energy of the multitude may be prepared; and that by the fury of the people the chains of the people may be broken.
>
> WORDSWORTH, *Letter to Mathetes*

> Look at the map of Europe and count the blood-stains on it between Arcola and Waterloo.
>
> JOHN RUSKIN

In the late eighteenth century the British parliamentary system was still unreformed, and could in no sense be described as democratic. Even though two parties had emerged, those who called themselves Tories or Whigs were more often guided by the interests of their family or their pocket than by loyalty to political principles. The real power lay outside the House of Commons, in the hands of a few rich magnates and aristocratic landowners.

Wordsworth's native region provides a good example. The western half of Cumberland was part of the preserve of the Lowthers, or Earls of Lonsdale. In the 1760s Sir James Lowther (1736–1802) owned large estates in the area and treated the industrial port of Whitehaven as a family investment. He had married the daughter of Lord Bute, who was First Lord of the Treasury, and therefore Prime Minister (1762–3). Soon nine seats in the House of Commons were in his gift: his M.P.s were referred to in Parliament as 'Sir James's ninepins'. One of these seats, or 'pocket-boroughs', was the small country town of Cockermouth, where William Wordsworth was born.

Sir James needed a man to run his political affairs, to manage the undercover campaigns of entertainment and bribery. He chose Wordsworth's father, John, probably because Richard Wordsworth had held a similar position a generation before. John is described

Wordsworth's birthplace, Cockermouth

as a 'law-agent', but at election time, as the Lowthers were usually against the Whigs, 'Tory agent' would be a more accurate title. Sir James set John Wordsworth up in the largest house in the High Street of Cockermouth, and later gave him the office of Coroner of Millom. John moved in with his eighteen-year-old bride in 1766, and kept up an appearance of middle-class solvency. How he was able to do this is a mystery, for he never seems to have been paid by Lowther, not even for the necessary expenses of entertainment called for by an election campaign. In addition to financial worries the job was not a pleasant one: in spite of many years of apparent conviviality, Dorothy realized after her father's death that 'he had not one real friend'.

Thirty-five years later, in 1818, William Wordsworth was helping the new Lord Lonsdale, Sir William Lowther, in the Westmorland elections. It would be a good idea, he pointed out to the noble lord, to buy a large freehold estate and divide it into twelve, creating twelve new freeholders who would be entitled to a vote each because of the property qualification; he hastened to add that he would personally make sure that only suitable Tory adherents were thus enfranchised. A superficial observer of this piece of jobbery might well be forgiven for commenting: 'like father, like son'.

But Wordsworth had not simply inherited his father's position. In the interval he had travelled to the extreme Left wing of English politics at that time, and swung back again to the Right with vigour and determination. Cynics have observed that Wordsworth's detestation of aristocracy and love of democracy coincide with the elder Lord Lonsdale's refusal to pay John Wordsworth's accumulated salary to the Wordsworth children:

If there is a single man in Great Britain who has no suffrage in the election of a representative, the will of the society of which he is a member is not generally expressed; he is a Helot in that society.

Letter to the Bishop of Llandaff, 1793

But after 1802, when the new Lord Lonsdale agreed to pay the money over, Wordsworth discovered the admirable nature of a feudal and paternalistic society! 'I now perceive many advantages in our present complex system of representation, which formerly eluded my observation' *Letter to James Losh*, 1821. Wordsworth's changing of sides has always laid him open to this sort of comment; later generations of poets regarded him as a moral coward or a fallen idol, attitudes best summed up in the first stanza of Robert Browning's poem *The Lost Leader*:

> Just for a handful of silver he left us,
>   Just for a riband to stick in his coat—
> Found the one gift of which fortune bereft us,
>   Lost all the others she lets us devote;
> They, with the gold to give, doled him out silver,

> So much was theirs who so little allowed:
> How all our copper had gone for his service!
> Rags—were they purple, his heart had been proud!
> We that had loved him so, followed him, honoured him,
> Lived in his mild and magnificent eye,
> Learned his great language, caught his clear accents,
> Made him our pattern to live and to die!
> Shakespeare was of us, Milton was for us,
> Burns, Shelley, were with us,—they watch from their graves!
> He alone breaks from the van and the freemen,
> He alone sinks to the rear and the slaves!

But a close examination of the facts makes such a simple reaction difficult to justify. Wordsworth's 'swing to the Left' may be regarded as part of a general sympathy on the part of English intellectuals towards the French Revolution, and it is extremely unlikely that he was ever regarded as a leader of opinion.

In the next chapters we shall see that Wordsworth's political ideas run parallel to and are often interwoven with his philosophical and religious beliefs; from whichever aspect we view it, the same pattern of development emerges, though which element is providing the motivation remains obscure. It is interesting that in his later years Wordsworth regarded himself as a statesman as much as a poet; he certainly annoyed his womenfolk by talking politics incessantly with Robert Southey, though one might have expected two writers to bore the company with literary theory. The plain fact is, surely, that Wordsworth was intensely politically conscious all his life; he may have changed sides, but he never lost interest in the battle. He is indeed 'the most political of all our poets' and this is hardly surprising when we remember that he grew up in an age of Revolution.

We can only speculate on Wordsworth's political beliefs before 1792—in *The Prelude* he attributes his awakening to a French soldier, Beaupuy—(see below). But there is some evidence of his association with liberals at Cambridge which must be mentioned briefly at this point, since it seems rather unlikely that he would have visited France in 1790 and again in 1791–2 if he had no sympathy with what was going on there.

It is significant that he studied Italian at Cambridge under Agostino Isola. Isola was a Milanese liberal who had been found in possession of an English book, and therefore banished, since England had been regarded on the Continent as a 'revolutionary' country ever since 1688. Coming to England as a political refugee, he had originally worked for Thomas Gray, the poet, who, as Professor of History, was responsible for modern languages in the University. Cambridge also contained a strong 'republican' group at this time, and while there is no proof that Wordsworth joined them at the University we find that he freely associated with ex-Cambridge liberals after his return from France in 1793. It seems reasonable to suppose that even before 1790 he would have learned to appreciate their attitudes towards recent history.

We have already noticed that England was considered a very advanced and progressive country by European standards. The English had removed the head of a king as early as 1649, and the Glorious Revolution of 1688 could be interpreted as an example of Rousseau's 'general will' of the people triumphing over the Divine Right of Kings. This was one of the reasons why Wordsworth and Jones were welcomed by the French in 1790—

> . . . we bore a name
> Honoured in France, the name of Englishmen,
> And hospitably did they give us hail
> As their forerunners in a glorious course.
> *Prelude* 1805, vi, 409–12

Political reality in England, as we have seen, did not exactly square with this European idealization. The English liberals studied their seventeenth-century predecessors with great attention—Wordsworth frequently refers with enthusiasm to Milton and Algernon Sidney—but for them the land of the free was on the other side of the Atlantic.

The American Rebellion and War of Independence (1775–82) were seen by the British Left as the first stages of the liberation of England. It was Tom Paine, an English radical, who encouraged the Americans to break the link with the crown and declare a republic. But support for the Americans came from a wider section of the English people than the intellectuals: the presence of discharged and wounded soldiers created a loathing of war itself on humanitarian grounds. This is seen in two characters in Wordsworth's early poems. The Female Beggar in *An Evening Walk*—the first of Wordsworth's deserted women—laments for her soldier 'Asleep on Bunker's charnel hill afar', and the Female Vagrant, having followed her husband across the Atlantic, loses him and her children and is reduced to destitution.

The Gordon Riots (1780, described by Dickens in *Barnaby Rudge*), in which the London mob sacked the houses of Catholics and released the inhabitants of Bedlam, frightened all sections of English society. (This helps to explain why so many English liberals ceased to support France when they heard that Paris had been taken over by the 'mob' in 1793.) The first stages of the French Revolution seemed to be more obviously under reasonable management and it was assumed that the French would set up some sort of parliamentary government under the control of gentlemen. When the Bastille fell in 1789 a wave of euphoria swept over Europe; William Blake, blending together millennial hopes and biblical imagery, demonstrates the emotional release provided by the success of two revolutions accomplished overseas and the hope of a third to follow in England itself:

> The morning comes, the night decays, the watchmen leave their
>   stations;

The grave is burst, the spices shed, the linen wrapped up;
The bones of death, the cov'ring clay, the sinews shrunk and dry'd
Reviving shake, inspiring move, breathing, awakening,
Spring like redeemed captives when their bonds and bars are burst.
Let the slave grinding at the mill run out into the field,
Let the inchained soul, shut up in darkness and in sighing,
Whose face has never seen a smile in thirty weary years,
Rise and look out; his chains are loose, his dungeon doors are open;
And let his wife and children return from the oppressor's scourge.
They look behind at every step and believe it is a dream,
Singing: 'The sun has left his blackness and has found a fresher morning,
And the fair Moon rejoices in the clear and cloudless night;
For Empire is no more, and now the Lion and the Wolf shall cease.'

Wordsworth recognized this mood of elation when he landed at Calais with Robert Jones on 13 July 1790:

> 'twas a time when Europe was rejoiced,
> France standing on the top of golden hours,
> And human nature seeming born again.
> *Prelude* 1805, vi, 352–4

Everywhere on their journey through France they found the people mad with celebration, for the king had agreed to observe the new constitution:

> From hour to hour the antiquated Earth
> Beat like the heart of Man; songs, garlands, mirth,
> Banners, and happy faces, far and nigh!
> *Sonnet: 'Jones, as from Calais'*

This long vacation tour provided the material for the poem *Descriptive Sketches*, which concludes with a rousing cry for the spread of Liberty, presumably by means of war and revolution. But it is also important to remember that the object of the 1790 visit was really Switzerland, traditionally the land of liberty; Wordsworth never retracted his belief in the ideals of Switzerland, which helps to explain why, when France threatened Swiss independence in the late 1790s, it was necessary for him to make a decisive choice.

Wordsworth returned to France in November 1791 to find himself in 'a theatre, of which the stage/Was busy with an action far advanced' (*Prelude* 1805, ix, 93–4). The king had tried to flee the country in June 1791, and had been ignominiously brought back under guard. He was regarded as a traitor. The Revolutionary leaders in the capital were divided into two main groups—the Girondins, under Brissot, who were supported by merchants and the middle classes, and the Jacobins, under Danton, Marat and Robespierre, who were supported by the *sansculottes* (the clerks and artisans of Paris). In the newly elected Legislative Assembly, which Wordsworth visited, the Girondins led by Brissot were in control. Robespierre had to make his speeches in the Jacobin Club, as he was not eligible for election to the Assembly. Wordsworth had some idea of what was going on, as he had prepared himself for this second visit by reading pamphlets, and probably had a letter of introduction to Brissot; but at first he was only sentimentally affected by the ideals of the Revolution. He stayed in Paris for a week, and spent the time looking at paintings and collecting souvenirs—a stone from the Bastille, for example; yet on his arrival in Orléans he met officers and members of Royalist clubs. This contradiction did not seem to matter, for he was as

> careless as a flower
> Glassed in a Green-house, or a Parlour shrub
> When every bush and tree, the country through,
> Is shaking to the roots.
>
> *Prelude* 1805, ix, 87–90

There was a lull in the progress of the Revolution, and for a little time Wordsworth associated with those sections of society where 'politics' were not discussed.

Yet Wordsworth tells us that he was by upbringing and inclination a natural Democrat (*Prelude* 1805, ix, 217 ff). His conversion to the wholehearted support of the Revolution was the result of his admiration for Captain Michel Beaupuy, who took upon himself Wordsworth's political education. So that, Wordsworth tells us,

> when we chanc'd
> One day to meet a hunger-bitten Girl,
> Who crept along, fitting her languid gait
> Unto a Heifer's motion, by a cord
> Tied to her arm, and picking thus from the lane
> Its sustenance, while the girl with her two hands
> Was busy knitting, in a heartless mood
> Of solitude, and at the sight my Friend
> In agitation said, ''Tis against *that*
> Which we are fighting', I with him believed
> Devoutly that a spirit was abroad
> Which could not be withstood.
>
> *Prelude* 1805, ix, 510 ff.

Wordsworth was so moved that he became 'a Patriot', that is, a Republican, and from that time, he says,

> my heart was all
> Given to the People, and my love was theirs.
>
> *Prelude* 1805, ix, 124–5

With some people this might be mere bravado, but when Words-worth was on his way back to England he seems to have lingered in Paris far longer than was necessary, and possibly considered active participation in practical politics (*Prelude* 1805, x, 129 ff). Wordsworth sided with the Girondins, who were still in control of the Assembly, and had declared war on Austria and Prussia in April 1792 to spread the Revolution abroad. But the *sansculottes* were capable of independent action; in August they had seized the king, and in September, fearing the advancing armies might use the prisoners in the Paris prisons, they began to murder them (September Massacres). By the end of the year the country had become a republic and the king was on trial for his life; the Girondins were losing their command of the situation, and some critics have seen Wordsworth's departure from the scene at this point as evidence that he foresaw their fall from power (which took place in the summer of 1793). Certainly he hated Robespierre and the Jacobins, and his subsequent disillusionment with the course of the Revolution makes sense if he is seen as an exiled Girondin. One should always bear in mind that he never went back on his sympathy for the early stages of the Revolution, and his statement in 1821, at the height of his Toryism, when he was accused of deserting France, has its own indestructible logic: 'You have been deluded by places and persons, while I have stuck to principles. I abandoned France and her rulers when they abandoned Liberty, gave themselves up to tyranny, and endeavoured to enslave the world.'

Shortly after his arrival in England, Wordsworth found himself in an impossible moral position. England and France were now at war. For a while Wordsworth retained his loyalty to the Girondin leaders of France, though this meant that he was in English eyes a 'Jacobin', that is, a revolutionary extremist who had actually visited the infected country twice. Wordsworth, for his part, longed to hear of British defeats:

> I rejoiced,
> Yea, afterwards, truth most painful to record!
> Exulted in the triumph of my soul
> When Englishmen by thousands were o'erthrown. . . .
>
> *Prelude* 1805, x, 259–62

Provoked by a sermon issued in January 1793 entitled *The Wisdom and Goodness of God in having made both Rich and Poor*, which was an attack on the French Revolution by Richard Watson, Bishop of Llandaff, Wordsworth countered with *A Letter to the Bishop of Llandaff on the Extraordinary Avowal of his Political Principles . . . by A Republican*. But his publisher persuaded him that it was not wise to print such an open attack on the Government.

It is ironical that Watson had at first supported the Revolution and then changed his mind. For as the Girondins fell from power and the Reign of Terror began Wordsworth felt that the ideals of the Revolution had been betrayed (*Prelude* 1805, x, 308–61). He was glad that the French had driven back the invading foreign armies, but this was no real comfort to the conflict in his mind. He still hoped that the Revolution would bring forth some good result, but could not suppress his fears:

> Most melancholy at that time, O Friend!
> Were my day-thoughts, my dreams were miserable;
> Through months, through years, long after the last beat
> Of those atrocities (I speak bare truth,
> As if to thee alone in private talk)
> I scarcely had one night of quiet sleep
> Such ghastly visions had I of despair
> And tyranny, and implements of death
> And long orations which in dreams I pleaded
> Before unjust Tribunals, with a voice
> Labouring, a brain confounded, and a sense,
> Of treachery and desertion in the place
> The holiest that I knew of, my own soul.
>
> *Prelude* 1805, x, 369–81

In fact he was identifying himself with his Girondin friends who were guillotined by the Jacobins in October and November 1793; although the story that Wordsworth visited France at this time to take help to the Girondins may be untrue, this is clearly what he would have wished to do if an opportunity had arisen.

In July 1794 the death of Robespierre brought a feeling of relief (*Prelude* 1805, x, 536 ff). Wordsworth returned to his former trust in France, and thought of the British Tory government as 'vermin' (*Prelude* 1805, x, 655); but when the French began to take away the liberty of other countries, Wordsworth saw that there was little to choose between the French and any other conquering nation (*Prelude* 1805, x, 792 ff).

De Selincourt, the editor of *The Prelude*, dates this phase as early as the end of 1794; after this time Wordsworth sought refuge in philosophy (see Godwin, p. 74) and had to be virtually nursed back to mental and moral stability by Dorothy amid rural surroundings. Wordsworth and Coleridge were further alienated from France by Napoleon's campaigns of conquest; the subjugation of Switzerland in 1798—Liberty suppressing Liberty—was the crowning irony which confirmed Wordsworth's group in their suspicions of Napoleon. We must of course remember that many English liberals continued to support Napoleon—see Gillray's cartoon of English liberals incensed by the naval victories of Nelson; one of these, William Hazlitt, was so amazed at the change in Wordsworth and Coleridge that he accused them later, of swinging over 'as on a pivot, to the unclean side'. But the movement to the Right took far longer than this implies; Wordsworth continued to admire Charles James Fox, the Whig leader, although Fox was in favour of making peace with

NELSON's Victory;— or — Good-News operating upon Loyal-Feelings.

Napoleon, but after visiting France in 1802 Wordsworth could not stomach the Whigs as a party. He watched them rushing through Calais on their way to pay court to Napoleon (*Sonnet: 'Is it a reed that's shaken by the wind'*), and decided, since he regarded the French leader as a despot and a menace to free institutions, that the only course open was to support that party in England which wanted to continue the war, namely the Tories. His patriotism became inflamed (*Poems Dedicated to National Independence and Liberty*) and when Napoleon crowned himself Emperor, he shared the disgust of Beethoven, who tore out the dedication of the *Eroica* symphony. Wordsworth felt that the wheel had indeed come full circle or rather, to use his own expression, that France was like a 'dog/Returning to his vomit' (*Prelude* 1805, x, 935). He continued to support the Tories through the very difficult war years, and after 1815 seems to have left that any popular demonstration or movement towards parliamentary reform would be the prelude to an English Revolution which would, in turn, throw up a 'Napoleon' to tyrannize over the British people.

After receiving a government post (in 1813) he seems to have felt bound to repay the debt of obligation by political services, especially at election times. There seems no point in pretending that he was reluctant to serve the Tory Party in this way, though it added to his unpopularity with the younger Liberals. To the new generation of Romantics he appeared to have become a fossilized appendage of a backward-looking Establishment, which was already, in 1815, in the process of restoring the eighteenth-century dynasties to the thrones of Europe, so that the French Revolution might never have taken place.

Wordsworth's later views on home affairs will be more appropriately discussed at the end of Chapter 2. In foreign affairs he was always a consistent supporter of the principle of national self-determination—'The nations shall be great and free' (*Sonnet: Sept. 1802; Near Dover*). This goes back to his championing of Switzerland; in 1809 he tried to challenge the Government with a tract *On the Convention of Cintra*. He considered that the Spanish nationalists had been betrayed, and the tract soon develops into an argument about nationalist aspiration—

> I weigh the hopes and fears of suffering Spain
> Sonnet: 'Not mid the World's Vain Objects'

At a much later stage he produced three sonnets about Italian freedom (*At Bologna, In Remembrance of the Late Insurrections, 1837*). One of the difficulties about snap judgments of the later Wordsworth is that the revolutionary in him would not lie down and die. Macaulay, the Whig historian, reviewing *The Prelude* in 1850, was shocked at what he found: we must remember that the book was not published until after Wordsworth's death, and had the effect of a carefully nurtured time bomb. Macaulay found *The Prelude* 'to the last degree Jacobinical, indeed Socialist': the linking of words that look far back into the past and equally far forward into the future shows that from the point of view of the Whig benches at any rate, Wordsworth's politics were lamentably consistent.

Appearance and character

> Mrs Wudsworth would say, 'ring the bell', but he wouldn't stir, bless ye. 'Goa and see what he's doing', she'd say, and we wad goa up to study door and hear him a mumbling and bumming through it. 'Dinner's ready, sir', I'd ca' out, he'd goa mumbling on like a deaf man, ya see. And sometimes Mrs Wudsworth 'ud say, 'Goa and brek a bottle, or let a dish fall just outside door in passage.' Eh dear, that maistly wad bring him out, wad that. It was nobbut that as wad, how-ivver. For ye kna that he was a verra careful man, and he couldn't do with brekking t' china.
>
> One of the servants, reported by H. D. RAWNSLEY,
> *Lake Country Sketches*

> I have wished to keep the Reader in the company of flesh and blood, persuaded that by so doing I shall interest him.
> WORDSWORTH, *Preface to Lyrical Ballads*

Many portraits of Wordsworth and Coleridge exist, though unfortunately Dorothy was only painted in her dotage. In Wordsworth's case, as we might expect, most of the paintings show him in middle or old age after he had become famous. In addition several verbal sketches have come down to us: William Hazlitt first met Wordsworth in 1798 and recorded this description:

The next day Wordsworth arrived from Bristol at Coleridge's cottage. I think I see him now. He answered in some degree to his friend's description of him, but was more gaunt and Don Quixote-like. He was quaintly dressed (according to the costume of that unconstrained period) in a brown fustian jacket and striped pantaloons. There was something of a roll, a lounge in his gait, not unlike his own 'Peter Bell'. There was a severe, worn pressure of thought about his temples, a fire in his eye (as if he saw something in objects more than outward appearance), an intense, high, narrow forehead, a Roman nose, cheeks furrowed by a strong purpose, and a convulsive inclination to laughter about the mouth, a good deal at variance with the solemn, stately expression of the rest of his face. . . . He sat down and talked very naturally and freely, with a mixture of the clear gushing accents in his voice, a deep guttural intonation, and a strong tincture of the northern *burr* like the crust on wine.

This last point is worth amplifying as it does affect the poetry. Wordsworth's accent frequently struck Southern ears as harsh:

even though suburban gentility had not yet forced all regional speakers to conform to the colourless vowel-sounds of the Home Counties if they wished to be socially acceptable, and even though Coleridge, like Sir Walter Raleigh before him, spoke broad Devon all his life without being taken for a peasant, it is clear that Wordsworth's accent did contribute to a general impression of roughness. In reading Wordsworth's poems aloud, a Northern speaker will have no difficulty in rhyming 'notes' with 'thoughts', or 'chatters' with 'waters', though these are obviously not true rhymes to a Southern ear. But Wordsworth does not use any *dialect* expression, so that this difficulty need not be exaggerated.

In 1802 Wordsworth produced eight stanzas in the manner of Thomson's *Castle of Indolence*, which give first a self-portrait and then a description of Coleridge:

> Within our happy Castle there dwelt One
> Whom without blame I may not overlook;
> For never sun on living creature shone
> Who more devout enjoyment with us took:
> Here on his hours he hung as on a book,
> On his own time here would he float away,
> As doth a fly upon a summer brook;
> But go to-morrow, or belike to-day,
> Seek for him—he is fled; and whither none can say.
>
> Thus often would he leave our peaceful home,
> And find elsewhere his business or delight;
> Out of our Valley's limits did he roam:
> Full many a time, upon a stormy night,
> His voice came to us from the neighbouring height:
> Oft could we see him driving full in view
> At mid-day when the sun was shining bright;
> What ill was on him, what he had to do,
> A mighty wonder bred among our quiet crew.
>
> Ah! piteous sight it was to see this Man
> When he came back to us, a withered flower,—
> Or like a sinful creature, pale and wan.
> Down would he sit; and without strength or power
> Look at the common grass from hour to hour:
> And often times, how long I fear to say,
> Where apple-trees in blossom made a bower,
> Retired in that sunshiny shade he lay;
> And, like a naked Indian, slept himself away.
>
> Great wonder to our gentle tribe it was
> Whenever from our Valley he withdrew;
> For happier soul no living creature has
> Than he had, being here the whole day through.

Some thought he was a lover, and did woo:
Some thought far worse of him, and judged him wrong;
But verse was what he had been wedded to;
And his own mind did like a tempest strong
Come to him thus, and drove the weary Wight along.

With him there often walked in friendly guise,
Or lay upon the moss by brook or tree,
A noticeable Man with large grey eyes,
(Coleridge) And a pale face that seemed undoubtedly
As if a blooming face it ought to be;
Heavy his low-hung lip did oft appear,
Deprest by weight of musing Phantasy;
Profound his forehead was, though not severe;
Yet some did think that he had little business here:

Sweet heaven forfend! his was a lawful right;
Noisy he was, and gamesome as a boy;
His limbs would toss about him with delight,
Like branches when strong winds the trees annoy.
Nor lacked his calmer hours device or toy
To banish listlessness and irksome care;
He would have taught you how you might employ
Yourself; and many did to him repair,—
And certes not in vain; he had inventions rare.

Expedients, too, of simplest sort he tried:
Long blades of grass, plucked round him as he lay,
Made, to his ear attentively applied
A pipe on which the wind would deftly play;
Glasses he had, that little things display,
The beetle panoplied in gems and gold,
A mailed angel on a battle-day;
The mysteries that cups of flowers enfold,
And all the gorgeous sights which fairies do behold.

(Coleridge & He would entice that other Man to hear
Wordsworth) His music, and to view his imagery:
And, sooth, these two were each to the other dear:
No livelier love in such a place could be:
There did they dwell—from earthly labour free,
As happy spirits as were ever seen;
If but a bird, to keep them company,
Or butterfly sate down, they were, I ween,
As pleased as if the same had been a Maiden-queen.

Further verbal pictures of Wordsworth at this period may be found in Dorothy Wordsworth's *Journals* (see p. 97); but 1805 may be considered as the end of his youth. The death of his brother John at the beginning of that year affected him physically. In 1809 'a whole

coachload of passengers', according to De Quincey, 'took Wordsworth [then aged thirty-nine] for a man of sixty'.

In his later years there was a tendency to treat Wordsworth as a
venerable sage: there is too much sentimental piety about some descriptions, while others give the impression of a strange, and slightly
dotty, old man of the mountains. In *Passages in a Wandering Life*,
Thomas Arnold the Younger tells us that between 1835 and 1850:

The poet's ordinary dress was a loose brown frock-coat, trousers
of shepherd's plaid, a loose black handkerchief for a neck-tie,
a green and black plaid shawl round the shoulders, and a
wideawake or straw hat, often with a blue veil attached to it.

The best account of his facial appearance, some time between 1830
and 1834, is by Sir Henry Taylor:

Wordsworth's was a face which did not assign itself to any class.
It was a hard weather-beaten old face which might have belonged
to a nobleman, a yeoman, a mariner, or a philosopher; for there
was so much of a man that you lost sight of superadded
distinctions. For my own part, I should not, judging by his face,
have guessed him to be a poet. To my eyes there was more of
strength than refinement in the face.... Perhaps what was wanting
was only *physical* refinement. It was a rough grey face, full of
rifts and clefts and fissures, out of which, someone said, you
might expect lichens to grow.

Haydon, who painted Wordsworth on Helvellyn in 1842, noted that
'His head is like as if it was carved out of a mossy rock, created before
the flood', and those who tried to penetrate to the character beneath
the face of the old man used the same 'stony' vocabulary. Carlyle, for
example, saw in 1840:

A fine wholesome rusticity.... His face bore the marks of much,
not always peaceful meditation; the look of it not bland or
benevolent so much as close impregnable and hard.

There is plenty of evidence for this impression of 'hardness'
throughout Wordsworth's life, frequently related to us by London
'witlings' whose smooth sophistication he was not likely to suffer
gladly. He was a North-countryman, and the bluntness of his approach
to many issues should be considered, I think, as a traditional North-
country attitude, exaggerated at times to the point of obtuseness;
it may have been merely a defence mechanism. His prose style bears
this out: half the trouble about the *Preface to Lyrical Ballads* was
caused by the dogmatic style of some of its assertions—Wordsworth
probably thought he was simply stating a point of view.

Most observers, therefore, saw him as a tough and humourless man
whose intransigent attitude had led to the quarrels with his friends;
Keats dubbed him 'the Egotistical Sublime'. But Coleridge, who knew
him well, saw him as a happy man, because he had one aim in life:

Wordsworth on Helvellyn, by Benjamin Robert Haydon, 1842

He is a happy man because he is a Philosopher, because he knows
the intrinsic value of the different objects of human pursuit,
and regulates his wishes in strict subordination to that knowledge;
because he feels . . . that we can do but one thing well, and that
therefore we must make a choice. He has made that choice from
his early youth, has pursued and is pursuing it; and certainly
no small part of his happiness is owing to this unity of interest
and that homogeneity of character which is the natural consequence
of it.

Coleridge was no doubt contrasting his own divided aims. Wordsworth's unity of purpose contributes to the directness of his poetry
and so strengthens the appearance of sincerity that some critics
have stated that Wordsworth, like the young George Washington,
'always tells the truth'. But this would be to postulate inhuman
perfections. It would be even more uncomfortable to associate with
a character like that than to feel at home with our previous assessment,
the hard man whose admirers compared him to a stone. Behind the
external appearance of harshness and reserve lay sensitivity, suffering,
even humour; Wordsworth took some time to get to know, but those
who dared to make the attempt were often agreeably surprised.
Greville, the society diarist, noted in 1831:

Wordsworth may be bordering on sixty; hard-featured, brown,
wrinkled, with prominent teeth and a few scattered grey hairs, but
nevertheless not a disagreeable countenance; and very cheerful,
merry, courteous and talkative, much more so than I should have
expected from the grave and didactic character of his writings.

No notice should be taken of the frequently reiterated statement
that Wordsworth lacked humour: of course he had a sense of humour
—'sly humour', Hazlitt called it in 1825, and added, 'he has a
peculiar sweetness in his smile'. Those who have met with Cumberland
jokes will realize that they are nearly always directly personal and
intended to deflate pretension: the victims may well feel that this is
not what passes for humour in 'polite society'. An example will serve
to illustrate this point: Leigh Hunt was a vegetarian, and praised
'in glowing words the cauliflower swimming in melted butter'; Wordsworth wryly asked whether 'if by chance of good luck they ever met
with a caterpillar, they thanked their stars for a delicious morsel
of animal food'.

This down-to-earth good sense has not been sufficiently stressed
in the past; there is a normality, a sanity, a state of psychological
health which is so often missing in the more obviously 'Romantic'
of Wordsworth's contemporaries. Wordsworth, Coleridge and
Dorothy have been too much revered by their admirers, and their
common humanity played down. When discussing a passage in
Dorothy's German journal, where she states that she 'carried *Kubla*
to a fountain in the neighbouring market-place, where I drank

some excellent water', one editor allowed himself to speculate upon the existence of a missing manuscript copy of *Kubla Khan*. In fact 'Kubla' was the name of their drinking-*can*, and the pun may strike some people as near-sacrilege; others may consider the whole thing quite trivial. But, speaking personally, I regard this passage as an illumination; the Wordsworths suddenly become *people* instead of rather vague and sublime presences; furthermore, they become people one would like to have met.

2 Economic history

The cultivation of poetry is never more to be desired than at periods when, from an excess of the selfish and calculating principle, the accumulation of the materials of external life exceeds the quantity of the power of assimilating them to the internal laws of human nature.

SHELLEY, *Defence of Poetry*

I have thought twelve hours about society for every one about poetry.
WORDSWORTH, 1833

Arkwright's cotton mills by day, by Joseph Wright of Derby

The Industrial Revolution

. . . the encreasing accumulation of men in cities . . .

WORDSWORTH, *Preface to Lyrical Ballads*

It is no longer fashionable to discuss the Industrial Revolution as if it were an event which happened between 1760 and 1840. In certain areas of the country industrialization had been a slow but continuous process since the seventeenth century or even earlier; and it is a process which has not finished yet. The first half of the eighteenth century had seen an increase in trade, which was paralleled by an increase in the population. The $5\frac{1}{2}$ million inhabitants of England and Wales in 1700 had swelled to nearly 7 million in 1760; in 1801 the first census revealed that there were over 9 million people; by 1811 there were $10\frac{1}{2}$ million. The increase was not uniformly distributed over the whole country; the population grew most rapidly in the North and West, especially where coal and iron were to be found, and supplied a convenient labour force for the manufacturing industries.

In the textile industry a number of technical inventions produced an increase in output; a way had been found of using coal, in the form of coke, to smelt iron; and the steam engine was so improved that it provided a new source of power. But we must not imagine that factory towns grew up overnight. The early factories depended on water power; in 1716 John Lombe built a silk mill in Derbyshire, recognizably an industrial building but situated in the country. In the later years of the eighteenth century it was still usual to build factories near water; the iron industry was similarly dispersed in a series of villages. The new industrial centres were, in fact, quite small at first, and as they were mainly out of the way in unfashionable parts of the country, many people ignored them completely; one or two distinguished men even had the impression that the population was declining.

But by the 1780s and 1790s—the years of Wordsworth's youth—the new advances in techniques of production began to provoke widespread comment. The transport system improved rapidly, and this was a source of pride to the whole country, besides enabling the different regions to exchange materials and goods. The roads were becoming a pleasure to travel on after centuries of neglect. The first canals were constructed between 1757 and 1761 in order to transport coal from the mines to the towns and factories; in the years 1791–7 the canal system expanded rapidly, and by 1815 covered most of England's transport requirements in the industrial field.

The age of steam was not established until 1800, when Wordsworth was thirty. The location of factories was changed so that they were situated near coal; more intensive exploitation of coal deposits and iron ore meant that either, as in the Black Country, the little villages began to merge and quite large areas of land were enveloped and spoilt, or that, as in the case of Manchester, a factory town emerged. The whole phenomenon of the Industrial Revolution must be seen as a cumulative process, resulting in an economic take-off at the end of the eighteenth century under the stimulus of the Napoleonic Wars.

Negative reactions were somewhat delayed, especially when the economists of the day preached the inevitability of 'progress'. At first the whole of society, including the poets, had welcomed the new industrial processes and the feeling of power which they encouraged. There was a phase of hope and widespread optimism, at least until the agricultural distress of 1795, when it became clear that there would sometimes be a problem in feeding such a vast population. Society had to consider its attitude to the 'new men'—the manufacturers— and also to the pressures of organized labour. It was also necessary to recondition the human mind to accept Change instead of Stability as the time-continuum against which one lived. The English people were the first to experience an industrial revolution, and nobody was conscious that this was what was happening to them. We may feel today that things might have been better planned, and that it is a great pity that what now looks like the decisive contribution of England to world history should have been carried through with so much muddle and mess.

These were comparatively abstract and long-term problems; what was immediately obvious was the effect of the new methods of production upon the *people* who were closely involved in them. The condition of the new 'working classes' gave more and more cause for anxiety after the turn of the century. Because of the division of labour, work soon became the perpetual repetition of a simple task, or the minding of a machine; such work often had to be done for fourteen hours a day, six days a week, and there were no special provisions for the women and very young children who were considered especially suitable for work in the textile industries. The question of leisure activities did not arise, and the cheap housing, poor diet, and squalid surroundings produced a total environment that had a depressing effect upon human endeavour: this was especially noticeable in Lancashire. To some observers, the new generations who were born into this environment appeared stunted and uncouth; their cheap clothing and strange variations on the English language made them seem like another species, almost subhuman. Disraeli was later to talk of the Two Nations, the Rich and the Poor, who could exist side by side in the same country with no knowledge of each other's way of life. With these human problems Wordsworth was deeply concerned, though it must be admitted that a superficial reading of his poetry gives the impression that he ran as hard as he could to get away from them.

Unless Wordsworth's poetry is studied in the context of the economic history of the time many important points will be missed, and the intention of whole poems may be misconstrued. Most of Wordsworth's readers who have left us their opinions were middle-

46

class, but we must remember that he addressed his poetry to readers of all classes and we do not know how much the choice of natural subject matter may have meant to urban dwellers who lived out of sight of flowers and trees. A poem about a daisy or a butterfly, however quiet in tone and however naive it may appear in isolation, may be read in this context as a hymn to battle against economic thinkers, who could find no place for such useless natural objects in their systems of ideas. Even Wordsworth's residence in the Lake District, a non-profit-making area compared to, say, Manchester, and his initial attempt to live off the profession of poetry, represent a challenge to the age.

Those who still feel that Wordsworth 'escaped' from social reality will hardly be impressed by the argument so far, and will ask to be shown Wordsworth's poems about factories, steam-engines and so on. It is not generally realized that he did write on such topics, though it must be admitted that a frontal attack on the factory system was not likely to be *poetically* successful. Nevertheless, *The Excursion* (1814) is partly about society during the Industrial Revolution. In his own time the Wanderer has seen the face of England changed:

> at social Industry's command,
> How quick, how vast an increase! From the germ
> Of some poor hamlet, rapidly produced,
> Here a huge town, continuous and compact,
> Hiding the face of earth for leagues—and there,
> Where not a habitation stood before,
> Abodes of men irregularly massed
> Like trees in forests,—spread through spacious tracts,
> O'er which the smoke of unremitting fires
> Hangs permanent . . .
>
> *The Excursion* viii, 117–26

The echo of Milton's Hell in the final image is significant. Gas-light, the factory bell and shift work seem to call up similar echoes, for at night-time:

> an unnatural light
> Prepared for never-resting Labour's eyes
> Breaks from a many-windowed fabric huge;
> And at the appointed hour a bell is heard
> Of harsher import than the curfew-knoll
> That spake the Norman Conqueror's stern behest—
> A local summons to unceasing toil!
> Disgorged are now the ministers of day;
> And, as they issue from the illumined pile,
> A fresh band meets them, at the crowded door—
> . . . Men, maidens, youths,
> Mothers and little children, boys and girls,
> Enter, and each the wonted task resumes

> Within this temple, where is offered up
> To Gain, the master-idol of the realm,
> Perpetual sacrifice.
>
> *The Excursion* viii, 167–76, 180–5

Wordsworth's comparison of mill and religious building is extremely apt as those who have seen some of these early industrial 'temples' will agree. They are often indistinguishable in external appearance from the larger nonconformist chapels in the next street. William Blake made good poetic use of this confusion of 'mill' and 'church', too.

In Wordsworth's note to this section of his poem—which also deals with improved roads and canals, and proffers hope that the new processes will bring ultimate good—he compares his work with that of a poet of the first half of the eighteenth century, John Dyer:

In treating this subject, it was impossible not to recollect, with gratitude, the pleasing picture, which, in his Poem of the Fleece, the excellent and amiable Dyer has given of the influences of manufacturing industry upon the face of this Island. He wrote at a time when machinery was first beginning to be introduced, and his benevolent heart prompted him to augur from it nothing but good. Truth has compelled me to dwell upon the baneful effects arising out of an ill-regulated and excessive application of powers so admirable in themselves.

The implication of this note is that most readers did not want to hear that anything was wrong, and that Wordsworth's doubts about the growth of industry show original thinking on his part.

Certainly Wordsworth is interested and concerned; but he has little to offer as a remedy, and is no machine-breaker or Luddite. He does see, though, that

> Our life is turned
> Out of her course, wherever man is made
> An offering, or a sacrifice, a tool
> Or implement, a passive thing employed
> As a brute mean . . .
>
> *The Excursion* ix, 113–17

anticipating the social criticism of John Ruskin and William Morris by more than thirty years.

The growth of the industrial proletariat convinced him that state education for all was essential, though in 1809 he asked: 'What can you expect of national education conducted by a government which for twenty years resisted the abolition of the Slave Trade?' He was impressed by the Madras or monitor system of Dr Bell, in which pupil teachers passed on one teacher's instruction to hundreds of junior pupils. Bell visited Wordsworth in 1811 and in the same year William, Dorothy and Mary taught 'Madras' in the village school at

Grasmere. It was shortly after this that the passage appealing for universal education was written:

> O for the coming of that glorious time
> When, prizing knowledge as the noblest wealth
> And best protection, this imperial Realm,
> While she exacts allegiance, shall admit
> An obligation, on her part, to *teach*
> Them who are born to serve her and obey;
> Binding herself by statute to secure
> For all the children whom her soil maintains
> The rudiments of letters . . .
>
> *The Excursion* ix, 293–301

It took another sixty years to achieve this; Forster's Education Act was not passed till 1870. Some of Wordsworth's other ideals—that children should be treated equally, and that education should be *devoid of competition*—have been rather slower in materializing.

Nevertheless, the attitudes which Wordsworth adopted towards industrialization were successfully transmitted to the later nineteenth century, and ultimately down to our own day, where they have sometimes been incorporated into the law of the land. Wordsworth contributed to the growth of 'Humanity', the climate of opinion in which Shaftesbury was able to proceed with factory legislation; and surely his attitude of reverence towards landscape formed public opinion, so that one now needs planning permission to site a factory and the line of a motorway has to be negotiated; certain areas have become National Parks, and one cannot help noticing how many of these were districts where Wordsworth lived or with which he was in some way associated (see Gazetteer).

Because we think we have tamed industrialism we no longer fear it; but in the age of *laissez faire*, when the power of the manufacturers seemed unbounded, it took a certain courage to think for oneself and run the risk of appearing ridiculous. Wordsworth's 'retirement' to the Lakes begins to look less like a retreat than a strategic withdrawal to ensure survival. Although he chose a contemplative life, he defined his occupation as 'activity in solitude for society'. The 'fair works' of Nature provided Wordsworth with a contrasting background which showed up more clearly 'what man has done to man'. Remembering that it was Wordsworth whom the Utilitarian John Stuart Mill turned to when he found that his philosophy produced nothing but visions of a grey and empty world, and that Matthew Arnold, after Wordsworth's death, believed that he alone could heal human nature in the 'iron time', the little poem that follows, written in 1833, seems a convenient summing-up of Wordsworth's mature attitudes.

C

To the Utilitarians

Avaunt this economic rage!
What would it bring?—an iron age,
When Fact with heartless search explored
Shall be Imagination's Lord,
And sway with absolute control
The god-like Functions of the Soul.
Not *thus* can Knowledge elevate
Our Nature from her fallen state.
With sober Reason Faith unites
To vindicate the ideal rights
Of Human-kind—the true agreeing
Of objects with internal seeing,
Of effort with the end of Being.

Agrarian distress

amid the gloom
Spread by a brotherhood of lofty elms,
Appeared a roofless Hut; four naked walls
That stared upon each other!
WORDSWORTH, *The Ruined Cottage (Excursion i)*

Enclosure like a Bounaparte let not a thing remain . . .
JOHN CLARE, *Remembrances*

In the 1790s Britain was still primarily an agricultural country; it still appears to be so in the novels of Jane Austen twenty years later, and, after all, even today one could choose a route from East Anglia to Cornwall which would give a foreigner this impression. Large areas of the South and West remained untouched by the growth of the manufacturing industries, and in spite of the stimulating effect of the Napoleonic Wars upon certain sections of the economy, most of those who worked on the land steadily became poorer. There is abundant evidence of this in the writings of William Cobbett, who observes well the results of a process without clearly understanding the causes. He says, for example, that the people are 'poor creatures about Great Bedwin and Cricklade' because

. . . Those countries, always but badly furnished with fuel, the desolating and damnable system of paper-money, by sweeping away small homesteads, and laying ten farms into one, has literally *stripped* of all shelter for the labourer.

In order to find out why things had not been going so well on the land as in the urban areas we must once again go back to the beginning of the eighteenth century.

In the year 1700 between 80 and 90 per cent of the population lived in the country, including the small market-towns (compared with about 10 per cent in the year 1900). Although 80 per cent of the land was already privately owned, 20 per cent, mainly in the Midland counties, was still divided up according to the open-field system: the inhabitants of a village held land in common, and this common land, if suitable for cultivation, was divided into strips. (One could compare the present system of allotment-holding, which certain pressure groups regard as uneconomic.) Even if he only held his cottage on a tenancy, a cottager could usually keep animals on the common pastureland, and collect fuel from the land unsuited to agriculture, known as the waste. Although the system had been modified in many villages so that the strips fell together instead of being widely separated, everybody, including squatters, had access to the common land and was able to earn some sort of a living from it, and this could be supplemented seasonally by labouring or harvesting for a bigger landowner.

As the eighteenth century wore on, an agricultural revolution took place, complementing the industrial take-off. Methods of cultivation were so improved that even relatively poor land could be intensively exploited; new crops were introduced, which involved new systems of rotation and made large units of farmland more economic than small-holdings. Farming became a fashionable occupation among the aristocracy, who had enough influence in Parliament to pass through Bills of Enclosure. The effect of these was to transfer the common land to private ownership; the dispossessed commoners were given small pockets of land or other compensation, but these were not necessarily equivalent to the rights they had lost. Squatters, who had no legal rights, were forced off the land. Even cottagers were frequently obliged to sell up, and those who did not remain as labourers went off to swell the population of the new towns.

After 1760 there were many Acts of Enclosure, and during Wordsworth's lifetime the new system of landownership became completely effective. Of course this contributed to Britain's ability to feed herself during the Napoleonic Wars, but in bad years, because of the lack of imported corn, most people could not afford bread. The result of the enclosures was that many countrymen lost what little security they had formerly possessed, including the sense of *belonging* to a particular village or cottage. John Clare testifies to the wholesale obliteration of landmarks, and the subsequent consciousness of alienation; *The Female Vagrant* is not so much a *poem* by Wordsworth as a case-history.

The cottagers also lost their economic independence in areas unaffected by enclosure, such as the Lake District. The new factories frequently centralized the processes of manufacture which had formerly been dispersed among the cottages, especially in the textile industries. Many had previously enjoyed a steady income from carding or spinning, which provided an occupation for women and children. Again, the choice was between following the work to the factory towns or eking out an existence by labouring.

Mere labourers, however, had no security at all. Although the farmers frequently made considerable profits, wages did not rise to correspond with the price increases brought about by the wars. When bad times came and wages were below the level on which they could support their families, the labourers found that they had to ask the authorities of the parish in which they lived for relief; in other words they became paupers, who could be sent to the workhouse.

In 1795, after a severe winter and the failure of many crops, the price of provisions soared to an unprecedented height; the price of wheat in London was 108 shillings a quarter: and this meant that it was impossible to buy bread, even if it were obtainable. There were not enough workhouses to cope with the problem. The magistrates at Speenhamland in Berkshire decided to supplement wages out of the poor rates, and this system of outdoor relief soon became general; years of demoralization and artificially low wages ensued, but there was no mass starvation and a revolutionary situation was avoided.

Wordsworth, like Dickens fifty years later, considered that all human beings had a claim upon each other, even though political economists thought that war and poverty were 'natural checks upon the species' and 'kept down the surplus population'. It is interesting to note that *Oliver Twist* and *A Christmas Carol*, which were attempts to make the middle classes *see* their fellow human beings and *notice* their problems, have been reduced by the English mind to children's books. Similarly, Wordsworth is commonly bowdlerized into a 'Nature poet', and his frequent accounts of human beings in economic difficulties are dismissed as his 'revolutionary growing-pains'—to be omitted from the safe anthologies in which he is commonly presented to the adolescent mind.

In the middle years of the 1790s Wordsworth observed what was happening to some of the cottagers and *cared* about it; like a good journalist, he called attention to outstanding cases in *The Female Vagrant* and *The Ruined Cottage*. The titles of both poems suffered change, and *The Ruined Cottage* is to be found incorporated in the first Book of *The Excursion*, where Wordsworth looks back from 1814 to the year 1795:

> Not twenty years ago, but you I think
> Can scarcely bear it now in mind, there came
> Two blighting seasons, when the fields were left
> With half a harvest. It pleased Heaven to add
> A worse affliction in the plague of war:
> This happy Land was stricken to the heart!

A Wanderer then among the cottages,
I, with my freight of winter raiment, saw
The hardships of that season: many rich
Sank down, as in a dream, among the poor;
And of the poor did many cease to be,
And their place knew them not . . .
            . . . shoals of artisans
From ill-requited labour turned adrift
Sought daily bread from public charity . . .
                The Excursion, i, 535–46, 559–61.

It is these economic stresses which bring about the tragedy of Margaret and her family and lead eventually to the Ruined Cottage, which remains as a symbol of these afflictions.

The Last of the Flock (see pp. 121) records a similar process of degradation and suffering, as a farmer's sheep are sold off one by one. These poems are probably set in Somerset, but as most of Wordsworth's social observation is directed towards the inhabitants of the Lake District, it would be as well to consider the economic history of that area in some detail before proceeding with Wordsworth's reactions to the poverty and despair around him.

The Lake District

These things are like the barbarism of two centuries ago. It is the railroad that must mend them.

HARRIET MARTINEAU, *Complete Guide To the English Lakes*

The Lake District in Wordsworth's youth was not a tourist centre, but an economic going concern. Penrith, Keswick, Kendal and Cockermouth were small country towns with a mixture of small-scale industrial activities. The farmers and shepherds in the valleys may seem to have lived an isolated existence, if one thinks of *Michael*, but the wool from the sheep would be carded and spun in the cottages, and ultimately sent to the towns. Along the Cumberland coast an industrial fringe was already well established, based on deposits of coal and iron ore: Whitehaven was in those days an important port. Inside the ring of mountains Wordsworth was not as isolated from industrial activities as some people like to think: a valley forge, driven by water power, 'thumps' in the closing lines of *An Evening Walk*,* among other 'natural' noises of Lakeland midnight—but this may be considered unusual, and the image may in fact be borrowed from Gray. For as the Industrial Revolution progressed and changed much of Northern England, the Lake District became more and more

---

*See Critical Survey, p. 118, for the text of this passage.

of an economic backwater, a comparatively poor district where, for example, people scraped the yellow lichen *Ochrolechia tartarea* from the rocks and sold it to dyers for a penny a pound. It seems wrong, therefore, to suggest, as some critics do, that the Lake District avoided the worst distresses.

While enclosure came later to the Lake District than the southern parts of England, there is plenty of evidence of rural depopulation in the later years of the eighteenth century. This was because the system of land tenure was remarkably different from other areas, and there were a large number of 'statesmen' or 'estatesmen' who were small freeholders. In 1766 a Cumberland man pointed out the difficulties of agriculture in the region—it was too wet to grow wheat— and estimated that a quarter of Cumberland was owned by thirty lords and gentlemen, and the remainder divided between 10,000 small landowners. He said:

These petty landowners work like slaves; they cannot afford to keep
a man servant, but husband, wife, sons and daughters all turn out
to work in the fields; they wear wooden shoes, shod like a horse's
foot with iron, sackcloth shirts, yarn stockings, homespun linsey,
and cloth that comes about 2s a yard, felt hats; their diet is whey,
potatoes, turnips, oatmeal bread and oatmeal and water; they very
seldom taste meat or wheat bread, and work very hard upon this
diet; they breed many children . . . and (as you may suppose) when
they grow up, they post away to happier climes, and make you
very good servants.

These were the natural democrats whom Wordsworth idealized in memory; in his *Guide to the Lakes* he says that

Toward the head of these Dales was found a perfect Republic
of Shepherds and Agriculturists, among whom the plough of each
man was confined to the maintenance of his own family. . . .
Neither high-born nobleman, knight, nor esquire was here; but
many of these humble sons of the hills had a consciousness that
the land which they walked over and tilled had for more than
five hundred years been possessed by men of their name and
blood.

We notice the past tense: Wordsworth has omitted here to mention that these small proprietors depended on the cottage industries, which were taken away when the factory system had become established. So that in Wordsworth's lifetime the statesmen declined; in other parts of the *Guide* he is more realistic about them:

These people participate in the general benefit which the island
has derived from the increased value of the produce of land,
brought about by the establishment of manufactories, and in the
consequent quickening of agricultural industry. But this is far
from making them amends; and now that home-manufactures are

nearly done away, though the women and children might, at many seasons of the year, employ themselves with advantage in the fields beyond what they are accustomed to do, yet still all possible exertion in this way cannot be rationally expected from persons whose agricultural knowledge is so confined, and, above all, where there must necessarily be so small a capital. The consequence then is—that proprietors and farmers being no longer able to maintain themselves upon small farms, several are united in one, and the buildings go to decay or are destroyed.

There was a need for a new source of wealth, and as the nineteenth century advanced this was provided by the tourist industry.

It is often assumed that Wordsworth himself was responsible for the fame of the area as a holiday centre, but this is only partly true. In the early eighteenth century all uncultivated districts were labelled 'wild' and 'horrid', and were therefore to be shunned. But by 1750 fashion had changed—look at the new style of English landscape garden—and artists and poets set out to explore their own island in search of the picturesque; in due course they arrived in Cumberland. At first they climbed to the heights to look down on Nature or to survey the scene—encouraging the building of 'stations' such as the Windermere Octagon; but after Thomas Gray's *Journal of a Tour in the Lakes* (written in 1769) artists began to take their views from the valleys. The rich began to build along the sides of Windermere, and fitted our boats with cannon; salvoes were fired in order to 'enjoy the echoes'. De Quincey tells us of:

an item in a bill at Patterdale (head of Ullswater)—

To an echo,	first quality	...	£0 10	0
To do.,	second quality	...	0 5	0

It seems the price of echoes varied, reasonably enough, with the amount of gunpowder consumed. But at Lowwood, on Windermere, half-crown echoes might be had by those base snobs who would put up with a vile Brummagem substitute for 'the genuine article'.

The Wordsworthian attitude of reverence for mountains had not yet appeared, and Wordsworth's two early poems, *Descriptive Sketches* and *An Evening Walk*, mainly purvey established eighteenth century taste. I say 'established' because in 1788 Wilberforce observed that a Lakeland holiday was already popular: 'The banks of Thames are scarcely more public than those of Windermere.'

While Wordsworth later adopted an attitude of hostility to tourists—he fought the coming of the railways in the 1840s tooth and nail—there is no doubt that he aided and abetted their holiday plans. Why else publish his own guide in 1822 and 1835— *A Description of the Scenery of the Lakes in the North of England with Views*, as it was first entitled. By the 1830s the next stage—the identification by the public of the Lakes with Wordsworth—had been reached. Thomas Arnold and Ruskin's father bought houses there, feeling that the scenery would be a good influence on their children; and the reading parties from Oxford and Cambridge soon followed. The mountains and lakes were now revered as a source of 'uplift'. With the invention of photography this attitude to Nature could be disseminated in book form. Wordsworth's name soon doubled with the Lakes in the titles—*The English Lake District as interpreted by Wordsworth* appeared in 1874, and in 1911 Eric Robertson produced a book simply called *Wordsworthshire*—the final apotheosis! But it took many years for the ordinary people of the area to benefit from tourism in any worthwhile economic sense. Meanwhile the factory towns and the mines were not far off as they were in the South, and the northern peasant was used to a hard life; he was not forced to stay on the land as a pauper, since employers and employed were in the same economic difficulties and regarded each other as of nearly the same status. As Dickinson, the Cumberland poet, put it:

> And o' fare't alike—beath maister and man
>   In eatin' and drinkin' or wark;
> They turn'd out at morn and togidder began
>   And left off togidder at dark . . .

It is in this inherited conception of the *equality* of all human beings that the people of the Lake District provided a contrast to the rest of England; Wordsworth therefore believed that 'humble and rustic' men were not yet corrupted. We can see why Michael was to be admired; but Michael's son, who left for the town, *was forced to do so* because his father had to find money in a hurry *and would not sell his land*. Though the industrial and agrarian revolutions may not have changed the appearance of the Lake District, they claimed the peasants' children. And the break-up of the family was a change which Wordsworth felt must be resisted.

Wordsworth's concern for the poor, the displaced and the beggars

> His master's dead,—and no one now
>   Dwells in the Hall of Ivor;
> Men, dogs, and horses, all are dead;
>   He is the sole survivor.

WORDSWORTH, Simon Lee, the Old Huntsman

So much was Wordsworth concerned for the apparent breakdown of the family as a unit that he embarked upon a course of action which seems incredibly naive and yet illustrates his downright belief in the social value of poetry. In January 1801 he wrote to

Charles James Fox, the Leader of the Whig Opposition, enclosing the two volumes of *Lyrical Ballads*, and asking him to read *Michael* and *The Brothers*, not for their poetic merit but because they illustrate 'the weakening of the bonds of domestic feeling among the poor'. The letter is worth quoting from at length:

It appears to me that the most calamitous effect, which has followed the measures which have lately been pursued in this country, is a rapid decay of the domestic affections among the lower orders of society. This effect the present Rulers of this Country are not conscious of, or they disregard it. For many years past, the tendency of society amongst almost all the nations of Europe has been to produce it. But recently by the spreading of manufactures through every part of the country, by the heavy taxes upon postage, by workhouses, Houses of Industry, and the invention of Soup-shops etc. etc. superadded to the increasing disproportion between the price of labour and that of the necessaries of life, the bonds of domestic feeling among the poor, as far as the influence of these things has extended, have been weakened, and in innumerable instances entirely destroyed. The evil would be less to be regretted, if these institutions were regarded only as palliatives to a disease; but the vanity and pride of their promoters are so subtly interwoven with them, that they are deemed great discoveries and blessings to humanity. In the mean time parents are separated from their children, and children from their parents.

Obviously Wordsworth thought that his poems would have some positive effect in this direction; it becomes clearer why so many of the poems written at this time deal with 'domestic affections', and in particular with the separation of mother and child. *The Cottager To Her Infant, Maternal Grief, The Childless Father, The Emigrant Mother*—so run the consecutive titles from a group of 'Poems Founded on the Affections'. Wordsworth hoped that the people who read these poems would cease to put forward such hardheaded schemes as the separation of husband and wife in workhouses, or the sale of children to be 'apprenticed' in the mills.

Wordsworth followed the rural child into the towns. *The Reverie of Poor Susan*, cast in the form of a popular song and working on the association of ideas, is not a sentimental ballad but a study of the uprooted personality, forced to live in an unnatural environment. Early reviewers were more upset by the social conscience which poems like this displayed than by the outlandish verses, and did not understand why a poet should be concerned with the study of 'low and rustic life'. Gentle readers did not want their poetry linked with what amounts to sociology; with his taste for 'interviewing' the practitioners of strange trades like the Leechgatherer and asking 'How is it that you live and what is it you do?' Wordsworth seems almost a hundred years ahead of his time. We are therefore not surprised to

Charles James Fox, by Karl Anton Hickel

find that it was this part of his work which most nineteenth-century readers chose to ignore, as any Victorian anthology will prove with its selection of passages relating to Nature. He also made a special study of the outcasts, the waifs and strays of industrial society—the vagrants and the idiots. People dismiss this aspect of Wordsworth's poetry as 'odd', forgetting that George Orwell became a tramp for six weeks and lived for a year as a down-and-out; and Shakespeare wrote a play about a mad old man who was also a vagrant! Perhaps it is because in isolation human beings achieve their true status; they are no longer tied to an economic process which dominates their existence.

Wordsworth thought he could learn from them; he regarded no man as his inferior. Indeed he approached the vagrants with feelings of reverence and holy fear; their very names seem more awe-inspiring than feudal titles: The Old Cumberland Beggar, The Pedlar, The Discharged Soldier, the Female Vagrant and The Beggarwoman. Their mere existence fascinated him—'an old man *was*'*—and the question addressed to the Leechgatherer: 'How is it that you live?'—is not really a question about sources of income. He had been interested in tramps since childhood—'I love a public road'; he had read Crabbe's description of a workhouse at school and had been shocked by the confinement of the mentally ill 'inasmuch as idiots and lunatics among the humbler classes of society were not to be found in Workhouses—in the parts of the North where I was brought up,—but were mostly at large'. (*The Idiot Boy* is intended to justify the retention of such a child in its mother's care, in the same way that Coleridge's *The Dungeon* pleads for humane treatment of criminals.) In his early twenties Wordsworth wandered the roads himself in search of case histories—see *Guilt and Sorrow* or *Old Man Travelling*—and when he settled at Grasmere he lived alongside a road which was used by travellers to Whitehaven and to Scotland in bad weather; Dorothy's *Journals* are full of encounters with wanderers.

It is not at first clear what these people had to offer Wordsworth, though he tried to help them. The Soldier in Book iv of *The Prelude* is an example of Wordsworth performing a Good Samaritan act; but what impressed Wordsworth and remains with us is the description of the Soldier's appearance:

> He was of stature tall,
> A foot above man's common measure tall,
> Stiff in his form and upright, lank and lean;
> A man more meagre, as it seem'd to me,
> Was never seen abroad by night or day.
> His arms were long, and bare his hands; his mouth
> Shew'd ghastly in the moonlight: from behind

---

*See Wordsworth's letter to Sara Hutchinson, 14 June 1802, for the emphasis on the verb 'to be' in the first version of *Resolution and Independence*.

> A milestone propp'd him, and his figure seem'd
> Half-sitting, and half-standing. I could mark
> That he was clad in military garb,
> Though faded, yet entire. He was alone,
> Had no attendant, neither Dog, nor Staff,
> Nor Knapsack; in his very dress appear'd
> A desolation, a simplicity
> That seem'd akin to solitude.
>
> *Prelude* 1805, iv, 405–19

Wordsworth continues to watch, but for a long time the figure refuses to move. The strangeness of the whole situation comes across very strongly, together with a certain emblematic quality. This is made clearer in the description of the London Beggar, whom Wordsworth did not help and yet who manifestly affected him considerably. Lost in the confusion of 'the moving pageant' of the streets, he tells us,

> 'twas my chance
> Abruptly to be smitten with the view
> Of a blind Beggar, who, with upright face,
> Stood propp'd against a Wall, upon his Chest
> Wearing a written paper, to explain
> The story of the Man, and who he was.
> My mind did at this spectacle turn round
> As with the might of waters, and it seem'd
> To me that in this Label was a type,
> Or emblem, of the utmost that we know,
> Both of ourselves and of the universe;
> And, on the shape of the unmoving man,
> His fixèd face and sightless eyes, I look'd
> As if admonish'd from another world.
>
> *Prelude* 1805, vii, 609–22

The religious implications of this are clear; but to our present purpose we notice that the vagrants and the beggars lead us away from 'economic man' towards other kinds of existence.

The Old Cumberland Beggar is more obviously a sermon addressed to the political economist, who believes that only 'people who show a profit' are important, and that people who are poor or old or ill should be shut away because they are 'useless to society'. Wordsworth defends the Beggar:

> deem not this Man useless—Statesmen! ye
> Who are so restless in your wisdom, ye
> Who have a broom still ready in your hands
> To rid the world of nuisances.

The middle class may shut themselves off from life in a mental suburb of self-righteousness,

But of the poor man ask, the abject poor;
Go, and demand of him, if there be here
In this cold abstinence from evil deeds,
And these inevitable charities,
Wherewith to satisfy the human soul?
No—man is dear to man; the poorest poor
Long for some moments in a weary life
When they can know and feel that they have been,
Themselves, the fathers and the dealers-out
Of some small blessings; have been kind to such
As needed kindness, for this single cause,
That we have all of us one human heart.

The refore the Beggar has a 'use' in his society:

May never HOUSE, misnamed of INDUSTRY,
Make him a captive—

He is not to be shut away in the workhouse.

Whether this sermon to the reader is successful has often been
debated, and it is worth contrasting at this point the more subtle
approach of the painter, John Constable, addressing a London audience. He is describing the fate of a tall and elegant ash-tree—

Many of my Hampstead friends may remember this *young* lady
at the entrance to the village. Her fate was distressing, for it is
scarcely too much to say that she died of a broken heart. I made
this drawing when she was in full health and beauty; on passing
some time afterwards, I saw, to my grief, that a wretched board
had been nailed to her side, on which was written in large
letters, '*All vagrants and beggars will be dealt with according to law!*'
The tree seemed to have felt the disgrace, for even then some of
the top branches had withered. Two long spike nails had been
driven far into her side. In another year one half became paralyzed
and not long after the other shared the same fate, and this
beautiful creature was cut down to a stump, just high enough
to hold the board.

This ironical amused stance, this little parable indicative of a society's
real values, was something Wordsworth was not able to do.

The older Wordsworth

He was always the poor man's friend.

Said of Wordsworth.

The later Wordsworth is usually presented as a very unattractive
figure; the case against his poetry will be examined separately, but

what annoys people even more than his apparent repudiation of the principles underlying *Lyrical Ballads* is his political attitude. In this section we continue the story from the point reached in the 'Politics' section in Chapter 1—the year 1815 and the illusion of the eighteenth century restored to Europe. The years immediately after the Napoleonic wars were years of extreme repression in England; there was also a slump in trade and manufacture after the wartime boom. The conditions seemed right for a repetition of the French Revolution on English soil. Since our history books are still largely written from the liberal side we are amazed to find Wordsworth on the side of the aristocracy and against the rising hopes of the people; as he himself put it: 'I cannot but be of opinion that the feudal power yet surviving in England is eminently serviceable in counteracting the popular tendency to reform.' Yet, in spite of his now professed Toryism, he continued to mix his poetry with social criticism and to the very end of his life insisted on making statements which show an intense involvement in the sufferings of the people.

Wordsworth dreamt of an alliance between the aristocracy and the common people—at any rate in the rural areas. He realized that he was supporting the weaker side, and was against the transfer of power to 'mere financiers and political economists.' He disliked industrialists, and successful merchants, preferring the company of 'gentry', who could be convinced of their duty to those they controlled on their landed estates. He felt that people without property were irresponsible, and that the manufacturers who would acquire power under the Reform Bill would only act out of self-interest. He stuck to these attitudes through the 1820s and after, and could see no reason to take up the new liberal and radical ideas, which aimed at further break-up of the existing order of things. He regarded the new ideas as a trick to give even more power to the manufacturers—and perhaps his political analysis was not at fault, since the exponents of these ideas were largely middle-class.

Nevertheless, in 1831, after a visit to Wordsworth, John Stuart Mill was impressed by the amount that he—a liberal Utilitarian by upbringing—agreed with the 'hardened Tory'. Wordsworth, he reported,

seems always to know the pros and cons of every question; and when you think he strikes the balance wrong it is only because you think he estimates erroneously some matter of fact. . . . If one's conclusions and his were at variance on every question which a minister or Parliament could tomorrow be called upon to solve, his is nevertheless the mind with which one would really be in communion; our principles would be the same and we should be like two travellers pursuing the same course on opposite sides of the river.

There is other evidence of a thawing-out during the 1830s. Of course he opposed the Reform Bill itself, yet said in a letter to Crabb

Robinson (5 Feb 1833): 'You mistake in supposing me an Anti-Reformer— *that* I never was, but an Anti-Bill man, heart and soul.' In 1836, the Bill now having been passed, he suggested to Gladstone that there ought to be *more* enfranchisement to cure the effects of it; if the pyramid were extended at the base and the lower classes given some power, this would counter the preponderance of the manufacturers.

In fact, Wordsworth's position begins to look surprisingly consistent, if one considers what he is *against*; he is prepared to use any weapon to attack liberal commercial values and the new affluent middle class. In the years 1815–27, when he was hated by the young Romantic poets for his apostasy, it is only fair to point out that many quite reasonable people were at panic stations because of incipient popular unrest. When the danger of revolution seemed to have passed he emerged with points of view that look forward to the emancipation of the working classes. For evidence of this, as well as of his continuing interest in the outcast and distressed, it is worth looking at the *Postscript* to *Yarrow Revisited and Other Poems* (1835). This shows how far Wordsworth has moved since the *Preface to Lyrical Ballads*, and on what subjects he feels compelled to address his readers; this time there is no discussion of the theory of poetry, but we begin with a review of the Poor Law Amendment Act (1834).

Wordsworth looks forward to an ideal Welfare State where all are entitled to 'maintenance by law' without a feeling of degradation. The State must act in relieving distress, for private charity and a change of heart among the rich are not enough. The law must be made more humane, for 'sights of abject misery, perpetually recurring, harden the heart of the community.' He then turns to 'the state of the workmen congregated in manufactories'. In order to prevent 'combinations of masters to keep down, unjustly, the price of labour' he suggests what we would call 'co-ownership schemes' in industry, and ends by recommending the study of certain of his verses to trade union members.

In the 1840s most working men supported the Chartists, who aimed at a secret ballot and adult male suffrage. Officially Wordsworth continued to dwell on the virtues of landed proprietors, but he made occasional remarks which surprised his companions. On one occasion he kicked at a fence which was *enclosing* a footpath, saying 'I have no respect for the Whigs, but I have a good deal of the Chartist in me'. He very much admired the poetry of Ebenezer Elliot, the Corn Law Rhymer, that is, a poet who helped to lead the opposition to the laws which kept the price of bread artificially high, and said 'None of us have done better than he has at his best'. When Thomas Cooper, a Chartist who had advocated extreme violence in 1842, visited him, he told him: 'You were right. . . I have always said the people were right in what they asked; but you went the wrong way to get it.' However, the Chartists did not receive any public support from him and were not conscious of his attitude; so that George Julian Harney wrote on Wordsworth's death: 'We are not impressed with any heavy sense of sorrow. . . . We had no tears for the salaried slaves of Aristocracy and pensioned parasites of Monarchy.'

His last campaign, in 1845, fought with pamphlet and sonnet, was against the projected Kendal and Windermere Railway, which would have brought tourists into the Lake District at the price of wrecking the scenery. This was not just an old man's hatred of change; the sonnet *Steamboats, Viaducts, and Railways* (1833) is surprisingly in favour of these evidences of man's ability, and concludes:

> Nature doth embrace
> Her lawful offspring in Man's art; and Time,
> Pleased with your triumphs o'er his brother Space,
> Accepts from your bold hands the proffered crown
> Of hope, and smiles on you with cheer sublime.

But Wordsworth had already proposed in his *Guide* that the Lake District should be made 'a sort of national property in which every man has a right and interest who has an eye to perceive and a heart to enjoy'; we can now see that, over a hundred years before his time, he had come up with the idea of a National Park.

However much, therefore, we may feel with the later Romantics that Wordsworth was 'a political apostate', his social interests will always remain as evidence of his humanity. If he ended up with a taste for feudalism and aristocracy it was because he believed that the old paternalism was better than the inhuman gulf between 'classes'—'One would wish to see the rich mingle with the poor as much as may be upon a footing of fraternal equality.' Actions speak louder than words: at the age of seventy he climbed to a house

high up Loughrigg side where dwells the good woman who lost her two children in the flood last winter. The wind was high when I knocked at her door, and I heard a voice from within that I knew not what to make of, though it sounded like the lullaby of a Mother to her Baby. After entering I found it came from a little sister of those drowned Children, that was singing to a bundle of clouts, rudely put together to look like a Doll, which she held in her arms.

Letter to Dora Wordsworth, 7 April 1840

Perhaps he still identified himself with the man who bought a duffle cloak for Alice Fell (see Critical Survey, p. 138); he instructed his daughter to buy the child a doll—'only let it be a good big one'.

Tintern Abbey, 1794 by J. M. W. Turner

3 Philosophy and religion

[Wordsworth] . . . a great poet by inspirations, and in moments of revelation, but a thinking, feeling philosopher habitually . . . his Poetry [is] his Philosophy under the action of strong winds of Feeling—a sea rolling high.

S. T. COLERIDGE

Locke and the sense of sight

> Locke's philistinism was in no sense an aberration. He wanted to get away from the imagination, away from the vague glamour of medieval things, from reverence for tradition, from mysticism, enthusiasm and *gloire*; away from all private visionary insights and down to the plain, measurable, publicly verifiable facts; and this desire was central to his whole mission as a philosopher and reformer.
>
> MAURICE CRANSTON, *John Locke*

> ... metaphysical systems, for the most part become popular, not for their truth, but in proportion as they attribute to causes a susceptibility of being seen, if only our visual organs were sufficiently powerful.
>
> S. T. COLERIDGE

As we have seen in the section on Education, Wordsworth grew up in a mathematical and scientific age, which still adhered to principles discovered in the seventeenth century. Isaac Newton (1642–1727) had demonstrated that natural phenomena were governed by universal laws; these were capable of experimental proof, whereas the 'truths' derived from books, mystical visions or revelations were not only incapable of mathematical proof but were often contradictory.

The late seventeenth century had seen a new departure in philosophic enquiry; philosophers abandoned metaphysical speculations and tried to pursue their studies in a scientific spirit. The change of attitude may not have appeared so dramatic since the word 'philosophy' was more general in its meaning than today, and scientists were called 'philosophers' or 'natural philosophers' down to the end of the eighteenth century. Between them the scientists and philosophers set out to explain a universe, which, after the muddle of the Dark or Middle Ages, seemed to be flooded with clear light.

In approaching philosophical problems John Locke (1632–1704) kept the temperature of discussion as low as possible; there was no point in reviving the interminable religious disputes which had produced the Wars of Religion in the earlier seventeenth century. Addressing an audience of sensible and clear-headed gentlemen—the sort of people who had produced the Bloodless Revolution of 1688—Locke pictured himself as 'an under-labourer in clearing the ground a little, and removing much of the rubbish that lies in the way of knowledge'. He proposed that we should test things by the evidence of our senses. 'Revelation must be judged by reason'; in this way one could avoid being misled by Fancy (a rather disorganized mental activity) into the dangers of 'Enthusiasm' (uncritical belief in a religious or political doctrine). Finally—a very neat blow at any remaining opposition—he pointed out that only people who were mentally ill allowed themselves to be guided by 'persuasions of immediate intercourse with the deity', so that prophetic or bardic inspiration was simply a delusion.

Between them Locke and Newton built up the mental picture of the universe which the educated classes in the eighteenth century absorbed as incontrovertible truth. The Great Architect, or the Watchmaker, had put together a mathematically perfect world. (God, or the Deity, existed because somebody had had to work out the mathematics in the first place.) In the created universe there was no room for divine operation; the biblical miracles presented a difficulty here, but perhaps rational explanations would soon be found. There was no need for God to intervene in his superbly designed universe, which was equipped to deal with all contingencies. The Watchmaker, having wound up the watch he had made, had retired elsewhere, presumably for contemplation. The Great Machine could be left to operate without interference.

The many *mechanical* analogies (in this admittedly crude summary) were all used to explain the world to simple people; but machines, though they may be perfect, are nevertheless quite *dead*. There was no real room for God in Newton's universe, and even living creatures were an untidy addition to the perfect geometry of stars, planets and rays of light. Similarly, in Locke's descriptions of mental activity, comparisons are made with *inanimate* objects, and the mind becomes, as at the beginning of the following extract, a sort of vast furniture warehouse.

All ideas come from sensation or reflection. Let us then suppose the mind to be, as we say, white paper, void of all characters, without any ideas, how comes it to be furnished? Whence comes it by that vast store, which the busy and boundless fancy of man has painted on it with an almost endless variety? Whence has it all the materials of reason and knowledge? To this I answer, in one word, from EXPERIENCE; in that all our knowledge is founded, and from that it ultimately derives itself. Our observation, employed either about external sensible objects, or about the internal operations of our minds, perceived and reflected on by ourselves, is that which supplies our understandings with all the materials of thinking. These two are the fountains of knowledge, from whence all the ideas we have, or can naturally have, do spring.

The objects of sensation one source of ideas. First, our senses, conversant about particular sensible objects, do convey into the mind several distinct perceptions of things, according to those various ways wherein those objects do affect them; and thus we come by those *ideas* we have of yellow, white, heat, cold, soft, hard, bitter, sweet, and all those which we call sensible qualities, which when I say the senses convey into the mind, I mean, they from external objects convey into the mind what produces there those perceptions. This great source of most of the ideas we have, depending wholly upon our senses, and derived by them to the understanding, I call SENSATION.

The operations of our minds the other source of them. Secondly, the other fountain, from which experience furnisheth the understanding with ideas, is the perception of the operations of our own mind within us, as it is employed about the ideas it has got; which operations, when the soul comes to reflect on and consider, do furnish the understanding with another set of ideas which could not be had from things without; and such are perception, thinking, doubting, believing, reasoning, knowing, willing, and all the different actings of our own minds; which we being conscious of, and observing in ourselves, do from these receive into our understanding as distinct ideas, as we do from bodies affecting our senses. This source of ideas every man has wholly in himself; and though it be not sense, as having nothing to do with external objects, yet it is very like it, and might properly enough be called internal sense. But as I call the other Sensation, so I call this REFLECTION, the ideas it affords being such only as the mind gets by reflecting on its own operations, within itself. By Reflection, then, in the following part of this discourse, I would be understood to mean that notice which the mind takes of its own operations, and the manner of them, by reason whereof there come to be ideas of these operations in the understanding. These two, I say, viz., external material things as the objects of Sensation, and the operations of our own minds within as the objects of Reflection, are, to me, the only originals from whence all our ideas take their beginnings. The term operations here, I use in a large sense, as comprehending not barely the actions of the mind about its ideas, but some sort of passions arising sometimes from them, such as is the satisfaction or uneasiness arising from any thought.

All our ideas are of the one or the other of these. The understanding seems to me not to have the least glimmering of any ideas which it doth not receive from one of these two. *External objects* furnish the mind with the ideas of sensible qualities, which are all those different perceptions they produce in us; and *the mind* furnishes the understanding with ideas of its own operations. These, when we have taken a full survey of them, and their several modes, combinations, and relations, we shall find to contain all our whole stock of ideas; and that we have nothing in our minds which did not come in one of these two ways. Let any one examine his own thoughts, and thoroughly search into his understanding, and then let him tell me, whether all the original ideas he has there, are any other than of the objects of his senses, or of the operations of his mind considered as objects of his reflection; and how great a mass of knowledge soever he imagines to be lodged there, he will, upon taking a strict view, see that he has not any idea in his mind but what one of these two have imprinted, though perhaps with infinite variety compounded and enlarged by the understanding, as we shall see hereafter.

LOCKE, Essay Concerning Human Understanding

This long extract gives one the general flavour of Locke's discourse, besides illustrating some of his main propositions. Earlier philosophers had thought that there were innate ideas, but Locke will have none of this. The operations of the mind which he describes are reduced to two fairly simple activities. We *passively* receive sense-impressions—'in bare, naked perception the mind is, for the most part, merely passive'; and all human thought and knowledge is reduced to rational generalizations derived from experience. There is little room for poetry—a product of the despised Fancy—in all this; yet Wordsworth was in the Locke tradition when he rejected the 'gaudy and inane phraseology' of the Fancy and devoted a long poem to the description of how Nature (in Locke's sense of the whole external world rather than simply mountains and lakes) formed his mental character.

Wordsworth also inherits from Locke an intense concern with the *visible* universe; although Locke tries to explain all kinds of sensory experience he is most at home with the sense of sight, which could most easily be related to Newton's optical discoveries. Therefore, as Ernest Tuveson points out in *Imagination as a Means of Grace*: 'From the nature of mind as described by Locke we could expect a new poetry to be highly visual in nature, for the faculty of sight came to monopolize the analysis of intellectual activity.' So that even in a passage like the following, which is moving away from Locke's philosophic teaching, Locke's influence is apparent.

> There is creation in the eye,
> Nor less in all the other senses; powers
> They are that colour, model, and combine
> The things perceived with such an absolute
> Essential energy that we may say
> That those most godlike faculties of ours
> At one and the same moment are the mind
> And the mind's minister.
>
> *Fragment* (1798–9)

Many explanations have been given for the careful measurements and statistical information so frequent in Wordsworth's early poetry, for example:

> And to the left, three yards beyond,
> You see a little muddy pond
> Of water, never dry;
> I've measured it from side to side;
> 'Tis three feet long, and two feet wide . . .
>
> *The Thorn* (1798)

but surely even this may ultimately go back to a desire to placate the scientific and Lockean tradition. The terminology of Locke is still considered valid to support the argument advanced in the *Preface to Lyrical Ballads*: we are referred to 'sensations' and 'ideas', and told that 'falsehood of description' has been avoided, for the object of poetry is 'truth'. In this way, Wordsworth insists, 'Poetry is the most philosophic of all writing'.

Rousseau and the education of the sensibility

The world has not seen more than once or twice in all the course of history a literature which has exercised such prodigious influence over the minds of men, over every cast and shade of intellect, as that which emanated from Rousseau between 1749 and 1762.

MAINE, *Ancient Law*

Rousseau, Sir, is a very bad man.

DR JOHNSON

The eighteenth century is often referred to as the Age of Reason; most people believed that the world that Newton and Locke had made *was the real world*. Later ages have tended to magnify the importance of those thinkers and poets who disagreed; there is no reason to think that the young Wordsworth would have taken any notice of them; he believed with his University that whatever Newton said, was right.

Nevertheless, he could not fail to have heard of the protest movement which originated with Jean Jacques Rousseau (1712–78). There is no evidence that Wordsworth ever studied Rousseau in a systematic way, but he would have met with his influence in France, if not well before. Rousseau's tactics in doing battle with 'Reason' were very simple; he rejected its validity altogether, and appealed to the emotions—he did not *feel* that the dictates of Reason and science were true. As Tennyson put it a century later: 'The heart stood up and answered "I have felt".' While the objections to this point of view are obvious—we can be led into all manner of belief by wishful thinking—it coincided with the beginnings of a general desire to re-open the discussion which Locke had apparently concluded for good and all.

Rousseau challenged the Christian doctrine of Original Sin; he believed that man was by nature good, and that he had been corrupted by civilization; savages were uncorrupted. In European countries virtue would be found to linger in remote and rural communities. This doctrine appears in an altered form in the *Preface to Lyrical Ballads* where Wordsworth tells us that he had written about 'low and rustic life . . . because in that situation the essential passions of the heart find a better soil in which they can attain their maturity'.

Civilized man could perhaps be saved by education. In *Émile* Rousseau suggested that it might be possible to recreate a system of 'natural education'. The child is to be brought up in the country, and should learn by experience; this is far better than sitting indoors, studying books. He would not be made to read, in fact, or to perform any formal educational exercises; nor would he be crammed with useless theorizing. On the other hand, his tutor would always tell him the truth, and he would never be allowed to hear stories or fairy-tales. He would learn morality by observing people's reactions when he performed unsocial actions; but he would never be punished. These teachings clearly influenced the early books of *The Prelude*, and it is worth digressing at this point to see how Wordsworth amended and yet clung to the spirit of Rousseau's ideals.

Wordsworth's views on education were remarkably ahead of his time. They were also consistent throughout his life. Whereas many otherwise 'progressive' disciples of Rousseau believed in controlling the entire environment of the child and programming its mind with carefully selected sense impressions, Wordsworth and Dorothy believed in complete freedom: 'Till a child is four years old he needs no other companions than the flowers, the grass, the cattle, the sheep that scamper away from him, when he makes a vain unexpecting chase after them, the pebbles upon the road etc.' Wordsworth hated 'model children' and 'infant prodigies' (*Prelude* 1805, v 291–349); he preferred 'real children, not too wise, too learned, or too good'. His writings were later able to save a model child, the philosopher John Stuart Mill, who had been brought up on a system of intensive reading and deprived of the 'culture of the feelings'. Although Wordsworth's own children, together with Basil Montagu and Hartley Coleridge, can hardly be called unqualified successes in their later life, this does not undermine Wordsworth's ideas, which anticipate the freedom of modern infant teaching.

Allied to Wordsworth's campaign for the free child was his campaign against 'edifying children's literature'; instead of, for example, Harriet Martineau's stories designed to illustrate economic principles, he asserted the child's right to works of imagination and fairy-tales. He continually stressed the value of out-of-school freedom, writing in 1845:

[is not] too little value . . . set upon the occupations of children out of doors. . . . I do not relish the words of one of the Reporters in which he would reconcile the Parents to the expense of having their Children educated in school by remarking that the wear and tear of clothes will be less; and an equivalent thus saved in shoe-leather.—Excuse this disagreement in opinion, as coming from one who spent half his boyhood in running wild among the Mountains.

It followed from Rousseau's theories that children, being nearer to nature, might 'know' more than adults, who had been miseducated. In Wordsworth's poetry we find adults 'learning' from children, and in the *Immortality Ode* the child is addressed as

Thou best Philosopher, who yet dost keep
Thy heritage, thou Eye among the blind,
That, deaf and silent, read'st the eternal deep
Haunted for ever by the eternal mind,—
     Mighty Prophet! Seer blest!
     On whom those truths do rest,
Which we are toiling all our lives to find.

These beliefs of Rousseau would have filtered down to Wordsworth in any case; like the cult of Feeling (see Jane Austen: *Sense and Sensibility*) they were part of the climate of opinion by the 1790s. But it is to be noted that the only doctrine of Rousseau's which Wordsworth uses *directly* after his return from France is that of 'the general will'—the 'will of the people' had produced the French Revolution, as Wordsworth explained in his *Letter to the Bishop of Llandaff*. By 1794 he seems to have had enough of undisciplined emotion and of the actions of Robespierre, Rousseau's fervent disciple; and therefore rushed to embrace a new philosophy of reason and nonviolence. 'Throw away your books of chemistry,' he tells a friend, 'and read Godwin on Necessity.'

Godwin, the philosophical anarchist

> The ideas of the author became more and more perspicuous and digested as his enquiries advanced.
>
> GODWIN, *Political Justice*

William Godwin (1756–1836) is now remembered chiefly as Shelley's second father-in-law and the author of *The Miner's Dream of Home*. In 1793 these attainments were far in the future, and his reputation was riding high: everyone was reading his recently published *Enquiry Concerning Political Justice*. The book had been written in haste, he charmingly tells us in the Preface, so that the first part was already at the printers before the second part was written. We are further disarmed by the lucid and persuasive style: surely the book has been much underestimated? Human beings have made so much progress since the beginnings of civilization, says Godwin, that nothing can now hinder the ultimate goal—the perfectibility of man. 'There is no science that is not capable of additions; there is no art that may not be carried to a still higher perfection.' Therefore the time would surely come when mind would control matter—he forecast a field being ploughed by remote control—and eventually Man would conquer sickness and become immortal.

Politically the book calls for the abolition of government, institutions, and also of private property. In the absolute reign of reason which is shortly to appear on earth anarchy will be a pleasant and co-operative state of affairs, since all men will be inspired to a joyful devotion to social duty and justice. Perhaps Godwin should be allowed to describe what would happen:

If justice reigned a state of equality would prevail. Labour would become light as rather to assume the appearance of agreeable relaxation and gentle exercise. Every man would have a frugal, yet wholesome diet; every man would go forth to that moderate exercise of his corporal functions that would give hilarity to the spirits. None would be made torpid with fatigue, but all would have leisure to cultivate the kindly and philanthropic affections and to let loose his faculties in the search of intellectual improvement. How rapid would be the advances of intellect, if all men were admitted into the field of knowledge. And the moral progress would be as great as the intellectual. The vices which are inseparably joined to the present system of property would inevitably expire in a state of society where all shared alike the bounties of nature. The narrow principle of selfishness would vanish. No man being obliged to guard his little store, or provide, with anxiety and pain, for his restless wants, each would lose his individual existence in the thought of general good. No man would be an enemy to his neighbour, for they would have no subject of contention, and of consequence philanthropy would resume the empire which reason assigns her.

Progress towards this happy state would be hindered by revolution; some of those who read his book might have been inspired to take some practical action, so in order to make clear his position Godwin produced a pamphlet in 1795 entitled *Considerations on Lord Grenville's and Mr. Pitt's Bills* in which he supported the government's repression of 'agitators and democrats'. This is not so hypocritical as it sounds for Godwin hated violence and war. His book was just the message that the English liberals were waiting for, now that they were disillusioned by Robespierre, frightened by Pitt's attempts to repress 'sedition', yet still unwilling to support the war with France. In June 1794 Wordsworth told his friend Matthews that

The destruction of those Institutions which I condemn appears to me to be hastening on too rapidly. I recoil from the bare idea of a Revolution. . . . Every enlightened friend of mankind . . . should diffuse by every method a knowledge of [the] rules of political justice. . . .

After this need I add that I am a determined enemy to every species of violence?

Godwin also offered guidance on moral problems; we must always look to the general good, calculate the consequences of the courses of action open to us, and arrive at an unbiased decision. We should never allow ourselves to be swayed by our feelings. This, again, sounds at first very attractive and in Wordsworth's mind 'found ready welcome' (*Prelude* 1805, x, 806 ff). Unfortunately, Godwin's illustrative examples give the game away. A house is burning down; it contains an intellectual and a chambermaid; which one should we save first? In this case an enlightened friend of mankind would save the intellectual because of his potential influence on thousands of human minds; the chambermaid is advised to devote herself willingly to the flames! Some are evidently more equal than others in this system of justice; let us consider another example. Let us imagine that I have the misfortune to be born or to have settled in Portugal; being an enlightened philosopher I dislike the institutions there; should I try to change them by political subversion? Godwin is not pleased with that idea: I might compromise my sincerity by acting in an underhand manner. Should I then speak out and invite martyrdom? Oh dear no! says Godwin: 'an enlightened person ought by no consideration to be prevailed upon to settle in Portugal; and, if he were there already, ought to quit the country with all convenient speed'. This is not just avoiding violence—it is simply avoiding the issue.

But Godwin's teaching on crime and punishment is years ahead of its time. If our actions are necessary, that is, the result of all the preceding circumstances, then the criminal is not 'guilty'; he is the inevitable product of an unenlightened social system. Wordsworth rewrote *Guilt and Sorrow* to conform to this teaching, and in *Lyrical Ballads* we are invited to contemplate *The Dungeon* and *The Convict* from a Godwinian viewpoint; criminals are to be re-educated and placed in surroundings conducive to this end.

Wordsworth soon became disillusioned with most of Godwin's ideas. They did not seem to square with his experience of real people; there was something inhuman about Godwin's conclusion that 'the virtuous man, in proportion to his improvement, will be under the constant influence of fixed and invariable principles'. Wordsworth's tragedy, *The Borderers*, shows what happens when one trusts to reason rather than the feelings. For Godwin taught that one should ignore even the most obvious emotions, such as filial piety and gratitude: 'Gratitude—a principle which has so often been the theme of the moralist and the poet, is no part of either justice or virtue.' Wordsworth later countered by writing *Simon Lee, the Old Huntsman*, of which the theme *is* gratitude:

> Alas! the gratitude of men
> Hath oftener left me mourning.

But in 1795 and 1796, after seeking the answers to his problems from Godwin's book and finding none, Wordsworth had come to a full stop: he had become 'Sick, wearied out with contrarieties' (*Prelude* 1805, x, 900–1) and finally 'yielded up moral questions in despair'.

It was about this time that Wordsworth met Coleridge (1772–1834), whom we are considering in this chapter as an important English philosopher rather than as a poet. Coleridge had not yet evolved his own system, and in many respects his development had run parallel to Wordsworth's. He had been so moved by reading *Political Justice* that in 1794 he had decided to found a Godwinian state in a remote part of America. Twelve males and twelve females—Godwin had objected to the ties of conventional marriage—would hold their property in common, as in the ideal republic described by Plato (whence Pantisocracy, which literally means 'all equal government'). But Coleridge's ideas were constantly changing; by 1797 he had finished with Godwinism, and during the time that he was constantly with Wordsworth at Alfoxden, his conversation (or 'monoversation') was full of references to Hartley, Berkeley and Spinoza. Of these the most important was Hartley, after whom he had named his first son.

Hartley and the association of ideas

> With my best efforts to be as perspicuous as the nature of language will permit on such a subject, I earnestly solicit the good wishes and friendly patience of my readers, while I thus go 'sounding on my dim and perilous way'.
>
> S. T. COLERIDGE, in *Biographia Literaria*, about to embark on a description of Hartley's 'system'

David Hartley (1705–57) was a disciple of Locke, and it is reasonable to assume that Wordsworth, like Coleridge, had read his work while studying at Cambridge, or just afterwards. Hartley's *Observations on Man, His Frame, His Duty and His Expectations*, first published in 1749, had recently been reprinted. His 'system' was founded on the principle of the Association of Ideas, a principle which had been recognized by the Greeks and by Locke, but which Hartley used to explain everything. Sense impressions produced vibrations within the brain; two impressions received simultaneously would be linked and a later stimulus which recalled one would also recall the other. (See Wordsworth's poem: *There was a Boy* for an illustration of this.) The mind was a machine which worked by association—'all reasoning, as well as affection, is the mere result of association'. Hartley's philosophy was in fact an early form of the twentieth-century scheme of mental association known as Behaviourism (Pavlov's dogs were taught to salivate at the sound of an electric bell), and if writing today he would presumably have compared the brain to a computer. The point to notice in this mechanistic philosophy is that the mind is thought of as *passive*:

> The eye it cannot choose but see,
> We cannot bid the ear be still;

Our bodies feel, where'er they be,
Against, or with our will.
Expostulation and Reply, 1798

Of course, when we test Hartley's philosophy against experience an immediate problem comes to mind: why is it that we are so often unable to link a face with a name or remember the title of a book we were reading only last week? If the brain is a machine, why do the most obvious associations sometimes escape us? Hartley tries to explain:

When a person desires to recollect a thing that has escaped him, suppose the name of a person, or visible object, he recalls the visible idea, or some other associate, again and again, by a voluntary power, the desire usually magnifying all the ideas and associations; and thus bringing in the association and idea wanted, at last. However, if the desire be great, it changes the state of the brain, and has an opposite effect; so that the desired idea does not recur, till all has subsided; perhaps not even then.

This curiously lame explanation seems not to have bothered Wordsworth, who adapted the system to his own purposes. The association of sense impressions with moral ideas forms the principle on which *The Prelude* is constructed. Wordsworth explains how the associations of early childhood help us in later life:

So feeling comes in aid
Of feeling, and diversity of strength
Attends us, if but once we have been strong.
Prelude 1805, xi, 326–8

The long extract, which is printed in the Critical Survey, p. 145, should be studied before embarking on the vivid descriptions of the first two books of *The Prelude*; it explains why the childhood memories are to be treasured.

Locke had thought that there were meaningless and trivial associations, but after Hartley's philosophy had been reinterpreted by Wordsworth, this objection was refuted. Nature, we shall see, chooses good associations for her children; even those which appear bad will ultimately be good. Association also influenced Wordsworth's poetic theory. He classified his poems on Hartleian principles, e.g. Imagination, Affection, Sentiment and Reflection, and in the *Preface to Lyrical Ballads* he explained that one of the functions of poetry is to show how 'we associate ideas in a state of excitement'; Wordsworth did not expect his poems to 'gratify certain known habits of association'—he will provide new associations and 'create the taste by which he is to be enjoyed'.

At the same time that Coleridge was discussing Hartley with Wordsworth he was also constantly urging him to write 'a philosophic poem'—'No man was ever yet a great poet without being at the same time a profound philosopher'. But it was never suggested that Wordsworth should simply versify Coleridge's ideas. The two poets were intellectual equals; if anything, Coleridge deferred to Wordsworth. Their views were only approximately the same, and they differed over Christianity. Coleridge was absorbed in discussing minute points of religion, and found Wordsworth's lack of interest in the subject difficult to understand—he called him a 'semi-Atheist'. Wordsworth, on the other hand, placed more value on Nature as a religious and moral agent; he began those speculations about the meaning and direction of his own life which eventually built up into *The Prelude*. A brief excursion in July 1798 provided Wordsworth with an opportunity to summarize these new ideas in *Lines Written a Few Miles Above Tintern Abbey, on Revisiting the Banks of the Wye During a Tour, July 13th 1798*. This poem was written immediately after the experience it describes—most unusual for Wordsworth—and owes its style and structure to Coleridge's *Frost at Midnight*. The ideas behind it are partly derived from Hartley's chapter on *The Pleasures and Pains of the Imagination*, which explained that— 'the grandeur of some [natural] scenes, and the novelty of others, by exciting surprise and wonder [makes] a great difference in the preceding and subsequent states of mind'; he also contrasted 'the offensiveness, dangers, and corruption of populous cities, and the health, tranquillity and innocence which the actual view, or *mental contemplation*, of rural scenes introduces'.

Hartley concluded his observations on natural beauty by stressing that although such scenes 'strike the young mind with pleasure', it is only '*after a considerable time*' that the responses rise to their maximum; the poem in fact deals with an interval of five years. In the end, said Hartley, 'the pleasures of imagination must decline'—but Wordsworth, although recognizing the possibility in *Tintern Abbey*—was not to face up to this fact until the time of the *Immortality Ode*.

Wordsworth's 'Creed' 1798–1805

> Egro vivida vis animi pervicit, et extra
> processit longe flammantia moenia mundi
> atque omne immensum peragravit mente animoque.

(Therefore the lively power of his mind prevailed and he journeyed far out beyond the flaming walls of the world, and traversed infinity in his intellect and imagination.)

LUCRETIUS, *De Rerum Natura*, i, 72–4.

There is, of course, far more in *Tintern Abbey* than Hartley. Wordsworth was already constructing his own philosophy in a series of blank verse effusions which were incorporated in *The Prelude*. Quite simply,

Wordsworth took the materialist philosophy of Locke and Hartley which had sufficed the eighteenth century, and changed round the terms, writing in positive instead of negative signs. Instead of a dead universe described in terms of machines from which the Creator had departed, he proposed a living universe called 'Nature' described in terms of growth and organic life, which was being continuously created by a God who was inextricably involved in all its parts. Whereas in Locke the mind at birth was 'a white paper', with no innate ideas, in Wordsworth the mind retains in early childhood some consciousness of a pre-existent state; in Locke the mind *passively* receives impressions from the senses, but in Wordsworth the mind *actively* perceives and a creative power within the mind organizes the multitude of chaotic sense impressions into a partial picture of the world. But it is necessary for the individual mind to cooperate with the external Mind in Nature; the two minds are related and together they create the world—in *Tintern Abbey* the beholder loves

> the mighty world
> Of eye, and ear,—both what they *half create*,
> And what perceive—
>
> lines 104–6

Finally, in moments of vision the internal mind 'goes out' into the external Mind; they communicate through new kinds of sense experience—this is what the 'sublime' passages in *Tintern Abbey* and *The Prelude* are about.

It is of course true that there are parallels to certain of these ideas in Greek and Roman philosophies, in Eastern religions, in the writings of mystics and in eighteenth century sublime poetry, and well-read and inquiring students like Wordsworth and Coleridge could not have avoided hearing about them. In Berkeley's *Siris*, for example—we know Coleridge was passing through a Berkeley phase as he named his second son, born in 1798, after him—we read that 'there is according to those philosophies (Platonic and Stoic) a life infused throughout all things'. The jump to 'interfused' is not difficult. But if we exaggerate the earlier parallels to the announcement made in *Tintern Abbey* and *The Prelude* we lose sight of Wordsworth's purpose and of his originality in terms of the philosophic situation in 1798.

Nor is there much to be gained from explanations of Wordsworth's ideas which imply that he was in some way different from ourselves. If we *begin* by saying 'Wordsworth was a mystic, therefore. . .', or 'Wordsworth was a poetic genius, therefore. . .' or, as in recent years, 'Wordsworth was psychologically abnormal, possibly mad, and certainly strange . . .' we deceive ourselves; it is flattering to think that we have *explained* Wordsworth, and need therefore pay no attention *to what he says*. We are hiding from the attack presented by the plain statements of a normal and intelligent human being.

Furthermore, I do not see that fastening a label from ancient philosophy upon Wordsworth—in this case to call him a 'Pantheist'—is particularly helpful; we are simply consigning him to a museum of dead ideas. To *label* anything, whether an idea or a person, is frequently a method of *blocking* inquiry, of avoiding the difficulty of actually looking for ourselves; it is a way of shunning mental adventure. And this is exactly the quality which Wordsworth excels in. In 1798 it took amazing moral courage to publish a poem which said 'the world is alive'.

Wordsworth's achievement has also been devalued by attributing all his ideas to Coleridge. But the first written reference to the new philosophy occurs in 1794, before the two poets had met. In preparing *An Evening Walk* for a possible new edition, Wordsworth writes of

> A heart that vibrates evermore, awake
> To feeling for all forms that Life can take,
> That wider still its sympathy extends
> And sees not any line where being ends;
> Sees sense, through Nature's rudest forms betrayed,
> Tremble obscure in fountain, rock and shade.

In *The Prelude*, (though one could argue that Wordsworth is writing *after* meeting Coleridge), he tells us that he felt these emotions as early as 1787:

> I felt the sentiment of Being spread
> O'er all that moves, and all that seemeth still,
> O'er all, that, lost beyond the reach of thought
> And human knowledge, to the human eye
> Invisible, yet liveth to the heart,
> O'er all that leaps, and runs, and shouts, and sings,
> Or beats the gladsome air, o'er all that glides
> Beneath the wave, yea, in the wave itself
> And mighty depth of waters. Wonder not
> If such my transports were; for in all things
> I saw one life, and felt that it was joy.
>
> *Prelude* 1805, ii, 420–430

At Cambridge he developed these ideas until

> To every natural form, rock, fruit or flower,
> Even the loose stones that cover the highway,
> I gave a moral life, I saw them feel,
> Or link'd them to some feeling: the great mass
> Lay bedded in a quickening soul. . . .
>
> *Prelude* 1805, iii, 124–8

The Prelude, which is, in fact, the nearest thing to the great philosophical poem which Coleridge hoped Wordsworth would produce, was mostly written while Coleridge was in Malta, and it is as an exposition of Wordsworth's ideas that we must read it; for Coleridge, as we shall see, had already begun to return to Orthodox Christianity and in 1803 was shocked at Wordsworth's irreverence: 'O dearest William! Would Ray or Durham have spoken of God as you spoke of Nature?'

The theme of *The Prelude* is the growth of the individual mind under the guidance of the Mind of external Nature. The Babe is

> An inmate of this *active* universe;
> From nature largely he receives; nor so
> Is satisfied, but largely gives again,
> For feeling has to him imparted strength,
> And powerful in all sentiments of grief,
> Of exultation, fear, and joy, his mind,
> Even as an agent of the one great mind,
> Creates, creator and receiver both . . .
>
> *Prelude* 1805, ii, 266–73

Wordsworth explains how his own mind slowly arrived at maturity, how he dedicated himself to poetry, and how after being diverted by Cambridge, France and Godwinism, his imagination was restored, a vision of the eternal Mind granted to him on Snowdon (*Prelude* 1805, xiii, 1–119) and his poetic vocation assured. It is a 'heroic poem', even though, as Wordsworth admitted, 'it was a thing unprecedented in literary history that a man should talk so much about himself'. The hero of modern times is *the individual*, and Wordsworth only knew one individual well enough to write about—himself!

The whole poem radiates a feeling of new life, of active exploration of a new-found universe. Wordsworth writes as if he is a new kind of human being, like Adam naming the creatures for the first time. This sense of exultation, of 'man's unconquerable mind', was not to last. Wordsworth lived by his beliefs for eight years, but in 1805 he was so shaken by the death of his brother John that his self-sufficiency collapsed. For a time he adopted a Stoical attitude to outface suffering, but this only brought on middle age prematurely. We shall follow his change of course towards religious belief in the next section.

But Wordsworth's achievement in these eight years cannot be written off, even though the poet himself tried, as the years went by, to minimize it. He had made an attempt to overthrow the eighteenth-century system of materialism and this attempt, with Coleridge's help, succeeded. In the effort of battering down the wall of the old order Wordsworth suffered some damage; very frequently the pioneers of new ideas hurt themselves in making the breach through which others will rush gaily (and take the credit!). Wordsworth had been exhausted by his efforts as early as 1804 (see *Ode to Duty*), and he would probably have returned to conventional pieties and religion even if his brother's death had not accelerated to process. After 1805 the flood of ideas poured on past Wordsworth, without him; for *The Prelude* was not published until 1850. It was left to Coleridge to schematize and to elucidate, to pilot through the new philosophy into the minds of the next generation.

Looking down on the clouds, Snowdonia

Coleridge's development after 1798 was roughly parallel to that of Wordsworth, though he was always more concerned to make his opinions square with Christianity. Coleridge tells us that after he 'had successively studied in the schools of Locke, Berkeley, Leibnitz, and Hartley and could find in none of them an abiding place for [his] reason' (*Biographia Literaria*, ix) he discovered in Germany the writings of 'the illustrious sage of Koenigsberg': Immanuel Kant. In March 1801 he announced that Hartley was 'overthrown' and that 'Newton was a mere materialist. *Mind*, in his system, is always *passive*—a lazy *Looker-on* on an external world.' Having cleared away the relics of the eighteenth century, Coleridge substituted the doctrine of the Imagination, the creative power within the mind, with which we actively perceive and make our world. In this way he saw that Man was truly made in the Image of God: 'The primary Imagination I hold to be the living power and prime agent of all human perception, and as a repetition in the finite mind of the eternal act of creation in the infinite I AM' (*Biographia Literaria*, xiii).

The way was now open to an Orthodox Christian philosophy which would contain psychology, history and poetry within it, and which would emphasize the Middle Ages; it would lead to the Gothic Revival, and, finally, the Oxford Movement (see 'Final religious position' below). Although Coleridge never produced the great metaphysical work which he had always intended, he passed on his ideas by lectures, journalism and conversation. John Stuart Mill's essay on Coleridge clearly indicates the wide extent of this influence, calling him one of the 'great seminal minds of England'.

But Wordsworth, 'having never read a word of German metaphysics, thank Heaven', travelled towards religious belief on a lonelier road, like Christian in the Valley of the Shadow of Death. It seems appropriate to bridge the transition into the next section with a long appreciation of Wordsworth written by John Keats in a letter of May 1818, in which he puts Wordsworth above Milton as a 'philosopher'; Keats's judgments are usually right!

I will return to Wordsworth—whether or no he has an extended vision or a circumscribed grandeur—whether he is an eagle in his nest, or on the wing. And to be more explicit and to show you how tall I stand by the giant, I will put down a simile of human life as far as I now perceive it; that is, to the point to which I say we both have arrived at. Well—I compare human life to a large Mansion of Many Apartments, two of which I can only describe, the doors of the rest being as yet shut upon me. The first we step into we call the infant or thoughtless Chamber, in which we remain as long as we do not think . . . we no sooner get into the second Chamber, which I shall call the Chamber of Maiden-Thought, than we become intoxicated with the light and the atmosphere, we see nothing but pleasant wonders, and think of delaying there for ever in delight. However, among the effects this breathing is father

of is that tremendous one of sharpening one's vision into the heart
and nature of Man—of convincing one's nerves that the world is
full of Misery and Heartbreak, Pain, Sickness and oppression—
whereby this Chamber of Maiden-Thought becomes gradually
darken'd and at the same time on all sides of it many doors are
set open—but all dark—all leading to dark passages. We see not
the balance of good and evil. We are in a Mist. *We* are now in that
state—We feel the 'burden of the Mystery'. To this point was
Wordsworth come, as far as I can conceive when he wrote 'Tintern
Abbey' and it seems to me that his Genius is explorative of those
dark Passages. . . . Here I must think Wordsworth is deeper than
Milton, though I think it has depended more upon the general and
gregarious advance of intellect, than individual greatness of Mind.
From the Paradise Lost and the other Works of Milton, I hope it
is not too presuming, even between ourselves to say, that his
Philosophy, human and divine, may be tolerably understood by
one not much advanced in years . . . He did not think into the
human heart, as Wordsworth has done.

Return to the Anglican Church 1805—20

> Nor will *they* implore
> In vain who, for a rightful cause, give breath
> To words the Church prescribes aiding the lip
> For the heart's sake. . . .

WORDSWORTH, Forms of Prayer at Sea

It is most unlikely that Wordsworth ever thought of his philosophical
ideas as a 'Creed'; later he said that we are not supposed to take literally
his reference to himself in *Tintern Abbey* as 'a worshipper of Nature'.
This, he points out in a letter of December 1814, was 'a passionate
expression uttered incautiously'. He goes on to explain that he was
never a follower of Spinoza (the seventeenth-century philosopher,
who identified God with Nature). It would be easy to put this 1814
statement down to the cowardice of a middle-aged civil servant
ashamed of his youthful indiscretion, were it not for the amazing
passage which follows. One would expect the older Wordsworth to
trot out the arguments of the Established Church at this point: instead
he says he does

not indeed consider the supreme Being as bearing the same
relation to the Universe as a watch-maker bears to a watch. In fact,
there is nothing in the course of religious education adopted in this
country, in the use made by us of the Holy Scriptures that appears
to me so injurious as the perpetually talking about *making* by God
—Oh! that your Correspondent had heard a conversation which I

had in bed with my sweet little boy, four and a half years old, upon this subject the other morning. 'How did God make me? Where is God? How does he speak? He never spoke to *me*.' I told him that God was a spirit, that he was not like his flesh, which he could touch; but more like his thoughts, in his mind, which he could not touch. The wind was tossing the fir trees and the sky and light were dancing about in their dark branches, as seen through the window. Noting these fluctuations, he exclaimed eagerly, 'there's a bit of him I see it there!' This is not meant entirely for Father's prattle. . . .

Perhaps what Wordsworth is trying to say is not as unorthodox as it may sound. We are used to the traditional emphasis placed in Christian teaching on the *transcendence* of God, on His detachment from the world which He has created. Wordsworth emphasizes the *Immanence* of God, that is, His presence in Nature; to say that Nature is *permeated* by God is perfectly orthodox—the Roman Catholic poet and Jesuit priest, Gerard Manley Hopkins, wrote a sonnet beginning 'The world is charged with the grandeur of God'.

In the letter quoted above Wordsworth reiterated that he never said that God is Nature, or that Nature and God are the same; what he (and Hopkins) stressed was 'the indwelling spirit'. Theologically-minded critics have pointed out the Christian precedents to Wordsworth's view of Nature. They say he was looking for evidence of *natura naturans*, 'all-creating nature', rather than *natura naturata*, 'the made world'; in certain seventeenth- and eighteenth-century writing of unimpeachable orthodoxy reference is made to *anima mundi*, a spirit pervading the world and supplying the continuing presence of God. What is this other than the 'Spirit far more deeply interfused' of *Tintern Abbey*, or *The Prelude's* 'Wisdom and Spirit of the Universe'?

In this way one could go on to save—or salvage—a number of Wordsworth's apparently unorthodox poems in the interests of Christianity. But difficulties arise which are inherent in the nature of poetry itself. Most Romantic poetry depends not on statement but on suggestion and metaphor, whether concise, concrete and verbal, as in Keats and Hopkins, or diffuse, abstracted and structural, as in Shelley and Wordsworth. And if Wordsworth is simply *describing one thing in terms of another*, then the case for a 'Christian' *Tintern Abbey* or 1805 *Prelude* breaks down. Surely the *language of religion* is being used to direct us towards a new kind of philosophy, for which no language of its own exists. Wordsworth's use of religious vocabulary may be ambiguous, to say the least.

This ambiguity of language helps to explain why so many interpretations of Wordsworth's philosophy and religion were able to arise. If one read the linguistic signs as pointing to something vaguely beyond the poem, to 'Something evermore about to be' (*Prelude* 1805, vi, 542), then the poetry could be used to support innumerable creeds. But if we study the use of religious language in Wordsworth's poems between 1798 and 1820 we see a gradual change from what might be

86

meant metaphorically or 'poetically' (Wordsworth said that he employed the pre-existence theme in the *Immortality Ode* 'as a Poet') towards language that is used *literally* and in an orthodox Christian sense. (The many later alterations to *The Prelude* move in this direction too.) In his poetry, Wordsworth uses the language of faith years before his 'prose mind' can accept Christian doctrine; this is why his 'conversion' is impossible to date, and why there is so much divergence between the poetic and prose statements he may make at any stage in his progress.

In 1798, then, at the conclusion of *Tintern Abbey*, we find phrases indicative of the future—'blessings', 'zeal of holier love', 'Shall e'er prevail against us'; in *Resolution and Independence* (1802) we hear of 'peculiar grace./ A leading from above, a something given', and 'a Man from some far region sent'. These point out of this world, but where *to* is not made clear. Later in 1802 on the way to France, 'Dear God!', in the penultimate line of the *Sonnet: Composed upon Westminster Bridge*, may be an exclamation, but in August 1802 his blessing on his daughter Caroline is undoubtedly surrounded by Christian references.

> It is a beauteous Evening, calm and free,
> The holy time is quiet as a Nun
> Breathless with adoration; the broad sun
> Is sinking down in its tranquillity;
> The gentleness of heaven is on the Sea;
> Listen! the mighty Being is awake,
> And doth with his eternal motion make
> A sound like thunder—everlastingly.
> Dear Child! dear Girl! that walkest with me here,
> If thou appear'st untouched by solemn thought,
> Thy nature is not therefore less divine:
> Thou liest in Abraham's bosom all the year;
> And worshipp'st at the Temple's inner shrine,
> God being with thee when we know it not.

How far is this to be taken simply as metaphorical language?

By 1804 Wordsworth had embraced an attitude usually described as Stoical—his poems refer more and more to the virtue of endurance in the face of suffering, age and death (*Michael, The Small Celandine, Resolution and Independence, Ode to Duty*). In the *Immortality Ode* (1804) he declares

> We will grieve not, rather find
> Strength in what remains behind;
> In the primal sympathy
> Which having been must ever be;
> In the soothing thoughts that spring
> Out of human suffering;

> In the faith that looks through death,
> In years that bring the philosophic mind.

In these lines 'the primal sympathy' seems to represent all that is left of the relation bwtween Man and Nature; 'the philosophic mind', on the other hand, is a direct reference to Roman Stoicism.

Nevertheless, the language of the *Immortality Ode* offended many liberal critics who had up to then been sympathetic to Wordsworth's poetry. They were not clear how to take lines like

> trailing clouds of glory do we come
> From God, who is our home:
> Heaven lies about us in our infancy!

Even though learned readers took this as a reference to Platonic, rather than Christian belief, there appeared to be something Biblical about the 'young lambs' and 'the tabor's sound'. And the *Ode to Duty*, with its opening lines

> Stern Daughter of the Voice of God!
> O Duty! if that name thou love
> Who art a Light to guide, a Rod. . .

sounds as if it might have been written by an Old Testament Prophet.

The death of Wordsworth's brother John in the spring of 1805 destroyed any remaining illusions. In the *Elegiac Stanzas* (see Critical Survey, p. 152) the picture of Peele Castle fronting the storm seems an apt image of Stoical defiance in a hostile universe:

> And this huge Castle, standing here sublime,
> I love to see the look with which it braves,
> Cased in the unfeeling armour of old time,
> The lightning, the fierce wind, and trampling waves.

Having stated that his earlier life was misdirected, and his poetry the product of 'fond illusion', Wordsworth concludes with a decision to

> welcome fortitude, and patient cheer,
> And frequent sights of what is to be borne!
> Such sights, or worse, as are before me here—
> Not without hope we suffer and we mourn.

The first three lines of this are exaggerated Stoicism; but what is the 'hope' of the casually thrown-in last line? 'Batter my heart, three-person'd God', wrote John Donne; it seems that Wordsworth has decided, his spirit broken, to try the Christian 'hope' of personal immortality.

The difficulty is that the letters written at the time by Wordsworth, while full of references to 'God' and 'fortitude', can hardly be described as pious. He contrasts the moral ideas of humanity with those of the deity, who is described in terms reminiscent of Voltaire: 'Why have we sympathies that make the best of us so afraid of inflicting pain and sorrow, which yet we see dealt about so lavishly by the supreme governor?' Nevertheless, in 1806, staying at the house of his friend Sir George Beaumont, Wordsworth began to go to church again, even though he was not a regular attender.

The next stage of his personal beliefs is obscure. *The White Doe of Rylstone* (written 1807–8) is a very difficult poem, containing a sympathetic account of the Catholic Rising in the North in 1569. The rebel banner is made by the one Protestant daughter of the Catholic Norton family, who endures a lonely life after the failure of the rising and the death of her brothers and father. She is visited by a Doe, which radiates sanctity; the point of the poem, says Wordsworth, is 'nothing less than the Apotheosis of the Animal'. I must confess that I have not the least idea what this phrase could mean in an orthodox Christian context. But the poem appears to commend long-suffering endurance and to suggest that mourners may be silently visited by Divine Grace. The relevance of this to Wordsworth's personal bereavement is clear.

While *The Excursion* (1814) contains a Pastor and a Churchyard, the Christianity it offers is still minimal; Wordsworth himself says that it illustrates 'the Bible of the Universe, as it speaks to the ear of the intelligent'. Yet it was the poem that brought Wordsworth to the notice of clerics in need of sermon material (his poems were used for this purpose throughout the last century, and I have heard them used in this). In 1820 Wordsworth saw that 'the Church was in danger' owing to the debates on Catholic emancipation, that is the restoration to Roman Catholics of full civil rights; he therefore produced the *Ecclesiastical Sonnets* (or *Sketches*) as a contribution to the controversy, a hymn in defence of the Established Church. He continued to give public support to the Church of England for the rest of his life. While there were clearly political motives involved, there seems no reason to doubt his sincerity.

Final religious position

> For I must tread on shadowy ground, must sink
> Deep—and aloft ascending, breathe in worlds
> To which the heaven of heavens is but a veil.
> All strength—all terror, single or in bands,
> That ever was put forth in personal form—
> Jehovah—with his thunder, and the choir
> Of shouting Angels, and the empyreal thrones—
> I pass them unalarmed.

> Preface to *The Excursion*

In general Blake loves the poems. What appears to have disturbed his mind, on the other hand, is the Preface to *The Excursion*. He told me, six months ago, that it caused him a stomach complaint, which nearly killed him. When I first saw Blake at Mrs Aders', he very earnestly asked me, 'Is Mr Wordsworth a sincere, real Christian?' In reply to my answer he said, 'If so, what does he mean by the worlds to which the heaven of heavens is but a veil? and who is he that shall pass Jehovah unalarmed?'

CRABB ROBINSON, Diary

Assessments of Wordsworth's final religious position are amazingly various; he has been called Atheist, Nature Worshipper, Stoic and Orthodox Anglican, besides being hailed as a precursor of the Anglo-Catholic Oxford Movement. One way of solving the difficulty is to postulate a Wordsworth who passed through all these stages in turn (and in this chapter I have described his beliefs in approximately this order); the progress from non-belief through paganism to Orthodoxy may be compared to the development from caterpillar to chrysalis to butterfly—to paraphrase the loaded remarks of one critic.

Such a neat pattern is useful to hold on to, and gives a tidy-minded impression; but while it agrees with the general weight of the evidence, it must be regarded with caution. The case for the young Wordsworth's 'nature religion' or 'Pantheism' will not stand up to deep probing; for example *Hartleap Well* (see Critical Survey, p. 130) was always taken to be a 'pagan document'; now that attention has been called to the parallel passage in *Home at Grasmere* (also in Critical Survey, p. 130), we find that it is about 'God' after all—and these poems date from 1800. On the other hand, the supposedly orthodox later Wordsworth will occasionally give utterance to the most surprising remarks, for example: 'Theologians may puzzle their heads about dogmas as they will, the religion of gratitude cannot mislead us' (1825). Nor does one expect to be told that the Church should not have committed itself to such 'needless and mischievous attempts at explanation as the Athanasian Creed, [which is] an unhappy excrescence'. Human beings are not, in fact, as consistent as they like to think. We could agree that Wordsworth was capable of holding all the above-mentioned beliefs in his mind at once, and state that one or other of them rose to the surface according to the circumstances, for example, Stoicism after his brother's death, and the 'religion of gratitude' passage just quoted, after a season of fine spring weather! But a more serious argument advanced by some critics is that Wordsworth only 'appears to travel' through a variety of religious experiences. In reality, according to this theory, Wordsworth was always a High Anglican deep down.

There is a great deal of evidence to support this viewpoint. Wordsworth was brought up in a Church of England environment; his earliest memories of his mother are about church ceremonies. He was destined for holy orders, and only abandoned the Church as a vocation in 1792; his brother Christopher's ecclesiastical career, ending as Master of Trinity, gives rise to interesting speculations—what might not Wordsworth have become? In 1802 he married an Anglican wife and had his children christened. So one might go on, piling fact on fact.

But, of course, it won't do. One has only to look at the poems of Wordsworth's great period (1798–1807); so many of them are concerned with religious themes—to use the word in the widest sense—with topics such as death, human survival, endurance, old age, childhood, joy, existence in its every meaning. And on all these points Wordsworth is a great teacher, trying to change basic attitudes, to refashion human nature. Yet nowhere is there any reference—worth taking seriously—to Christ or the Cross. This is not difficult to explain; Wordsworth shared the general Romantic belief, inherited from Rousseau, in the natural goodness of Man; there is no room in this philosophy for the doctrines of Original Sin and of Christ's atoning Sacrifice. As late as 1815 Wordsworth maintained that he himself had no need of a Redeemer.

I prefer, therefore, to go along with what I have already referred to as the general weight of the evidence. In the preceding section we traced Wordsworth's return to a 'minimal Christianity' which is the nearest thing I can detect to a consistent religious position. We must now glance at the background of religious controversy in the first half of the nineteenth century, and examine Wordsworth's attitude towards the contending parties.

It seems appropriate to list the many Christian sects of the time and outline Wordsworth's attitude towards them, starting with the Roman Catholics and ending with the extreme Protestant movements. Where no special comment is made, it is to be assumed that the position of each denomination is roughly the same as today.

At the beginning of the nineteenth century the Roman Catholic Church was not officially recognized in England and its members had been second class citizens since the Reformation. To readmit the English Catholics to public life was not really the problem; there was the difficulty of the Anglican Church of Ireland. If its official position as the State Church were compromised, this would be a defeat for Protestantism. In 1808 Wordsworth said that he was 'not prepared to see the Catholic religion as the Established Church of Ireland'. This contrasts with the sympathy shown in *The White Doe of Rylstone*, and also with the following passage from a letter of 1829 (the year of Catholic emancipation); while living in Ireland Wordsworth observed a mother dipping her child in St Kevin's pool;

What would one not give to see among Protestants such devout reliance on the mercy of their Creator, so much resignation, so much piety, so much simplicity and singleness of mind, purged of the accompanying superstitions!

Wordsworth is, for his time, surprisingly tolerant of Roman

Catholic ideas. It is difficult to decide from where this sympathy springs, unless perhaps from his memories of Annette and Caroline Vallon. Who would expect to find in 1821 a Protestant writing a sonnet in praise of the Virgin Mary:

> Mother! whose virgin bosom was uncrost
> With the least shade of thought to sin allied;
> Woman! above all women glorified,
> Our tainted nature's solitary boast;
> Purer than foam on central ocean tost;
> Brighter than eastern skies at daybreak strewn
> With fancied roses, than the unblemished moon
> Before her wane begins on heaven's blue coast;
> Thy Image falls to earth. Yet some, I ween,
> Not unforgiven the suppliant knee might bend,
> As to a visible Power, in which did blend
> All that was mixed and reconciled in Thee
> Of mother's love with maiden purity,
> Of high with low, celestial with terrene!
> *Ecclesiastical Sonnets XXV: The Virgin*

Later Wordsworth was rightly to claim that he had anticipated the Oxford Movement, which aimed to reassert the Catholicity of the Church of England, by twenty years.

His sympathy with monasticism and the contemplative life is similarly remarkable. In 1837, in *The Cuckoo at Laverna*, he anticipated the modern revival of interest in St Francis of Assisi. In *The Tuft of Primroses*, a poem probably written in 1808, he discusses the call to the monastic life and translates passages of the letters of St Basil. Tintern Abbey is mentioned, and Fountains Abbey, Yorkshire, which will

> outlive the ravages of Time
> And bear the Cross till Christ shall come again.

It is perhaps appropriate that a later nineteenth-century poet, Aubrey de Vere, on visiting Gracedieu monastery in Leicestershire, found a portrait of Wordsworth placed among those of the Saints; the Abbot had chosen his way of life after reading *The Excursion*.

In the 'politics' of the Church of England, Wordsworth sided with the High Church party, in whose beliefs he had been brought up. This group looked back to the seventeenth-century era of Archbishop Laud, and had effectively controlled the chief offices (and the financial power) of the Establishement since the days of Queen Anne. His brother's rapid rise was the result of his support for this party. In the 1830s and 40s Keble, Pusey and Newman, stressing the Catholic aspect of the English Church, tried to convert the High Church party to their point of view; they were referred to as the Oxford Movement, the Tractarians, or the Anglo-Catholics. In spite of the fact that 'poetically' he had so often seemed to support them, Wordsworth would not give prose assent to their doctrines by writing a pamphlet on their behalf.

But the Anglo-Catholics made full use of Wordsworth. John Keble's *The Christian Year* (1827) has been aptly described as 'Wordsworth and water'; in 1842 an Oxford Movement Anthology appeared, called *Contributions of William Wordsworth to the Revival of Catholic Truths*; John Henry Newman, later Cardinal Newman, paid tribute to the work of Wordsworth, Scott and Coleridge in preparing the ground for his ideas, and in 1886 Gerard Manley Hopkins, a later product of the movement, praised the *Immortality Ode* as one of the very deepest insights 'in all history'.

Yet those who associated with Wordsworth in his later years were often liberal Christians, members of the Broad Church party of the Church of England. It is significant that Dr Thomas Arnold of Rugby, one of the main liberal spokesmen, chose to live near Wordsworth during the school holidays. The liberals wished to remove from the Anglican Church the theological lumber of the past and substitute modern and progressive ideas; they were also in favour of making up the quarrel with the nonconformists. In the later years of the nineteenth century the liberals discarded more and more Christian dogma: some became agnostics, and others developed a set of beliefs about Nature which became known as 'Wordsworthian'. The Wordsworthians are responsible for creating the image of the saintly but vague nature mystic—a picture of Wordsworth which leaves out so much that is important. Wordsworthianism grew in strength until it became a serious rival to orthodox Christianity. Like many of the gentler Victorian beliefs it never survived the Battle of the Somme.

So far we have ignored what is to most historians the most important movement of the age—Methodism, as it was termed outside the Church of England; within it, the party of the Evangelicals. In a generation English society was largely changed by the emotional religion of the Wesleys; the career of William Wilberforce, who was converted from a frivolous card-playing existence and devoted his energies to abolishing the slave trade, illustrates its effect on a single life. The Evangelicals were serious and earnest about all matters; they revived and revitalized the nonconformist churches besides strongly influencing a portion of the Church of England. To this movement Wordsworth was always antipathetic; but on their side they had no love for him. He made no reference to the Saving Blood of Christ; *The Excursion*, said one, was 'quite contrary to Christianity'. Wordsworth, in his turn, tried to keep Evangelicals out of the Lake District parishes.

The Lake Counties had always had a strong link with the Quakers (or Society of Friends) because it was there that their founder, George Fox, made some of his earliest converts. Ann Tyson, who looked after Wordsworth while he was at school, frequently took him to Quaker meetings, since the church at Hawkshead was a long way from the house. In later years Wordsworth became friendly with Thomas Wilkinson, a Quaker from Yanwath, near Penrith; he is commemorated in the poem which begins: 'Spade! with which Wilkinson hath tilled his lands. . .' This shows the Quaker directness of approach, even if it is not poetry! But the twenty-ninth sonnet of *The River Duddon* sequence, describing a lonely Quaker burial place, shows the later Wordsworth at his best:

> Yet, to the loyal and the brave, who lie
> In the blank earth, neglected and forlorn,
> The passing Winds memorial tribute pay;
> The Torrents chant their praise, inspiring scorn
> Of power usurped; with proclamation high,
> And glad acknowledgement, of lawful sway.

One cannot leave Wordsworth's religion without a glance at his final years. The visitor to Rydal Mount, after bumping into a boulder with the following inscription:

> Wouldst thou be gathered to Christ's chosen flock,
> Shun the broad way too easily explored,
> And let thy path be hewn out of the Rock,
> The living Rock of God's eternal Word

would find himself in a conventional household, where the master read morning and evening prayers to the assembled family and servants. One might be excused for wondering what the aged poet *really* believed. It is significant that what appears to be his last autograph, written in a shaky hand in a young girl's album, is the final passage of the *Immortality Ode*, which teaches us to live by 'the human heart'. These words recur so often in Wordsworth's work that they seem to represent an unwavering core of faith. 'All religions', he wrote in 1824, 'owe their origin or acceptation to the wish of the human heart to supply in another existence the deficiencies of this.' 'If my writings are to last,' he said in 1835, '. . . they will please for the single cause, "That we have all of us one human heart".' Keats, as we saw in the last chapter, concluded with the same emphasis. It seems only fair to allow Wordsworth the last word.

> The Clouds that gather round the setting sun
> Do take a sober colouring from an eye
> That hath kept watch o'er man's mortality;
> Another race hath been, and other palms are won.
> Thanks to the human heart by which we live,
> Thanks to its tenderness, its joys, and fears,
> To me the meanest flower that blows can give
> Thoughts that do often lie too deep for tears.

4 Wordsworth and his audience

I will not take upon me to determine the exact import of the promise which by the act of writing in verse an Author, in the present day, makes to his Reader; but I am certain it will appear to many persons that I have not fulfilled the terms of an engagement thus voluntarily contracted.

WORDSWORTH, *Preface to Lyrical Ballads*

Dorothy Wordsworth, from a portrait at Dove Cottage

Introductory note

Wordsworth could have done little without the help of Dorothy and Coleridge: they also formed, for some years, the innermost circle of his readership. Although Wordsworth is often thought of as an isolated individual, he needed the emotional support of his friends. Indeed, one might argue that the intense personal relationships of the small 'set' were too strong, verging on the abnormal; after the breakdown of the group, the subsequent loneliness and deprivation must have affected each of its members considerably, and probably contributed to Coleridge's retreat into drugs and Dorothy's ultimate neurosis. In Wordsworth's case his 'retirement', at first a positive idea, became more obviously a seclusion, making his relations with his reading public more difficult than they need have been. It is the purpose of this chapter to trace this development, after sketching in the characters of the other two protagonists.

Dorothy Wordsworth and her Journals

... her taste a perfect electrometer ...

S. T. COLERIDGE

Dorothy was born in 1771, and was about a year and a half younger than William Wordsworth. When their mother died in 1778 she was sent away to Halifax, to stay with her mother's cousin, Miss Elizabeth Threlkeld, for nine years; she then lived at Penrith with her grandparents, seeing William for only a short time, and from 1789 to 1794 was away from the Lake District again, in the care of her uncle and aunt at Forncett in Norfolk. Brother and sister were not therefore reunited until later in that year when they lived at Windy Brow, Keswick—'We find our own food. Our breakfast and supper are of milk, and our dinner chiefly of potatoes and we drink no tea.' Dorothy's liking for long country walks upset the neighbours and her aunt tried to intervene; Dorothy replied that her brother's virtues were 'sufficient protection'. In October 1795 they settled together at Racedown Lodge, Dorset, a house which had been offered them rent-free by a Bristol family, the Pinneys. 'We plant cabbages,' said Wordsworth in a letter, 'and if retirement in its full perfection be as powerful in working transformations as one of Ovid's gods, you may perhaps suspect that into cabbages we shall be transformed.' Retirement and Dorothy's influence did in fact restore Wordsworth after the period of revolutionary storm and stress. After this time they were never really separated for any long period, and the course of Dorothy's life can be regarded as the same as Wordsworth's. They went to Germany together in 1798 and to Calais in 1802. After Wordsworth's marriage she continued to live in the same house; in 1829 she became seriously ill, suffering from arteriosclerosis. Soon her mental health began to deteriorate, and after 1835 there were few lucid intervals; nevertheless she outlived her brother and died in 1855.

Her monument consists of her Journals, which record the ordinary details of day-to-day life with her brother and help us to understand how the poems were created, for frequently the first idea for a poem is to be found in them. The most important records are the *Alfoxden Journal* (1798) and the *Grasmere Journals* (1800–3), but there are also accounts of the tours and visits which the Wordsworths made—not all these are complete, though, and the *Hamburg Journal* (1798) breaks off shortly after their arrival in Germany.

Dorothy began the Alfoxden Journal with an entry which one editor, H.Eigerman, has printed in free verse as if it were an Imagist poem:

ALFOXDEN, January 20th, 1798. The green paths down the hill-sides are channels for streams. The young wheat is streaked by silver lines of water running between the ridges, the sheep are gathered together on the slopes. After the wet dark days, the country seems more populous. It peoples itself in the sunbeams. The garden, mimic of spring, is gay with flowers. The purple-starred hepatica spreads itself in the sun, and the clustering snow-drops put forth their white heads, at first upright, ribbed with green, and like a rose bud when completely opened, hanging their heads downwards, but slowly lengthening their slender stems. The slanting woods of an unvarying brown, showing the light through the thin net-work of their upper boughs. Upon the highest ridge of that round hill covered with planted oaks, the shafts of the trees show in the light like the columns of a ruin.

We know that Wordsworth thought highly of this entry, for he began to copy it into a notebook, and used its phrases in a fragment of poetry:

> these populous slopes
> With all their groves and with their murmurous woods,
> Giving a curious feeling to the mind
> Of peopled solitude.
>
> *Alfoxden Notebook*

Dorothy went on with her Journal at his request. The observations of the moon are particularly remarkable, for example: '*January 25th.* . . . She sailed along, followed by multitudes of stars, small, and bright, and sharp'. And when we read '*March 23rd.* Coleridge dined with us. He brought his ballad finished', we hardly need to be reminded that *The Rime of the Ancient Mariner*, *Christabel*, and other poems were being written at this time. Coleridge also kept notebooks which parallel Dorothy's Journals in their observation of nature.

The impression of the *Grasmere Journals* is less literary; William is seen as a person enjoying retirement, occupied in his garden or in 'rural pursuits'. Although the Wordsworths are not well off they are charitable to the really poor, the beggars and the wanderers. The

Dove Cottage, Grasmere

following entry is taken at random, but illustrates this well.

[1800, June] *9th, Monday*. In the morning W. cut down the winter cherry tree. I sowed French Beans and weeded. A coronetted Landau went by, when we were sitting upon the sodded wall. The ladies (evidently Tourists) turned an eye of interest upon our little garden and cottage. We went round to R. Newton's for pike floats and went round to Mr Gell's Boat, and on to the Lake to fish. We caught nothing—it was extremely cold. The Reeds and Bullrushes or Bullpipes of a tender soft green, making a plain whose surface moved with the wind. The reeds not yet tall. The lake clear to the Bottom, but saw no fish. In the evening I stuck peas, watered the garden, and planted Brocoli. Did not walk, for it was very cold. A poor Girl called to beg, who had no work at home, and was going in search of it to Kendal. She slept in Mr Benson's, and went off after breakfast in the morning with

7d. and a letter to the Mayor of Kendal.

We also see the Wordsworths as part of a community of neighbours, and Dorothy is good at recording details of people and of local speech:

[1800, June] *22nd, Sunday*. . . .In the evening we walked for letters—no letters. No news of Coleridge. Jimmy Benson came home drunk beside us.
Monday. . . . An old man saw me just after I had crossed the stepping stones and was going through a copse—'Ho, wherever were you going?' 'To Elterwater Bridge'—'Why', says he, 'it's well I saw you; ye were gane to Little Langdale by Wrynose', and several other places which he ran over with a mixture of triumph, good-nature and wit—'It's well I saw you or you'd ha' been lost.'

Sometimes these meetings with strangers become the material for a poem by Wordsworth, for example, 10 June 1800 (*Beggars*); 3 October 1800 (*Resolution and Independence*); 15 April 1802 (*I wandered lonely as a cloud*), and so do the narratives of other people's experiences which Dorothy records:

[1802, February] *16th, Tuesday*. . . . Mr Graham said he wished Wm. had been with him the other day—he was riding in a post-chaise and he heard a strange cry that he could not understand, the sound continued, and he called to the chaise driver to stop. It was a little girl that was crying as if her heart would burst. She had got up behind the chaise, and her cloak had been caught by the wheel, and was jammed in, and it hung there. She was crying after it. Poor thing. Mr Graham took her into the chaise, and the cloak was released from the wheel, but the child's misery did not cease, for her cloak was torn to rags; it had been a miserable cloak before, but she had no other, and it was the greatest sorrow that could befal her. Her name was Alice Fell. She had no parents, and belonged to the next Town. At the next Town, Mr G. left money with some respectable people in the town, to buy her a new cloak.

In the poem, *Alice Fell*, (see Critical Survey p. 138) this is transformed into an experience in which Wordsworth takes the place of Mr Graham. A similar change of person takes place in *The Solitary Reaper*, whose song was originally heard by Mr Wilkinson (of the *Spade* sonnet). Some people have felt that this borrowing from Dorothy and others shows a certain egotism on Wordsworth's part, but it was his method as an artist to absorb things into himself, and think of them for a long period before writing them down; nor is it necessary to maintain, in any case, that the 'I' of a Wordsworth poem is necessarily the poet himself—it may stand as a universal shorthand symbol with which the reader can equally identify.

The Journals also contain accounts of literary composition:

[1802] *April 28th, Wednesday.* A fine sunny but coldish morning. I copied *The Prioress's Tale*. Wm. was in the orchard. I went to him; he worked away at his poem though he was ill and tired. I happened to say that when I was a child I would not have pulled a strawberry blossom. I left him, and wrote out *The Manciple's Tale*. At dinner time he came in with the poem of *Children Gathering Flowers* [*Foresight*], but it was not quite finished, and it kept him long off his dinner. It is now done. He is working at *The Tinker*. He promised me he would get his tea and do no more, but I have got mine an hour and a quarter, and he has scarcely begun his.

Again we notice that the initial stimulus comes from a memory of Dorothy's. The poems may almost be considered as examples of literary collaboration, and, though her own attempts at verse were not successful, the originality and freshness of perception in the Journals and her letters make a clear case for assessing her as a 'poet' in her own right.

Collaboration with Coleridge

Great in his writings, he was greatest in his conversation. In him was disproved that old maxim, that we should allow everyone his share of talk. He would talk from morn to dewy eve, nor cease till far midnight, yet who ever would interrupt him? . . . Never saw I his likeness, nor probably the world can see again.

CHARLES LAMB

Samuel Taylor Coleridge, more simply S.T.C., was born in 1772, the tenth child of a Devonshire clergyman; he was educated at Christ's Hospital in London and then at Jesus College, Cambridge. After a curious military episode—he ran away from Cambridge to join the 15th Dragoons*—he arrived in Bristol in 1795 full of plans to establish a new system of society, called Pantisocracy; this word is explained on p. 77, but what it meant in practice was the rather grandiose idea of founding a new American colony. One of the partners in the scheme was Robert Southey, at that time a poet and rebel against established ideas like Coleridge himself; married couples were needed for the venture, which of course fell through, leaving Coleridge rather unsuitably married to Southey's sister-in-law. He first met Wordsworth in 1795 and corresponded with him thereafter; meanwhile he dedicated himself to Left-wing political and religious propaganda,

* See the short account by E. M. Forster in *Abinger Harvest*, entitled 'Trooper Silas Tomkyn Comberbacke'.

Samuel Taylor Coleridge, by P. Vandyke

writing and lecturing in provincial towns. He had written *The Fall of Robespierre*, a verse drama, with Southey in 1794, and published *Poems on Various Subjects* in 1796, the year in which his first son, Hartley Coleridge, was born. At that time, like Wordsworth, he had no career, and depended on the generosity of friends; he had planned to live quietly in the country, but by the middle of 1797 was already beginning to get bored with rural solitude. On June 5th of that year he suddenly appeared at Racedown—'he did not keep to the high road, but leaped over a gate and bounded down the pathless field'. The description might be an allegory of Coleridge's journey through life.

After staying for three weeks at Racedown, Coleridge invited the Wordsworths to his cottage at Nether Stowey, Somerset; their visit coincided with that of Charles Lamb (see Coleridge's poem *This Lime-Tree Bower My Prison*). Living in close proximity in such a small cottage may have caused difficulties; one gathers that Coleridge's domestic arrangements included benevolent toleration of mice, whom he had not the heart to kill. But the Wordsworths' desire to continue the acquaintance was so strong that on July 14th they rented Alfoxden House, in a village three miles off. Racedown seems to have been given up without regret; what was important was 'Coleridge's society'.

Alfoxden was not a cottage, but a country house with considerable room for visitors. When John Thelwall, a well-known democrat and agitator, who had recently been on trial for treason, happened to call and then decided to stay for some time, the strange community fell under suspicion. The Home Office sent a detective to report on the movements of 'the French people'—they were assumed to be foreign as they did not have a Somerset accent. (It is all very much the same story as D. H. Lawrence's persecution in Cornwall during the First World War.) At first the spy thought he had stumbled on something worth investigating: Wordsworth carried a telescope, and Coleridge was surveying the river (he was in fact making notes for a projected long poem, *The Brook*); furthermore, Coleridge's oft-repeated references to 'Spy Nosy' were assumed by the Home Office spy to be aimed at him personally—he had presumably never heard of Spinoza, the philosopher of the moment.

After a while the poets were left alone. In the year July 1797 to June 1798 Coleridge produced most of the verse for which he is now remembered, including *Kubla Khan*, *Christabel*, and *The Ancient Mariner*—for which Wordsworth suggested the albatross and the theme of the guilty wanderer which had so often appeared in his own recent work. Meanwhile Wordsworth wrote all the poems, with the exception of *Tintern Abbey*, which subsequently appeared in the first volume of *Lyrical Ballads*. In Dorothy's *Alfoxden Journal* (20 January—22 May 1798) there is plenty of evidence of the interaction of the three minds in the creation of poetry.

At the same time a revolution in mental attitudes was taking place: disillusioned by Napoleon's conquests and the threat of invasion,

Coleridge was beginning that slide or jump to the Right which angered and puzzled his liberal associates, though it is fair to say that his revolutionary sympathies, unlike Wordsworth's, had never been more than superficial. 'I have snapped my squeaking baby-trumpet of sedition,' he wrote in April 1798, 'and the fragments lie scattered in the lumber-room of penitence. I wish to be a good man and a Christian, but I am no Whig, no Reformist, no Republican.' In fact, as we have seen in Chapter 3, he was beginning to evolve a new kind of conservative philosophy, and this was in no sense a time-serving decision, so that when Coleridge returned to 'orthodox' religion, his interpretation of Christian doctrine was strikingly original.

Coleridge had developed an apparently relaxed, but in fact extremely clever style of blank verse. The tradition of writing 'effusions' in blank verse had a long history in the eighteenth century, culminating in *The Task* by William Cowper. Cowper's poem was still under the shadow of Milton's *Paradise Lost*, and it is to Coleridge's credit that he was able to avoid Miltonic diction and write true 'conversational' poems. Wordsworth had also been experimenting with blank verse, and with the example of Coleridge's *Frost at Midnight* before him, was able to reproduce 'the movement of the mind' in *Tintern Abbey*. The same 'conversational' blank verse is used in much of *The Prelude* and it is noticeable that after Coleridge's influence lessened (during the next decade) Wordsworth's blank verse begins to revert to eighteenth-century and Miltonic mannerisms.

Although Wordsworth had produced more poems than Coleridge for their joint volume, *Lyrical Ballads*, honour was satisfied by giving the long *Ancient Mariner*—or *Ancyent Marinere* as it was originally spelt—pride of place. (Its position at the front of the volume was later regretted by Wordsworth as some readers were put off.) *Tintern Abbey* was given the other important position—it was printed at the end of the volume. The book appeared anonymously in September 1798, just as the authors and Dorothy departed for Germany.

The best description of this journey is to be found in *Satyrane's Letters*, writen by Coleridge and reprinted at the end of *Biographia Literaria*. The war continued but the German states were still neutral, and it seems that the travellers had illusions that Liberty, suppressed in England by Tories and in France by Jacobins, still lingered farther north. In Hamburg they visited the aged poet Klopstock, who had welcomed the Revolution but subsequently renounced the French. Originally Wordsworth and Coleridge had invited more English people to accompany them, perhaps envisaging a new Pantisocratic colony; but Mrs Coleridge and the children had remained behind, Coleridge being accompanied by only one disciple, Chester of Stowey. At the end of September the group split up; determined to get away from things English, they now decided to explore different areas, thinking they would learn more German if they gave up each others' company. The German poets and philosophers were becoming fashionable; perhaps Wordsworth and Dorothy could make a living by translating. Coleridge wished to study at a university; he went to Ratzeburg and Göttingen, enjoying himself immensely, and stayed till July 1799. But Wordsworth and his sister, after arriving at Brunswick, went on to Goslar because the local coach happened to go there. They were then immured in Goslar for five months by the coldest weather of the century.

Left to themselves by the German bourgeoisie—because in German usage 'sister' was the accepted genteelism for 'mistress'—the Wordsworths declined into misery and homesickness. Books were few, but there was ample time to write; as Coleridge, proficient in German after two months, put it: 'He seems to have employed more time in writing English than in studying German.' In fact, Wordsworth produced some of his greatest poetry; the descriptive passages in the early books of *The Prelude*, and the 'Lucy' poems, which are significantly about the North of England. Wordsworth felt that he wanted to return to England, settle down, and never go abroad again; as he stated in the last of the 'Lucy' poems, written two years later:

> I travell'd among unknown Men,
>> In Lands beyond the Sea;
> Nor England! did I know till then
>> What love I bore to thee.
>
> 'Tis past, that melancholy dream!
>> Nor will I quit thy shore
> A second time; for still I seem
>> To love thee more and more...

It was also remarkable that Germans—thought to be so liberal—now looked to England as the last refuge of Liberty; they applauded Nelson's recent victories—the political wheel had turned full circle. The Wordsworths returned to England in May; their money had in any case run out. They rushed back to the North, staying with the Hutchinson family at Sockburn-on-Tees, Yorkshire; it is significant that the poem quoted above continues with an image of domestic love—Wordsworth would soon be married to Mary Hutchinson. It was Coleridge who returned from Germany in triumph, clutching the works of Immanuel Kant.

Coleridge was under contract to the *Morning Post*, and had to spend some time in London; but in October 1799 he walked in the Lake District with William and John Wordsworth, and after a certain period of indecision arrived at Greta Hall, Keswick, with his wife and family in August 1800. A second time of close companionship now began, though of course the group had kept in close touch by correspondence and short visits in the interval.

In the spring of 1802 there was another phase of mutually influenced poetic production; Wordsworth wrote over thirty important poems at this time, and though Coleridge had already announced—in March 1801—that 'The poet is dead in me', he was able to contribute the main theme of the dialogue, which is, put simply, what happens to 'young Romantic poets' after the age of thirty when the visionary period of youth comes to an end. The following poems should be read in sequence:

Oct. 1800	— Coleridge: *The Mad Monk*
27 March 1802	— Wordsworth begins *Immortality Ode*
4 April 1802	— Coleridge writes first version of *Dejection*, called *A Letter to . . .* (Sara Hutchinson)
3 May 1802	— Wordsworth begins *The Leechgatherer* i.e. *Resolution and Independence*
17 June 1802	— Wordsworth continues *Immortality Ode*
4 Oct. 1802	— Final version of *Dejection* published by Coleridge.

A final comment is provided by Wordsworth in the *Prelude* 1805, xi 329 ff. (see Critical Survey p. 145).

The theme of the poems was hardly a happy one; Coleridge was now frequently ill with complaints which, though genuine enough, must surely have been complicated by psychosomatic factors. He was sufficiently recovered to begin a Scottish tour with William and Dorothy on 15 August 1803, but separated from the Wordsworths on the 29th. Dorothy's Journals provide a record of the tour, which involved the use of a vehicle described as 'an Irish jaunting car'; they made a pilgrimage to the grave of Burns and visited Sir Walter Scott, whose *Lay of the Last Minstrel* was to introduce the new metre of *Christabel* to a public who had never heard of the source. This is a typical example of Coleridge's influence, which extended to many other writers of the age; but in the case of Wordsworth the period of any real exchange of ideas was rapidly coming to an end. Coleridge, after many delays, left for Malta on 2 April 1804.

He had a semi-official position as assistant to the Governor, with many chances to travel in the Mediterranean area. There were delays in correspondence owing to the war, and Wordsworth decided to finish, as a tribute to his friend, the 'poem to Coleridge' which we now know as the 1805 *Prelude*. The news of the death of Wordsworth's brother John, who was drowned in Weymouth Bay on 5 February 1805, had a profound effect on the group. Coleridge fainted when told at a reception in Malta, and tried to get leave to return. But he was not able to do so until the following year, and when he met the Wordsworths again, at Kendal on 26 October 1806, they were shocked by his changed appearance. His fatness seems to have been largely the result of good living rather than ill-health; he had decided to separate from his wife, yet he was obviously in need of looking after. In 1808 he moved into the Wordsworths' new house, Allan Bank, together with his two sons, and after the usual long preliminaries embarked on his new periodical venture, *The Friend*. But this depended on keeping Coleridge away from 'stimulants' (i.e. brandy), and when Wordsworth happened to mention his difficulties to a friend, the final quarrel was inevitable.

Caricature of Wordsworth and Hartley Coleridge, by J. P. Mulcaster, 1844

This took place in 1810, and though a reconciliation was arranged in 1812 things were never the same again. Coleridge lived in London, and never returned to the North of England, so that meetings only took place on rare occasions.

After Coleridge died in 1834, his son Hartley, who lived at Ambleside, would frequently walk with Wordsworth in the Grasmere area. They were sometimes accompanied by Wordsworth's daughter Dora, who to some extent replaced Dorothy after her illness; at times this must have seemed like a re-enactment of the earlier years, when Dorothy, William and Coleridge were inseparable.

The recluse of Grasmere

> Fair, shining mountains of my pilgrimage
> And flow'ry vales, whose flowers were stars!
> The days and nights of my first happy age,
> An age without distaste or wars!
>
> HENRY VAUGHAN

> Mountains—I deny any grandeur to the spectacle. There is more emotion for me in a furlong of Cheapside than in the contemplation of mere elevated bodies.
>
> Attributed to DR JOHNSON

In our own times the idea of a poet living in the country, usually in a rural slum which the local residents have gladly abandoned for a council house, is so commonplace as to be unremarkable. In the late eighteenth century it was an extremely odd thing for a young professional poet to do, though there were precedents; for example, Cowper had used the countryside as a therapy for madness, and Hayley, a gentleman-amateur, lived in a gentleman's residence. The usual journey of the poet was in the opposite direction—from the country to the metropolis; one thinks of the young Crabbe, who travelled from Aldeburgh to London in 1780 with £3 which he had borrowed— he was about to abandon the project after twelve months of useless applications to publishers when he was saved by the generosity of Edmund Burke, who introduced him to 'polite society' and found him 'a place'. The age of patronage was passing, but in the aristocratic social ambience of the Regency the poet was still a society entertainer, dependent on the goodwill of publishers and the new magazines; if a writer played to this concept of the licensed fool, there was plenty of scope for personal enrichment, let alone making a living; the careers of Scott and Tom Moore bear this out, and certain aspects of Byron's success are comparable. This was a conception of the poet which Wordsworth despised; he lived out his protest, like a true disciple of Rousseau, by rejecting the corrupted metropolis and deliberately choosing the innocence of the country.

For a time, indeed, he succeeded in attracting his own circle to the Lakes—Southey, Coleridge and De Quincey lived there; Lamb, Keats and Shelley paid visits. He had set up his tent in the wilderness and the great went out to hear him. He nearly transferred the literary capital from London to Keswick; the 'Lakers' were an object of derision to the London élite, because people sneer at that which they really think may be superior to themselves. Even when the circle broke up, Wordsworth could still keep in touch; the recent improvement in communications was the foundation of this new literary republic— there were frequent exchanges of correspondence and books, and Wordsworth regularly visited all his friends, besides making extended tours in Britain and on the Continent. It is therefore wrong to think of him as mentally isolated.

Nevertheless, he did sever himself from much of interest in his own times, and there were moments when he regretted his decision. But the positive reasons for his withdrawal overweighed these occasional doubts. In choosing the life of a hermit he qualified himself for consideration as a *sage*, the new image of the poet which he wished to fulfil and which he transmitted to the Victorians.

There was an element of religious retreat about his gesture, which bears comparison with the similar deliberate withdrawal of the seventeenth-century poet, Henry Vaughan. (The parallel is worth exploring, and a comparison of Vaughan's *Retreat* and Wordsworth's *Immortality Ode* raises many questions. A copy of Vaughan's *Silex Scintillans* was found among Wordsworth's books after his death.) Wordsworth himself called his way of life a 'retirement', but in his case the flight from the centre to the periphery of England served also to cement a pact which he had made with his own childhood. The man of thirty-two recognized the child brought up in the Lake District as his 'father':

> The Child is father of the Man;
> And I could wish my days to be
> Bound each to each by natural piety.

By returning to the unchanging physical setting, he allowed Child and Man to confront each other; he set himself to 'live it all again'. He rediscovered for himself the significance of his childhood environment and the part it had played in his upbringing. Surely the visionary experiences of his youth would return.

'Visionary' is of course the keyword and links us to the clearer picture of the *living* landscape, the 'active universe' of *The Prelude*, where Wordsworth heard in the storm 'the ghostly language of the ancient earth' and received 'the visionary power'. But most people would say that this is impossible: the landscape does not make the poet or the painter, but 'Imagination: the Divine Vision' as Blake pointed out; or as Coleridge forlornly realized:

> Oh Lady, we receive but what we give
> And in our lives alone does Nature live.

This subjective position was one which Wordsworth was unwilling to admit; in his childhood, he tells us in *The Prelude*, Nature had granted him 'visitations' through the scenery of the Lake District and so made him a poet; he would not believe that 'the visionary character' was entirely bestowed on the landscape by his own mind.

It is hardly surprizing that this reverent attitude to the Lake District has since been questioned. Is a lake surrounded by mountains more sublime than a stagnant canal among factory chimneys? Is it more beautiful? A modern photographer would not necessarily agree. And do we now believe that people brought up among mountainous scenery are more virtuous than people from an industrial environment? It may have appeared so in the nineteenth century, but the reasons were economic in the first instance. The children of the inhabitants of remote mountain valleys are not always as healthy as has been supposed, and may even be inbred cretins. Dr Johnson was not impressed by mountains—though even he went to the Hebrides— and Charles Lamb in a well-known letter from London consigned 'hills, woods, lakes, and mountains to the eternal devil'. 'I must confess,' he added 'that I am not romance-bit about *Nature*. The earth, and sea, and sky (when all is said) is but as a house to dwell in.' In another letter he told Wordsworth that

Separate from the pleasure of your company, I don't much care if I never see a mountain in my life. . . . The lighted shops of the Strand and Fleet Street, the innumerable trades, tradesmen and customers, coaches, waggons, playhouses, all the bustle and wickedness round about Covent Garden, the very women of the town, the Watchmen, drunken scenes, rattles,—life awake, if you awake, at all hours of the night. . . . The wonder of these sights impells me into night-walks about her [London's] crowded streets, and I often shed tears in the motley Strand from fulness of joy at so much life. . . . I have no passion (or have had none since I was in love, and then it was the spurious engendering of poetry and books) to groves and vallies.

But then Wordsworth, apart from the vision on Westminster Bridge, rejected London as a 'blank confusion' and a 'hubbub'. Each to his taste, perhaps.

Yet obviously this will not do. Whatever other people may or may not like about their surroundings, Wordsworth himself was *peculiarly* influenced by the Lake District. The fact that the Victorians—and often Wordsworth himself—thought that the influence of mountains was one of vague moral uplift is only part of the truth. As we read the poems we cannot help noticing how many passages seem to re-create and then to grow out of the scenery they describe. *The Prelude* is especially to the point here; Wordsworth was trying to explain *why* certain things observed in childhood remained with him and strengthened him in later years. The first two books have many examples of these memories. Less well known is the incident (see Critical Survey, p. 148, which happened when Wordsworth's father died. He sat by a wall:

> Upon my right hand was a single sheep,
> A whistling hawthorn on my left, and there,
> With those Companions at my side, I watch'd . . .

At the time the father's death had appeared as a kind of punishment, yet

> . . . afterwards, the wind and sleety rain
> And all the business of the elements,
> The single sheep, and the one blasted tree,
> And the bleak music of that old stone wall,
> The noise of wood and water, and the mist
> Which on the line of each of those two Roads
> Advanced in such indisputable shapes,
> All these were spectacles and sounds to which
> I often would repair and thence would drink,
> As at a fountain; and I do not doubt
> That in this later time, when storm and rain
> Beat on my roof at midnight, or by day
> When I am in the woods, unknown to me
> The workings of my spirit thence are brought.
>
> *Prelude* 1805, xi, 359–61 and 376–89

It is the working-over of the Lake District scenery and its associations in *the memory* that is important, not the immediate impression. We see more clearly why Wordsworth could not describe these experiences in his earliest poems. What he was really concerned with was the effect of the experience when transmuted by recollection and made part of the mature mind. And this of course is the point of the hackneyed *I wandered lonely as a cloud*.

In other poems, such as *Michael*, Wordsworth confesses that he loved the hills and fields *first*, and the men who worked in them as a result. Humanity is sometimes reduced, one feels, to an object in the landscape; the Leechgatherer seems like 'a huge stone', and his endurance seems more important than his economic difficulties which Wordsworth has difficulty in comprehending. Earlier, in the section on Economic History, we have noted evidence of Wordsworth's concern for the plight of the poor; but it is frequently the wanderers through the Lake District, not its inhabitants, whom he pities. The Lake District people who survived him regarded him as a curious old man, mooning about the hills mouthing verse, and usually disregarding or looking through them as if they were not there. Even the outlandish

Scafell and Scafell Pike

wanderers had usually been noticed by Dorothy in the first instance, and we have seen how William worked up the poems about them from entries in her Journals. On the other hand he had a strange sympathy for large stones, frequently inscribing verses on them or even simply carving initials: one feels that he would have appreciated the sculpture of Henry Moore, and the ending of his greatest epitaph,

> Roll'd round in earth's diurnal course,
> With rocks, and stones, and trees.
> *'A slumber did my spirit seal'*

describes a human being translated into a stony landscape. It is almost a premonition. Wordsworth has been absorbed into his native earth in just this way, and perhaps it is right that we should think of him first when we visit the Lake District.

The reading public

We have our Haircutter below stairs. William is reading the Leech-gatherer to him.

DOROTHY WORDSWORTH

The Whale is followed by waves.

COLERIDGE (on the impact of great writers)

Although Wordsworth retired to Westmorland he was not forgotten, however much he might be attacked and reviled. Even those who attacked him assumed that they were dealing with a pernicious influence on the nation's poetry, and he was never downgraded to the status of a regional poet. The battle over his reputation was fought out in the columns of reviews, such as *The Edinburgh Review*, which had a very wide circulation, covering most of the aristocratic and middle-class reading public. People took their opinions from the great reviews without bothering to read the poetry itself. The tiny sales figures of Wordsworth's volumes are evidence of this.

The original small editions of *An Evening Walk* and *Descriptive Sketches* were not exhausted until 1805 when De Quincey purchased the remaining copies. Five hundred copies of *Lyrical Ballads* were printed in 1798; when Longman took over the stock of Joseph Cottle in 1800, the remaining copies were considered worthless. But the reviews had not been unfriendly, so that a second volume was published in 1800 and further editions in 1802 and 1805. In an attempt to establish communication with his readers Wordsworth added the explanatory *Preface*; this may have been a tactical mistake, and later Wordsworth said that 'the prefaces were written to gratify Coleridge'.

In 1807 all reviews of the *Poems in Two Volumes* were bad except Montgomery's. Wordsworth was so inhibited by this unfavourable reception that he delayed publication of subsequent poems, so that

E

his work in progress, *The Excursion*, did not appear till 1814, *The White Doe of Rylstone* (written 1807–8) till 1815, and *Peter Bell* (written 1798) till 1819.

After Coleridge's departure in 1810 Wordsworth seems to have temporarily lost contact with a truly critical audience (an audience of one can be just as effective as a larger group). As he had alienated the Whig critics of *The Edinburgh Review* his reputation fell to its lowest point and his poetry was laughed at for the next decade. It took five years to sell five hundred sets of the 1815 collected edition of Wordsworth's poetry.

Twelve years later, after two years' negotiation, only seven hundred and fifty sets of the 1827 collection were printed. Yet although Wordsworth the man still aroused so much antagonism, and although his later poetry seemed disappointing, his earlier works fought heroic battles on his behalf in the minds of successive generations. 'Up to 1820 the name of Wordsworth was trampled underfoot; from 1820 to 1830 it was militant; from 1830 to 1835 it has been triumphant'— so said De Quincey in 1835. It is certainly true that after the death of Byron in 1824, Wordsworth's fame and influence steadily increased. 1831 saw the first selection for schools, and in 1832 two thousand copies of a cheap edition were published—but only eight hundred copies were sold in two years. Although poetry has never sold well, there was a boom in the sales of certain kinds of verse in these years: Scott's *Lay of the Last Minstrel* (1805) sold 44,000 copies over a twenty-five year period, and the first edition of Byron's *The Corsair* (10,000 copies) was sold out on the day of publication in 1814.* Wordsworth finally achieved national recognition in 1842 when he received a Civil List pension of £300 per annum from Sir Robert Peel, followed by the office of Poet Laureate in April 1843.

The disappointing sales are understandable if we consider that Wordsworth was looking for a new class of readers; he knew that 'he would have to create the taste by which he would be enjoyed'. He was exceptionally pleased by any evidence that 'the folk' enjoyed his poetry—they would in any case have been unable to afford to buy it. Some of the *Lyrical Ballads* did find their way into the hearts of the people, and there is evidence to show that *Goody Blake and Harry Gill* was taken up by children as a new nursery rhyme. But the dalesmen of the Lake District were not impressed, and twenty years after the poet's death Canon Rawnsley could not find many copies of the poems in the cottages of Grasmere—Wordsworth's poetry was 'deep' and required 'a lot of figuring', not like 'lil' Hartley' (Hartley Coleridge) whose verse was much loved. If they remembered Wordsworth for anything it was his taste in chimneys—he insisted on the traditional style for new buildings—and his zeal for the preservation of ancient trees.

*(All these sales figures are from S. H. Steinberg's *Five Hundred Years of Printing* (Pelican Books) which contains a great deal of information about the contemporary reading public.)

Part Two

Critical Survey

Stonehenge by John Constable

Early poems, 1784–93

For many years little notice was taken of Wordsworth's writings before 1798, but even the *School Exercise* written at the age of fourteen (*Poetical Works*, i, 259–61) is useful as an illustration of the faults of eighteenth-century style; it is written in heroic couplets, in imitation of the work of Alexander Pope, and contains an excessive use of personification:

> Science with joy saw Superstition fly
> Before the lustre of Religion's eye;
> With rapture she beheld Britannia smile,
> Clapp'd her strong wings, and sought the cheerful isle.

Wordsworth produced a long poem in 1787 entitled *The Vale of Esthwaite* (*Poetical Works*, i, 270–83). The poem is remarkable for its Gothic horrors and its energy, for example:

> But he, the stream's loud genius, seen
> The black arch'd boughs and rocks between
> That brood o'er one eternal night,
> Shoots from the cliff in robe of white . . .

This is not a 'Wordsworthian' view of Nature, but it helps to explain what the poet meant when he told us in *The Prelude* that he was haunted by mysterious 'presences' during childhood and youth; *The Vale of Esthwaite* anticipates *The Prelude* in other ways—the interest is in the mind of the poet, and the effect of the imagination on landscape.

Wordsworth's first publications, *An Evening Walk* and *Descriptive Sketches*, appeared in 1793; the aim was to bring his name before the public as he felt he had done nothing at university—and, of course, the faint hope of making money. We might therefore expect these works to conform in some way to established taste, but it does not follow, as many of Wordsworth's later disciples were prone to assume, that anything in heroic couplets is *necessarily* bad; in fact, many passages from these poems compare quite favourably with Wordsworth's eighteenth-century predecessors. The common idea that Wordsworth disowned all his eighteenth-century 'beginnings' may perhaps need correcting. He went on 'improving' this poem over a long period of years so that the text usually printed shows many alterations from the original.

An Evening Walk is a topographical poem, that is, it describes the scenery of a limited locality. The area delimited can be very restricted indeed. The precedents for this kind of poem go back to the seventeenth century, and one could usefully look at Pope's *Windsor Forest* or Dyer's *Grongar Hill*. Wordsworth describes the Lake District in a series of pictures; in the last paragraph of the poem the evening walk is almost over, and culminates in a night-piece.

From *An Evening walk*

The song of mountain streams unheard by day,
Now hardly heard, beguiles my homeward way.
All air is, as the sleeping water, still,
List'ning th' aëreal music of the hill,
Broke only by the slow clock tolling deep,
Or shout that wakes the ferry-man from sleep,
Soon follow'd by his hollow-parting oar,
And echo'd hoof approaching the far shore;
Sound of clos'd gate, across the water born,
10   Hurrying the feeding hare thro' rustling corn;
The tremulous sob of the complaining owl;
And at long intervals the mill-dog's howl;
The distant forge's swinging thump profound;
Or yell in the deep woods of lonely hound.

TEXT.   The extract consists of lines 433–46 of the 1793 edition. It is the last paragraph of the poem.

CONTENT.   The sounds of night, picked out one by one, are imitated in the carefully constructed lines; yet the pauses between the sounds are also conveyed in the slowness and tranquillity of the whole passage, so that the general effect is one of intense stillness, with the ear strained to catch the least noise. Wordsworth describes silence by pointing away from it.

VERSE.   Heroic couplets, the typical verse form of the Augustan age, were brought to perfection by Alexander Pope. Notice that Wordsworth can play off speech-rhythm against the iambic pattern; if one reads the extract aloud 'List'ning' and 'Broke', for example, are heard to run counter to the expected rhythm and help the verse to mime what is being described. There are many similar examples of skilful writing, so that it is hardly possible to think of Wordsworth as abandoning traditional forms in 1798 because he was unable to write in the accepted manner. If anything this piece of writing is too competent, too clever.

POSTSCRIPT.   Coleridge admired the early poems, with reservations, and one of his many projected schemes was: 'to analyse the pleasures received from Gates, in corners of fields, at twilight' (*Notebooks 1794–1804*: 1707 with a reference to this extract from *An Evening Walk*).

Revolutionary Wordsworth 1793–98

This is a period of storm and stress, at any rate to begin with; Wordsworth's obscure and apparently purposeless wanderings are reflected in *Guilt and Sorrow* (also called *Salisbury Plain*, and, in truncated form, *The Female Vagrant*). In this extract the hero approaches Stonehenge:

> All, all was cheerless to the horizon's bound;
> The weary eye—which, wheresoe'er it strays,
> Marks nothing but the red sun's setting round,
> Or on the earth strange lines, in former days
> Left by gigantic arms—at length surveys
> What seems an antique castle spreading wide;
> Hoary and naked are its walls, and raise
> Their brow sublime: in shelter there to bide
> He turned, while rain poured down smoking on every side.
>
> Pile of Stone-henge! so proud to hint yet keep
> Thy secrets, thou that lov'st to stand and hear
> The Plain resounding to the whirlwind's sweep,
> Inmate of lonesome Nature's endless year;
> Even if thou saw'st the giant wicker rear
> For sacrifice its throngs of living men,
> Before thy face did ever wretch appear,
> Who in his heart had groaned with deadlier pain
> Than he who, tempest-driven, thy shelter now would gain?

lines 109–126

Some critics have called the human sacrifice image 'juvenile', and it is reminiscent of the general level of *The Vale of Esthwaite*; but in Wordsworth's defence one must point out that everybody believed that Stonehenge had been the scene of human sacrifice, and continued to do so until this century (see, for instance, Hardy's *Tess of the D'Urbevilles*). The rest of the poem is concerned with the *social* causes of human misery: the Female Vagrant tells us that

> homeless near a thousand homes I stood,
> And near a thousand tables pined and wanted food.

This is dismissed by many critics as 'tainted with Godwinism', but I cannot myself see that lines like these are ever likely to become out of date. They affront the 'enlightened reader' because they are about reality and because they demand sympathy, compassion and remedial action, qualities which are always in short supply.

Wordsworth's next work, *The Borderers*, appears at first to be a pseudo-Shakespearean tragedy, one of many that the Romantic poets produced. It is in fact an argument about Godwin's ideas, and critics are undecided whether to assign the vistory to Godwin or to the more conservative philosophy which Wordsworth was now beginning to embrace. The story of the play is simple; the hero 'goes into the world and is betrayed into a great crime'. The betrayer, Oswald, believes that it is possible to cut oneself off from the past (compare the argument between Tom Paine and Burke about the British constitution; is it desirable to imitate the French and abolish the past by Revolution?). If one reads nothing else, the account of Oswald's voyage (in Act iv, lines 1682–1882) should be compared to *The Ancient Mariner*.

During these years Wordsworth also began *The Ruined Cottage*; this was later incorporated into Book i of *The Excursion* and suffered considerable modification. In 1797 he was also producing shorter poems like *The Old Cumberland Beggar* (see p. 61). The point to notice is that while all these poems deal with problems of society and justice, the emphasis is changing from explaining the causes of criminal behaviour to understanding and defending the outcasts.

Lyrical Ballads

The first volume of *Lyrical Ballads* was published in 1798. It conveniently marks the beginning of nineteenth-century poetry, though not of course the end of eighteenth-century readers, who lingered on till after 1832, so that in the first three decades of the new century a great battle of taste was fought out, largely over Wordsworth's 'simple' poetry. Because of this certain ideas have passed into critical legend; Wordsworth's own *Preface* has encouraged modern readers to believe that the reading public of the 1790s were completely unprepared for the new poetry, and that *Lyrical Ballads* was a complete failure from the point of view of communication and also of financial success.

An article by Mayo* brought new facts into consideration. The first point which everybody had overlooked was that Wordsworth hoped 'to make money' with *Lyrical Ballads*, and presumably thought that he had gone some way in making concessions to popular taste. The magazine poetry of the 1790s frequently deals with similar subject-matter, and poets were already using a wide variety of metrical forms, including ballads. There were many reviews of Wordsworth and Coleridge's joint volume, and *Goody Blake and Harry Gill* was the most popular poem. If *Lyrical Ballads* was as unpopular as legend would have it, why would Wordsworth have added a second volume in 1800, and why would both volumes be reprinted in 1802 and again in 1805? The real onslaught on Wordsworth was delayed until after the publication of the 1807 *Poems*.

*Robert Mayo, 'The Contemporaneity of the *Lyrical Ballads*', *Publications of the Modern Language Association of America*, vol. 69, 1954, pp. 486–522.

Lyrical Ballads nevertheless remains a very strange publication, the full effect of which can only be appreciated by studying a facsimile edition, or one of the reprints of the first edition. One can see why *The Ancyent Marinere* prejudiced the success of the volume, and the 'simplicity' of many poems can be seen to emerge from a background of rather precious cleverness. *Tintern Abbey*, which, on the surface, appears more eighteenth-century than the other poems, is not typical of the volume. *The Idiot Boy* and *Simon Lee, the Old Huntsman* are true Lyrical Ballads, and are poems which remain alive because they continue to provoke such intense disagreement. Since most readers' first reaction to such poetry is unfavourable, one has to look hard for critics who have something positive to say. J. F. Danby's *The Simple Wordsworth* is particularly to be recommended here—he is very good on *Simon Lee*, for example. One of the easier Lyrical Ballads will serve to bring out the main points of critical debate.

The Last of the Flock

In distant countries I have been,
And yet I have not often seen
A healthy man, a man full grown
Weep in the public roads alone.
But such a one, on English ground,
And in the broad high-way, I met;
Along the broad high-way he came,
His cheeks with tears were wet.
Sturdy he seemed, though he was sad;
10 And in his arms a lamb he had.

He saw me, and he turned aside,
As if he wished himself to hide:
Then with his coat he made essay
To wipe those briny tears away.
I follow'd him, and said, 'My friend
'What ails you? wherefore weep you so?'
—'Shame on me, Sir! this lusty lamb,
He makes my tears to flow.
To-day I fetched him from the rock;
20 He is the last of all my flock.

'When I was young, a single man,
And after youthful follies ran,
Though little given to care and thought,
Yet, so it was, a ewe I bought;
And other sheep from her I raised,
As healthy sheep as you might see,
And then I married, and was rich
As I could wish to be;
Of sheep I number'd a full score,
30 And every year encreas'd my store.

E*

'Year after year my stock it grew,
And from this one, this single ewe,
Full fifty comely sheep I raised,
As sweet a flock as ever grazed!
Upon the mountain did they feed;
They throve, and we at home did thrive.
—This lusty lamb of all my store
Is all that is alive:
And now I care not if we die,
And perish all of poverty.

'Ten children, Sir! had I to feed,
Hard labour in a time of need!
My pride was tamed, and in our grief
I of the parish ask'd relief.
They said I was a wealthy man;
My sheep upon the mountain fed,
And it was fit that thence I took
Whereof to buy us bread:
"Do this; how can we give to you,"
They cried, "what to the poor is due?"

'I sold a sheep as they had said,
And bought my little children bread,
And they were healthy with their food;
For me it never did me good.
A woeful time it was for me,
To see the end of all my gains,
The pretty flock which I had reared
With all my care and pains,
To see it melt like snow away!
For me it was a woeful day.

'Another still! and still another!
A little lamb, and then its mother!
It was a vein that never stopp'd,
Like blood-drops from my heart they dropp'd.
Till thirty were not left alive
They dwindled, dwindled, one by one,
And I may say that many a time
I wished they all were gone:
They dwindled one by one away;
For me it was a woeful day.

'To wicked deeds I was inclined,
And wicked fancies cross'd my mind,
And every man I chanc'd to see,
I thought he knew some ill of me.
No peace, no comfort could I find,
No ease, within doors or without,
And crazily, and wearily,
I went my work about.
Oft-times I thought to run away;
80 For me it was a woeful day.

'Sir! 'twas a precious flock to me,
As dear as my own children be;
For daily with my growing store
I loved my children more and more.
Alas! it was an evil time;
God cursed me in my sore distress,
I prayed, yet every day I thought
I loved my children less;
And every week, and every day,
90 My flock, it seemed to melt away.

'They dwindled, Sir, sad sight to see!
From ten to five, from five to three,
A lamb, a wether, and a ewe;
And then at last, from three to two;
And of my fifty, yesterday
I had but only one,
And here it lies upon my arm,
Alas! and I have none;
To-day I fetched it from the rock;
100 It is the last of all my flock.'

TEXT. The version given here is taken from the 1798 edition of *Lyrical Ballads*. Wordsworth later made changes in the text—as in most of his early poems—mainly to please Coleridge. For example, he altered the number of children (line 41) from ten to six, to avoid describing an extreme case of misery; but by making this alteration he weakened the point of the poem.

GENERAL IMPRESSIONS. The first impression of the true Lyrical Ballads (i.e. *Simon Lee* or *Goody Blake and Harry Gill*) is one of amusement. We laugh at what is incongruous, and also I suspect, as a defence mechanism against something strange and unusual. Yet 'Wordsworth was of opinion that posterity will value most those Lyrical Ballads which were most laughed at'—(Crabb Robinson). The second impression is probably one of childishness and simplicity; we seem to have strayed into a non-adult world—is it comparable, as some have suggested, to the world of Blake's *Songs of Innocence* and *Songs of Experience*? Surely not, because we feel that we are listening to a true story of a real person, and if we grant this, then feelings connected with relieving distress are more likely to arise in us than purely poetic emotions.

SUBJECT. The social problem is the apparent occasion for the poem, and some people feel that it is an intrusion. But even the theme of agricultural distress is subordinate to the attack on Godwin's belief that property is evil. The peasant has identified himself with his flock. The poem was classified in 1815 as a Poem founded on the Affections. This is supported by Wordsworth's defence of his choice of the common people as subject matter—'Low and rustic life was generally chosen, because in that condition the essential passions of the heart find a better soil in which they can attain their maturity...' (*Preface to Lyrical Ballads*). Wordsworth worked from observation— 'The incident occurred in the village of Holford, close by Alfoxden', —but in a letter of 1836 he makes it clear that it was a friend who actually *saw* the man. (Compare *Alice Fell*, *The Solitary Reaper*, and many other poems where Wordsworth assimilates other people's experiences and tells them as if they were his own).

DICTION. Sometimes, for many lines together, we can say with Wordsworth—'the words, and the order of the words, in no respect differ from the most unimpassioned conversation' (*Preface to Lyrical Ballads*). Some early critics of Wordsworth's 'simple' style thought that he was stupid and incompetent; but we have already seen that he could write with due regard to eighteenth-century decorum. One can only conclude that we are presented here with a deliberately *unpoetical poem*, an assault upon the cultivated reader's exquisite sensibility. The cultivated reader sensed that he was being teased, and reacted accordingly —'Whatever is too original will be hated at first' (De Quincey).

BALLAD FORM. There was a literary vogue for pseudomedieval ballads following the publication of Bishop Percy's *Reliques of Ancient Poetry*, 1765, and Coleridge in *The Ancient Mariner* is trying to imitate the diction and manner of an earlier age. But Wordsworth's intentions here are more difficult to follow. Presumably he is trying to write a popular street ballad; if so, it looks as if the stylistic crudities are an imitation of 'the idiom of the people'. Perhaps the 'I' of the poem is not William Wordsworth but a rustic narrator—compare the old sea-captain who tells the story of *The Thorn*. This is not a very convincing solution, since most readers don't feel that this a dramatic monologue, and take the 'I' of the poem to be Wordsworth himself.

CONCLUSION. Hazlitt said of the *Lyrical Ballads*—'Fools have laughed at, wise men scarcely understand them'. Coleridge said that Wordsworth's object was 'to give the charm of novelty to things of everyday, and to excite a feeling analogous to the supernatural'. Certainly the feeling excited here is strange and unusual, and this may be due to the confusion in the man's mind between his sheep and his children (lines 21–30, 81–90). Even the numerical counting-down is uncanny: there are ten children in line 41 and the flock dwindles 'from ten to five, from five to three' (line 92). We are reminded of a well-known nursery rhyme—'Then there were none'. Which is more important—children or property, especially when the property is identified with one's hold on life? We think of Michael who sent away his son, Luke, rather than give up his land; and surely the picture of the man weeping with a lamb in his arms, which he has fetched 'from the rock', calls up a wealth of Old and New Testament imagery? In this way the man and his sheep may linger in our minds, even if we do not remember the economic difficulties so clearly—'The Last of the Flock' would make a good title for a Victorian narrative painting. But already we are moving away from the source of the poem—the real man on an actual road in Somersetshire—who obstinately refuses to turn into a symbol. However hard we try to make him into a *literary* archetype he remains firmly rooted in life, in nonliterary experience. Perhaps Wordsworth intended to break down the cultivated reader's protective distinction between literature and life: he certainly succeeded in confusing people, in 1798 and ever since. 'If the author be a wealthy man', said a reviewer in 1799, 'he ought not to have suffered the poor peasant to part with the last of the flock'.

Germany, 1798–9

The meteorological aspects of the German winter have already been discussed, and could perhaps be reread at this point (p. 105). Wordsworth was forced into using his own past as material for poetry and the first attempts of a writer in a new vein are frequently the best. The autobiographical narratives of this period are saved from per-sonal triviality by the force of visionary insight. Wordsworth discover-ed and established those kinds of poetry which would best suit him; it is in the German period that we travel to the furthest limits of the 'Wordsworthian' vision, in poems such as the 'Lucy' and 'Matthew' sequences, which are at one level blindingly clear, but in terms of prose exposition almost impossible to 'explain'.

The first two books of *The Prelude* must be read at this point, and if the reader finds more at this stage in the narrative sections this is entirely appropriate since they appear to have been written as separate entities at this time and only later blended into 'the Philosophical poem'. The 'Lucy' poems have received a great deal of critical atten-tion (see, for example, F. R. Leavis in *Revaluation*); it is because the 'Matthew' poems are so frequently ignored that I have chosen one of them for special comment.

We walked along, while bright and red
    Uprose the morning sun;
And Matthew stopped, he looked, and said,
    'The will of God be done!'

A village Schoolmaster was he,
    With hair of glittering gray;
As blithe a man as you could see
    On a spring holiday.

And on that morning, through the grass,
10   And by the steaming rills,
We travelled merrily, to pass
    A day among the hills.

'Our work,' said I, 'was well begun;
    Then, from thy breast what thought,
Beneath so beautiful a sun,
    So sad a sigh has brought?'

A second time did Matthew stop;
    And fixing still his eye
Upon the eastern mountain-top,
20   To me he made reply:

'Yon cloud with that long purple cleft
    Brings fresh into my mind
A day like this which I have left
    Full thirty years begind.

'And on that slope of springing corn
    The self-same crimson hue
Fell from the sky that April morn,
    The same which now I view.

'With rod and line my silent sport
30   I plied by Derwent's wave;
And, coming to the church, stopp'd short
    Beside my daughter's grave.

'Nine summers had she scarcely seen,
    The pride of all the vale;
And then she sang;—she would have been
    A very nightingale.

'Six feet in earth my Emma lay;
    And yet I loved her more,
For so it seemed, than till that day
40   I e'er had loved before.

'And turning from her grave, I met
    Beside the church-yard Yew
A blooming Girl, whose hair was wet
    With points of morning dew.

'A basket on her head she bare;
    Her brow was smooth and white:
To see a Child so very fair,
    It was a pure delight!

'No fountain from its rocky cave
50   E'er tripped with foot so free;
She seemed as happy as a wave
    That dances on the sea.

'There came from me a sigh of pain
    Which I could ill confine;
I looked at her and looked again:
    —And did not wish her mine.'

Matthew is in his grave, yet now
    Methinks I see him stand,
As at that moment, with his bough
60   Of wilding in his hand.

NOTE. This poem is part of a cycle and will become clearer if *The Fountain* is studied in conjunction with it.

TEXT. The earliest printed text—from *Lyrical Ballads* (1800)—is given here. Later versions are 'improved' in several places, and I would agree that the later reading of the penultimate line—'With *a* bough'—is a real improvement.

FIRST IMPRESSION. This is another attempt to imitate true ballad style, but this time it is more like a medieval ballad—'bright and red /Uprose the morning sun' sounds like *The Ancient Mariner*. Although graves and a dead girl are at the centre of the poem, no melancholy feelings can completely overlay the initial impression of life and good health, conveyed by 'bright', 'glittering', 'blithe', 'spring', 'steaming', 'merrily', and the jerky jogtrot of the first verses.

STORY. The ballad tells an apparently simple story; in fact it is a tale within a tale within a memory—as in many of Wordsworth's poems, for example *The Rainbow* and *Tintern Abbey*, there is a backward and forward movement in time. At first the narrator (whom we take to be the Boy of the parallel poem, *The Fountain*), joins the old Schoolmaster on a joyful excursion to the hills. Suddenly, the old man stops short; the peculiar shape and colour of a cloud brings back into his mind a similar day thirty years before—a true Hartleian touch, this! On the earlier occasion, the old man had also 'stopp'd short' while on a holiday fishing expedition; at that time his daughter Emma was already dead, but we flash back even further for a moment to recall her voice. He then goes on to say that after her death he loved her more than when she was alive—this leads us into a trap, for we begin to feel that the old man was a ghoulish sentimentalist. As he turns away from the grave (symbolically as well as literally) he meets, beside the yew-tree (traditional symbol of death) a Girl whose appearance is strikingly unusual. Some critics feel that she is either Emma returned from the grave, or a supernatural vision; though both these interpretations make some sense, I feel that the most obvious possibility is the true one. She is another child, an ordinary human being over whose appearance Wordsworth has thrown a 'supernatural charm' (see previous poem for the purpose of the *Lyrical Ballads*). Her *life* is over-emphasized—'blooming', her freshness—'dew', and her exceeding fairness; the 'fountain', clearly made a symbol of life in the poem of that title, 'trips' 'from its rocky cave'—possibly in association with 'basket' a reference to the return of Proserpine from the underworld, combining the idea of spring and the return of a daughter. These multitudinous associations—and more could easily come to mind—prepare us for a sentimental reunion scene (if it is Emma) or an adoption scene ('Let me be your father', etc.). Instead, with an unexpected unsentimental twist, the Girl is rejected—'I did not wish her mine' and allowed to remain free and unpossessed—we must not use others as emotional fodder. 'Mine' is an example of the heavy loading of a simple word—'With Wordsworth, words mean *all* of their possible meaning', says Coleridge. In *The Fountain* the Boy's offer of sonship had been similarly rejected; perhaps Matthew is peculiarly honest and telling us that there are no *substitutes*, but we still have the 'sigh of pain' and the persistence of the memory to account for. At any rate, his strange story, told thirty years later, forges another link in the chain of associations, so that Wordsworth, years afterwards, in the last stanza, can still see Matthew 'at that moment' of finishing his story, though he too, at the time of writing the poem, is also 'in his grave'. The 'bough of wilding' remains, perhaps an accidental association, but with some symbolic force of mystery, like the mythical Golden Bough, in communicating with the dead. And Wordsworth was always concerned, as we shall see in the extract from *The Prelude* (p. 145), in keeping open communications with the important moments of his past, which are used to fortify the present. It is this sense of fortification which the final lines of this poem give us. (See Danby, *The Simple Wordsworth*, 79–88, for further discussion of the poem.)

INFORMATION, PROBABLY IRRELEVANT. Since the Matthew poems are mysterious, a good deal of speculation has arisen, mainly biographical. For example, Matthew is usually thought to be William Taylor (see p. 22), but Taylor died at thirty-two. He was traditionally responsible for Wordsworth's early verse, encouraging his pupils to imitate the 'Graveyard school' of eighteenth-century poetry. We might therefore expect a commemorative poem in his honour to contain melancholy, death and a churchyard, but the whole mood of Wordsworth's poem is different from, say, Gray's *Elegy*, a stanza of which was inscribed on Taylor's tomb. The dead girl links *The Two April Mornings* to the 'Lucy' poems, and since Emma is used as another name for Dorothy Wordsworth in yet another group of poems, it has been suggested that the Lucy/Matthew cycle is connected with a sublimated brother-sister relationship. I cannot see that any of this speculation helps us to understand the poem; but if we must guess, it seems more to the point to look for an eight-year-old girl. In 1799 Wordsworth's own daughter, Caroline, would be almost the same age as Emma; he had, of course, never seen her.

CONCLUSION, POINTING FORWARD. Notice the hints of Stoicism; of facing experiences, not shirking them; of enduring and continuing to the end, six years before the *Elegiac Stanzas* (p. 152). At the beginning of the poem Wordsworth is a Boy, at the end a mature man, capable of recognizing adult experience, even the experience of middle and old age.

The decision to go home, 1799

The importance of this decision has already been discussed (p. 105); the experience is given its full poetic record in *Home at Grasmere*, that is the First Book of the uncompleted *Recluse*, to be found in *Poetical Works*, v, p. 313–39. In the earlier draft of this poem the following passage occurs, describing an incident on the journey from Yorkshire to Grasmere:

> Stern was the face of Nature: we rejoiced
> In that stern countenance, for our Souls thence drew
> A feeling of their strength. The naked Trees,
> The icy brooks, as on we passed, appeared
> To question us. 'Whence come ye? To what end?'
> They seemed to say; 'What would ye,' said the shower,
> 'Wild Wanderers, whither through my dark domain?'
> The sunbeam said, 'be happy'. They were mov'd
> All things were mov'd, they round us as we went,
> We in the midst of them. And when the trance
> Came to us, as we stood by Hart-leap Well,
> The intimation of the milder day
> Which is to be, the fairer world than this,
> And rais'd us up, dejected as we were,
> Among the records of that doleful place,

By sorrow for the hunted Beast who there
Had yielded up his breath, the awful trance
The vision of humanity, and of God
The Mourner, God the Sufferer, when the heart
Of his poor Creatures suffer wrongfully—
Both in the sadness and the joy we found
A promise. . . .

The passage goes on to say that the Hart-Leap Well experience made
William and Dorothy feel that their decision to settle at Grasmere was
justified. If nothing else, the Hart provided a forceful illustration
of the homing instinct.

Hart-Leap Well

Hart-Leap Well is a small spring of water, about five miles from
Richmond in Yorkshire, and near the side of the road which leads
from Richmond to Askrigg. Its name is derived from a remarkable
Chase, the memory of which is preserved by the monuments
spoken of in the second Part of the following Poem, which
monuments do now exist as I have there described them.

The Knight had ridden down from Wensley moor
With the slow motion of a summer's cloud;
He turned aside towards a Vassal's door,
And, 'Bring another Horse!' he cried aloud.

'Another Horse!'—That shout the Vassal heard,
And saddled his best steed, a comely gray;
Sir Walter mounted him; he was the third
Which he had mounted on that glorious day.

10 Joy sparkled in the prancing Courser's eyes;
The Horse and Horseman are a happy pair;
But, though Sir Walter like a falcon flies,
There is a doleful silence in the air.

A rout this morning left Sir Walter's Hall,
That as they galloped made the echoes roar;
But Horse and Man are vanished, one and all;
Such race, I think, was never seen before.

Sir Walter, restless as a veering wind,
Calls to the few tired Dogs that yet remain:
Brach, Swift, and Music, noblest of their kind,
20 Follow, and up the weary mountain strain.

The Knight hallooed, he chid and cheered them on
With suppliant gestures and upbraiding stern;
But breath and eye-sight fail; and, one by one,
The Dogs are stretched among the mountain fern.

Where is the throng, the tumult of the Chase?
The bugles that so joyfully were blown?
This race it looks not like an earthly race;
Sir Walter and the Hart are left alone.

The poor Hart toils along the mountain side;
I will not stop to tell how far he fled,
Nor will I mention by what death he died;
But now the Knight beholds him lying dead.

Dismounting then, he leaned against a thorn;
He had no follower, Dog, nor Man, nor Boy:
He neither smacked his whip, nor blew his horn,
But gazed upon the spoil with silent joy.

Close to the thorn on which Sir Walter leaned,
Stood his dumb partner in this glorious act;
Weak as a lamb the hour that it is yeaned,
And foaming like a mountain cataract.

Upon his side the Hart was lying stretched:
His nose half-touched a spring beneath a hill,
And with the last deep groan his breath had fetched
The waters of the spring were trembling still.

And now, too happy for repose or rest,
(Was never a man in such a joyful case!)
Sir Walter walked all round, north, south, and west,
And gazed and gazed upon that darling place.

And climbing up the hill—(it was at least
Nine roods of sheer ascent) Sir Walter found
Three several hoof-marks which the hunted Beast
Had left imprinted on the verdant ground.

Sir Walter wiped his face and cried, 'Till now
Such sight was never seen by living eyes:
Three leaps have borne him from this lofty brow,
Down to the very fountain where he lies.

'I'll build a Pleasure-house upon this spot,
And a small Arbour, made for rural joy;
'Twill be the Traveller's shed, the Pilgrim's cot,
A place of love for Damsels that are coy.

'A cunning Artist will I have to frame
A bason for that Fountain in the dell;
And they who do make mention of the same
From this day forth, shall call it HART-LEAP WELL.

30

40

50

60

'And, gallant brute! to make thy praises known,
Another monument shall here be raised;
Three several pillars, each a rough hewn Stone,
And planted where thy hoofs the turf have grazed.

'And in the summer-time when days are long,
I will come hither with my Paramour;
And with the Dancers, and the Minstrel's song,
We will make merry in that pleasant Bower.

'Till the foundations of the mountains fail
My Mansion with its Arbour shall endure;
The joy of them who till the fields of Swale,
And them who dwell among the woods of Ure!'

Then home he went, and left the Hart, stone-dead,
With breathless nostrils stretched above the spring.
And soon the Knight performed what he had said,
The fame whereof through many a land did ring.

Ere thrice the moon into her port had steered,
A Cup of Stone received the living Well;
Three Pillars of rude stone Sir Walter reared,
And built a House of Pleasure in the dell.

And near the fountain, flowers of stature tall
With trailing plants and trees were intertwined,
Which soon composed a little sylvan Hall,
A leafy shelter from the sun and wind.

And thither, when the summer-days were long,
Sir Walter journeyed with his Paramour;
And with the Dancers and the Minstrel's song
Made merriment within that pleasant Bower.

The Knight, Sir Walter, died in course of time,
And his bones lie in his paternal vale.—
But there is matter for a second rhyme,
And I to this would add another tale.

Part Second

The moving accident is not my trade:
To freeze the blood I have no ready arts;
'Tis my delight, alone in summer shade,
To pipe a simple song to thinking hearts.

As I from Hawes to Richmond did repair,
It chanced that I saw standing in a dell
Three Aspens at three corners of a square,
And one, not four yards distant, near a Well.

What this imported I could ill divine:
And, pulling now the rein my horse to stop,
I saw three Pillars standing in a line,
The last Stone Pillar on a dark hill-top.

The trees were gray, with neither arms nor head;
Half-wasted the square Mound of tawny green;
So that you just might say, as then I said,
'Here in old time the hand of man has been.'

I looked upon the hills both far and near,
More doleful place did never eye survey;
It seemed as if the spring-time came not here,
And Nature here were willing to decay.

I stood in various thoughts and fancies lost,
When one, who was in Shepherd's garb attired,
Came up the Hollow. Him did I accost,
And what this place might be I then inquired.

The Shepherd stopped, and that same story told
Which in my former rhyme I have rehearsed.
'A jolly place,' said he, 'in times of old!
But something ails it now; the spot is curst.

'You see these lifeless Stumps of aspen wood—
Some say that they are beeches, others elms—
These were the Bower; and here a Mansion stood;
The finest palace of a hundred realms!

'The Arbour does its own condition tell;
You see the Stones, the Fountain, and the Stream,
But as to the great Lodge! you might as well
Hunt half a day for a forgotten dream.

'There's neither dog nor heifer, horse nor sheep,
Will wet his lips within that Cup of Stone;
And oftentimes, when all are fast asleep,
This water doth send forth a dolorous groan.

'Some say that here a murder has been done,
And blood cries out for blood: but, for my part,
I've guessed, when I've been sitting in the sun,
That it was all for that unhappy Hart.

'What thoughts must through the creature's brain
        have passed!
From the stone upon the summit of the steep
Are but three bounds—and look Sir, at this last—
—O Master! it has been a cruel leap.

110

120

130

140

'For thirteen hours he ran a desperate race;
And in my simple mind we cannot tell
What cause the Hart might have to love this place,
And come and make his death-bed near the Well.

'Here on the grass perhaps asleep he sank,
150   Lulled by this Fountain in the summer-tide;
This water was perhaps the first he drank
When he had wandered from his mother's side.

'In April here beneath the scented thorn
He heard the birds their morning carols sing;
And he, perhaps, for aught we know, was born
Not half a furlong from that self-same spring.

'But now here's neither grass nor pleasant shade;
The sun on drearier Hollow never shone:
So will it be, as I have often said,
160   Till Trees, and Stones, and Fountain all are gone.'

'Gray-headed Shepherd, thou has spoken well;
Small difference lies between thy creed and mine:
This Beast not unobserved by Nature fell;
His death was mourned by sympathy divine.

'The Being, that is in the clouds and air,
That is in the green leaves among the groves,
Maintains a deep and reverential care
For them the quiet creatures whom he loves.

'The Pleasure-house is dust:—behind, before,
170   This is no common waste, no common gloom;
But Nature, in due course of time, once more
Shall here put on her beauty and her bloom.

'She leaves these objects to a slow decay,
That what we are, and have been, may be known;
But, at the coming of the milder day,
These monuments shall all be overgrown.

'One lesson, Shepherd, let us two divide,
Taught both by what she shows, and what conceals,
Never to blend our pleasure or our pride
180   With sorrow of the meanest thing that feels.'

TEXT. This is the second published version, from the second volume of *Lyrical Ballads* (1802). There were several later alterations, which look like attempts to make certain lines more elegant; surely the occasional clumsiness of expression suits the ballad style.

TYPE OF POEM. This raises an important question: with what type of poem, what *genre*, are we faced here? We could argue, from the title of the volume, that this is a Lyrical Ballad: if so, it is a further development of this kind of poem, in the same way that *The Two April Mornings* was an intensification of the basic method of *The Last of the Flock*. Here, too, a certain 'colouring of the imagination' is thrown over an incident on Wordsworth's journey home; but is this enough to explain the strange story and the even more mysterious 'Part Second'? Another approach would start from the medieval subject matter: is this a Gothic tale? The Gothic side of Wordsworth is usually played down, and he is thought of as reacting against the overstimulation of the imagination which medieval fantasy so frequently provided. But Wordsworth shares the interest in the Middle Ages common to his Romantic contemporaries, and such poems as the *Song at the Feast of Brougham Castle* and *The White Doe of Rylstone* are by no means negligible.

Personally, while admitting its close relation to the 'true' Lyrical Ballads, I prefer to describe this as a *commemorative poem*, related to the large number of poems 'On the Naming of Places' and the poems 'written on tour' (see p. 142). The story tells us, at a literal level, how Hartleap Well received its name; the curious prose preface emphasizes this and also conveys the idea of commemorating and preserving a tradition for posterity. But note that Wordsworth classified it as 'A poem of the Imagination' in collected editions.

METRE AND VERSE-FORM. The slow-moving five-foot lines are unexpected; the dignified quatrains make for a cumbrous narrative style, which is alien in spirit to that of a medieval ballad. This stanza form has an eighteenth-century history, and was used in Gray's *Elegy written in a Country Churchyard*:

> Yet ev'n these bones from insult to protect
> Some frail memorial still erected nigh,
> With uncouth rhimes and shapeless sculpture deck'd,
> Implores the passing tribute of a sigh.

In Gray's *Elegy* there is also a 'hoary-headed Swain', who addresses a 'kindred spirit' (to the dead poet) 'led by lonely contemplation'; there may be other parallels, but it must be conceded at this point that it is only at the close of *Hartleap Well* that Wordsworth approaches closely to Gray's verse movement:

> Never to blend our pleasure or our pride
> With sorrow of the meanest thing that feels.

These lines illustrate the sententious moralizing that the eighteenth-century reader would associate with the stanza, and look forward to its even more emphatic use in *Elegiac Stanzas* (p. 152).

THE STORY. The first part of the poem deals with Sir Walter's attempts to impose his mastery on the natural environment. Although he controls other animals—horses and dogs—he is never able to catch the hart alive, and it escapes him in the moment of death. Sir Walter is man enough to recognize the nobility of his victim, but does not see that he has challenged his real adversary—the forces of Nature. To be fair to Sir Walter, it is he who begins the commemoration of the event by building the 'Pleasure-House'; he also imposes 'a cup of Stone' upon 'the living Well'. (At this point notice the parallels to the first part of Coleridge's *Kubla Khan*, with its Dome of Pleasure and Sacred River, and its order imposed by an all-mighty ruler.) He degrades the nobility of the place by turning it into a weekend retreat; the human beings firmly under his sway—the Damsels, and the Artist—do not question his purpose, and he announces that his achievement will last for ever:

> Till the foundations of the mountains fail
> My Mansion with its Arbour shall endure.

But already, before Sir Walter's death, the gentler powers of Nature have begun to assert themselves:

> flowers of stature tall
> With trailing plants and trees were intertwined.

The second part of *Hartleap Well* is set in the present. (As in *Michael*, *The Ruined Cottage*, and other poems, Wordsworth is moved to visionary experience by the landscape surrounding a ruin.) The poet begins by disclaiming any intention to indulge in Gothic suspense and relate a tale 'packed with thrills':

> The moving accident is not my trade;
> To freeze the blood I have no ready arts . . .

We are readily persuaded to postpone any criticisms we may have of his mode of telling the story, and the next two lines make it clear that the tale is only there to bring out a moral. Many readers take the moral to be the last two lines of the poem, which seem to mean 'Be kind to animals'. On a very literal level this is true, and at this point one might compare the 'obvious moral' of *The Ancient Mariner*:

> He prayeth well, who loveth well
> Both man and bird and beast.

But *The Ancient Mariner* is really concerned with what happens when a man upsets the powers of Nature—

> with my crossbow,
> I shot the Albatross.

Sir Walter, who hunted down the hart, is therefore a lesser Ancient Mariner. Because of the Hart's death, 'the spot is curst'. Nearly all Sir Walter's monuments of pride have disappeared, but enough remains to commemorate the great event. Nature is alienated, and animals, including dogs and horses, refuse to drink at the well. The shepherd, 'sitting in the sun', hardly distinguishable from the poet, 'alone in summer shade', guesses that the place was of particular importance to the Hart: he was born there, and returned instinctively to his true home. The poet follows with more abstract interpretation of the event, but it is clear that his ideas are not opposed to the shepherd's: 'Small difference lies between thy creed and mine'. Nature observed the death of the Hart, and 'the Being', variously interpreted as Nature, God, or God-in-Nature, because of his 'reverential care', has allowed the place to decay as an example of 'What we are, and have been'. But at a later date, slowly and quietly, the beneficent powers of Nature will reassert themselves; there is no dramatic reversal of fortune, no catastrophe—'at the coming of the milder day the monuments will disappear, engulfed in new growth of beauty and of bloom'.

RELIGIOUS AND OTHER INTERPRETATIONS. The deeper meaning of the poem has always been a puzzle. Clearly there are a number of images which reveal a hinterland of religious suggestion. The hart, to begin with, recalls

> As pants the hart for cooling streams
> When heated in the chase . . .
>
> (NICHOLAS BRADY 1696)

This is from Psalm 42:1: 'Like as the hart desireth the water-brooks, so longeth my soul after thee, O God.' Is it possible to follow this symbolism in our poem? The poet tells us that 'This race it looks not like an earthly race', but it is not made clear what kind of chase we are witnessing. Sir Walter thinks he has captured something (the soul, the imagination?) which he associates with joy and his kind of pleasure. His life of action is surely contrasted with the contemplative life of the shepherd and poet, who realize that Man's past and present state ('what we are, and have been') is doomed, because it is based upon cruelty and the confining of imagination—surely this is the Cup of Stone, almost a Cap of Stone, laid upon 'the living well'. At this point we might call in evidence William Blake's teaching:

> He who bends to himself a Joy
> Doth the winged life destroy;
> But he who kisses the Joy as it flies
> Lives in Eternity's sunrise.

The 'milder day' remains a puzzle which cannot be solved from within the poem. We have the additional reference in *The Recluse* (see p. 129) and a further reading of that poem shows that the Wordsworths approached Grasmere in a mood of mystical elation verging on trance. At this time the poet's 'Creed' included belief in a new state of being, a redemptive process brought about in slow tranquileity without sudden conversions or a Last Judgment. The small community at Grasmere would be the first to experience 'the milder day' which would eventually include the whole of mankind.

A poet in retirement 1800–7

During these years we are still on the high plateau of Wordsworth's poetic achievement. Certain aspects of his retirement have already been discussed—see 'Collaboration with Coleridge' (p. 101) and 'The Recluse of Grasmere' (p. 108). These were years of simple pursuits and steady writing; personal and domestic themes predominate—Wordsworth was married in 1802. It was a firm belief of the poet that his way of life was right for him, and that his poems should arise naturally from it; as he himself said: 'I speak of what I know'.

Nevertheless, it is obvious that by limiting himself to his own observations in a remote valley, he would soon exhaust his material: he therefore drew on Dorothy's Journals and upon other people's experiences, for example in *Alice Fell*, *The Solitary Reaper* (observed by Wilkinson who 'Passed a female who was reaping alone'), and *The Kitten and Falling Leaves* (rough draft by Coleridge printed in *Notebooks*, vol. i, 1813). He received additional stimulation from holiday excursions and tours, so that his visit to France (combined with a reading of Milton) encouraged him to explore the possibilities of a new form—for him—the sonnet. Seeing that a French invasion was a possibility in 1803, he joined the Volunteers, and used the sonnet as 'a trumpet' to encourage national resistance, for the principle of national self-determination led logically to the defence of one's own country.

Most of his work for this period was published in *Poems In Two Volumes* (1807); many important poems, such as *Resolution and Independence* and the *Immortality Ode*, which were included in these volumes, have received a good deal of critical attention elsewhere. But three of the poems which follow were published in 1807—*Alice Fell, Stepping Westward* and *Elegiac Stanzas*—and when we consider that the major part of *The Prelude* dates from this time there seems no reason to challenge the usual critical dictum that this was Wordsworth's major creative period. Yet it is a pity that, as a corollary, his earlier and later poetry is left unread.

Alice Fell

The Post-boy drove with fierce career,
For threat'ning clouds the moon had drown'd;
When suddenly I seem'd to hear
A moan, a lamentable sound.

As if the wind blew many ways
I heard the sound, and more and more:
It seem'd to follow with the Chaise,
And still I heard it as before.

At length I to the Boy call'd out,
He stopp'd his horses at the word;
But neither cry, nor voice, nor shout,
Nor aught else like it could be heard.

The Boy then smack'd his whip, and fast
The horses scamper'd through the rain;
And soon I heard upon the blast
The voice, and bade him halt again.

Said I, alighting on the ground,
'What can it be, this piteous moan?'
And there a little Girl I found,
Sitting behind the Chaise, alone.

'My Cloak!' the word was last and first,
And loud and bitterly she wept,
As if her very heart would burst;
And down from off the Chaise she leapt.

'What ails you, Child?' She sobb'd, 'Look here!'
I saw it in the wheel entangled,
A weather beaten Rag as e'er
From any garden scare-crow dangled.

'Twas twisted betwixt nave and spoke;
Her help she lent, and with good heed
Together we released the Cloak;
A wretched, wretched rag indeed!

'And whither are you going, Child,
To-night along these lonesome ways?'
'To Durham' answer'd she half wild—
'Then come with me into the chaise.'

She sate like one past all relief;
Sob after sob she forth did send
In wretchedness, as if her grief
Could never, never, have an end.

'My Child, in Durham do you dwell?'
She check'd herself in her distress,
And said, 'My name is Alice Fell;
I'm fatherless and motherless.

'And I to Durham, Sir, belong.'
'And then, as if the thought would choke
Her very heart, her grief grew strong;
And all was for her tatter'd Cloak.

The chaise drove on, our journey's end
50 Was nigh; and, sitting by my side,
    As if she'd lost her only friend
    She wept, nor would be pacified.

    Up to the Tavern-door we post;
    Of Alice and her grief I told;
    And I gave money to the Host,
    To buy a new Cloak for the old.

    'And let it be of duffil grey,
    As warm a cloak as man can sell!'
    Proud Creature was she the next day,
60 The little Orphan, Alice Fell!

TEXT. The poem is given here in its 1807 version, since this provoked
the controversy over it. An earlier text of the poem occurs in a notebook kept by Sara Hutchinson (see *Poetical Works* ii, p. 542). Later
versions contain more 'dignified' phraseology. A close study of the
textual variants of this poem makes one wonder how much value
Wordsworth really put on the *words* of a poem as opposed to its
'message' (see THE CONTROVERSY OVER POETIC DICTION below).

TITLE. In 1815 Wordsworth added a subtitle—*or Poverty*. In the same
way the ballad *Lucy Gray* became *Lucy Gray, or Solitude* and *The Leechgatherer* was renamed *Resolution and Independence*. One may speculate
whether these new titles were designed to help the reading public, or
whether the older poet himself felt the lack of dignity. The new titles
limit the poems to the field of moral tracts, and make one wonder
exactly what Wordsworth thought his poems were about.

TYPE OF POEM. Clearly a Lyrical Ballad; but is it, as some say, an
improvement on the earlier ballads, or a last attempt at an exhausted
manner, a tired self-parody? There are very few poems of this type in
the 1807 volume, for Wordsworth was now more interested in literary
verse forms, such as elegy, ode and sonnet.

STORY. According to a note dictated by Wordsworth to Isabella
Fenwick, the incident happened to a 'Mr Graham of Glasgow . . . a
man of ardent humanity'; it is recorded in Dorothy Wordsworth's
Journals, 16 February 1802. (The relevant passage is quoted in the
section 'Dorothy Wordsworth and her Journals' p. 100.) At first reading the tale seems simple enough; it is a modern version of the parable
of the Good Samaritan, and a slightly unpleasant air of self-con-
gratulation surrounds the 'I' of the poem, however worthy his actions
may be. (This may be unfair, but how much did this charitable act
really cost the narrator? I expect Alice Fell—the real one—thought
him a pompous busybody, but she was probably used to being
ordered about by 'men of ardent humanity'.)

Further readings are more favourable; the strange cry and the endless sobbing remain in our minds, and it seems that Alice is weeping for far more than she or her unimaginative protector can understand. To misquote Gerard Manley Hopkins: 'It is Alice Fell you mourn for.' This poem and *The Last of the Flock* exhibit a pathetic clinging to a single idea or possession which must not be destroyed: I mean something far removed from a simple love of property. The cloak, in this case, represents a last hold upon life, and however disproportionate the child's grief may appear, it is still explicable in terms of human psychology. One might even guess that the orphan thought of 'the wretched rag' as a mother substitute—such things are not unknown among young children. The phrase 'as if she'd lost her only friend' bears this out. There are no replacements in these deeply held relationships (compare Matthew and his daughter in *The Two April Mornings*). One gathers that the 'I' of the poem, seeing that the old cloak was a complete write-off, assumed that the new cloak, which he bought with cash, had completely solved the problem. Compare: 'I'm sorry I've run over your dog. Here's the money to buy a new one', and incidentally, notice the textile-trade insistence on the best cloth that money can buy! The last two lines are not based on Mr Graham's observation, since he travelled on to another destination; they were put in 'to gratify Mr Graham', as the Fenwick note has it.

CHILD AS VICTIM. For the use of the child as a vehicle for social commentary in the nineteenth century, see Peter Coveney, *The Image of Childhood*. Wordsworth's other poetic children may be compared—see for example *The Idiot Boy*, *Lucy Gray*, and *We Are Seven*. The last-named poem has caused a great deal of controversy and amusement.

THE CONTROVERSY OVER POETIC DICTION. At the time of writing this poem (11–14 March 1802) Wordsworth was preparing a new edition of *Lyrical Ballads* and revising his famous *Preface*. He said that 'there is no essential difference between the language of prose and that of metrical composition', and declared that poetry should be concerned 'with incidents of common life'. *Alice Fell* provides a fair illustration of these *dicta*.

The reviewers of the 1807 *Poems in Two Volumes* disagreed with these principles. In common with most readers they expected poetry to deal with elegant, or at any rate, elevated topics; they also believed that there was a special language for poetry which was quite different from the language of prose—and certainly far removed from that of daily conversation. *The Edinburgh Review* (Oct. 1807) was openly abusive: 'If the printing of such trash as this be not felt as an insult on the public taste, we are afraid it cannot be insulted'. At this time the reviews controlled 'the public taste', and the 1807 *Poems* were widely ridiculed. *Alice Fell* was such a stumbling-block that Wordsworth withdrew it from the 1820 edition of his poems. It was restored at the request of some of his friends in 1836.

The whole controversy was surely settled by Coleridge in *Biographia*

Literaria (1817), but it has remained a hardy perennial in critical studies of Wordsworth. Modern readers are likely to be pragmatic; if a poem like *Alice Fell* is still convincing as poetry, it matters little what theories it was designed to illustrate; if it does not succeed, no amount of special pleading can save it. I have therefore devoted little space to the problem in this study, but those who feel that it is important might well look at Dr Johnson's comments on *Macbeth*—he disliked 'the butcher's knife', and also at the correspondence between Gerard Manley Hopkins and Robert Bridges. The twentieth-century preference for 'the colloquial' in poetry may well be a temporary phenomenon; Donald Davie's *Purity of Diction in English Verse* (1952), together with his admiration for the late Augustans, represent one attempt to revive an interest in the use of a 'civilized' diction; it is interesting that he has to go back to the age before Wordsworth. Meanwhile, here are two remarks by Wordsworth which can be applied to *Alice Fell* as well as to the whole problem:

1. 'Language is not thought's dress, but its incarnation'—implying, surely, that one should not, at a later date, alter the text.
2. 'The voice which is the voice of my poetry, without imagination, cannot be heard'—which is a nice snub to the critics, but could, I suppose, be used to justify any amount of bad writing.

On tour

In 1803 William and Dorothy visited Scotland together with Coleridge (see p. 106); many poems were written to commemorate the experiences of this holiday. A quick glance through the contents of Wordsworth's *Poetical Works* might well give the impression that he was more frequently 'on tour' than at home and several of his later sonnet sequences and other groups of poems are entitled *Memorials of a Tour* . . . to this place and that. He preferred walking to other forms of locomotion, and De Quincey calculated that Wordsworth must have walked between 175,000 and 180,000 miles in his lifetime. He remained physically active far into old age, riding from Westmorland to Cambridge at the age of sixty, and walking in the hills in his seventies. No wonder, then, that the poet described himself as 'a wanderer', supporting the literal sense of the next poem's conclusion.

Stepping Westward

While my Fellow-traveller and I were walking by the side of Loch Ketterine, one fine evening after sunset, in our road to a Hut where, in the course of our Tour, we had been hospitably entertained some weeks before, we met, in one of the loneliest parts of that solitary region, two well-dressed Women, one of whom said to us by way of greeting, 'What, you are stepping westward?'

'What, you are stepping westward?'—'Yea,'
—'Twould be a *wildish* destiny,
If we, who thus together roam
In a strange Land, and far from home,
Were in this place the guests of Chance:
Yet who would stop, or fear to advance,
Though home or shelter he had none,
With such a sky to lead him on?

10
The dewy ground was dark and cold;
Behind, all gloomy to behold;
And stepping westward seemed to be
A kind of *heavenly* destiny;
I liked the greeting; 'twas a sound
Of something without place or bound;
And seemed to give me spiritual right
To travel through that region bright.

The voice was soft, and she who spake
Was walking by her native lake:
The salutation had to me
20
The very sound of courtesy:
Its power was felt; and while my eye
Was fixed upon the glowing Sky,
The echo of the voice enwrought
A human sweetness with the thought
Of travelling through the world that lay
Before me in my endless way.

TEXT.   Though there is little difference between the text of 1807 and
Wordsworth's final version, I have printed the final version of this
poem, since the tidying up in matters of punctuation is in all cases
justifiable.

LITERAL BASIS.   Dorothy Wordsworth describes the incident which the
poem records (*Journals* i, pp. 367–8). Those who despise fictions will
presumably admire Wordsworth's fidelity to fact in line 1.

SUBJECT.   A glorious sunset is a standard Romantic thrill: the greet-
ings which human beings exchange are usually meaningless, and the
woman's strange expression was presumably the usual one in that part
of the country. Wordsworth's power as a poet is seen in what he can do
with such material, so that after reading *Stepping Westward* these
commonplaces, while retaining universality, are made new for us.

In fact Dorothy tells us more about the sunset and the landscape
than William—and yet he is traditionally thought of in association
with such moments of natural grandeur. Wordsworth is often considered to be cold, egotistical and self-sufficient, but what he writes
about here is the warmth of a stranger's greeting and how it increased
his pleasure in the sunset. The salutation seemed to open infinite

possibilities, and expressed a recognition of his right to travel; he felt welcomed, and also saw that he had been given something of inestimable value.

Exactly what is arguable. Obviously a good deal more could be read into the poem if one really tried. The 'endless way' of the last lines extends the travelling into a metaphor for the journey we make through life (compare *The Pilgrim's Progress*). '*Heavenly*' and 'spiritual' may simply be suggestive exaggerations, but if 'stepping westward' is a '*heavenly* destiny' surely the pilgrimage towards death is meant. But Wordsworth only says 'seemed to be a kind of' (lines 11, 12)—not, incidentally, an example of that precise use of language which one is taught to admire. Yet perhaps he *is* being precise, because to say more than he does would be inaccurate.

Notice how the sunset and the greeting are welded together in the last stanzas and are transformed into the endless journey and 'human sweetness' of the last three lines. Many of Wordsworth's poems are attempts to show how we associate ideas (see 'Hartley', p. 77), and he often points out how the second idea—'the echo of the voice' in this case—is blended with the first idea on which our conscious attention is fixed—'my eye / Was fixed upon the glowing Sky.'

Dorothy tells us that Wordsworth wrote the poem 'long after', as was his usual custom. The phrase reminds us of the conclusion to *The Solitary Reaper*:

> —The music in my heart I bore,
> Long after it was heard no more.

In the extract from *The Prelude* we shall see how 'spots of time', especially those connected with 'power' of feeling (line 21), are the source of 'future restoration'.

USE OF LANGUAGE. Notice how much of the poem is written in simple vocabulary, even strings of monosyllables (stanza 1). Pomposity has been avoided, and yet a monument has been erected. The total impression is a nice balance between the colloquial, which might have led to bathos, and an overpolished style which would not have been appropriate to the subject. Wordsworth chooses a neutral style, yet the total effect is somehow magnificent.

CRITICISM. The learned reviewers—and their successors in all ages— might regard this poem as too trivial to bear much discussion, but the fact remains that *Stepping Westward* is much *liked*—if one may be allowed to use such a term in criticism. The judgment of the common reader should never be ignored, though I realize that this poem is easier to follow than most. The best critical account of the poem is to be found in Donald Davie's *Articulate Energy*, p. 154 ff, where it is compared with *The Gypsy* by Ezra Pound. Professor Davie's further remarks (on pp. 164 and 165 of the same book) must not be missed; they seem to me one of the high points of modern appreciation of Wordsworth's greatness.

The great philosophical poem

The Prelude, 1805

Wordsworth's greatest poem was not published till after his death, and even then was slow in achieving recognition. Its position as the Epic of the Romantic Age is still not beyond question, firstly because it is treated simply as a verse autobiography, and secondly because it combines poetry and philosophy.

Wordsworth never wrote more than one book of *The Recluse*, which was to have been 'the great philosophical poem'. *The Prelude* was meant to illustrate the growth of his own mind, so as to show his fitness for such a project. On this level it may be read simply as an account of his own life, and though its evidence is selected there seems no reason to doubt its general accuracy.

It is at a more abstract level that problems arise: we no longer expect poetry to do the work of history, psychology and the novel, or to find 'the spirit of the age' expressed in poetic medium. Nor do we ask the poet to combine the roles of priest and sage, or to enlighten us with revelations, or teach us the morality on which we should base our lives.

In the nineteenth century many readers found—or thought they had found—a system of philosophy in Wordsworth's work; in our own time what Wordsworth offers as philosophy is largely ignored. It is of course true that our view of the function of philosophy has completely changed; we no longer expect philosophy to provide a world view or a metaphysical system, that is, a complete explanation of the universe. But even in the nineteenth century Wordsworth's early readers differed in their estimates of the meaning and value of the philosophy which his poetry was thought to contain; many of the books on Wordsworth's philosophy are simply expositions of the peculiar theories held by the authors. It looks as if whatever the poet had to say is so vague that it will hardly repay investigation.

In *Revaluation* F. R. Leavis followed Arnold in dismissing Wordsworth's philosophy as an 'illusion'; with this initial discouragement from such authorities the new reader is hardly likely to trouble himself with thirteen or fourteen books of blank verse. I can only ask him to sample the following extract and then make up his mind for himself.

From *The Prelude*

258   There are in our existence spots of time,
        Which with distinct pre-eminence retain
260   A vivifying Virtue, whence, depress'd
        By false opinion and contentious thought,
        Or aught of heavier or more deadly weight,

In trivial occupations, and the round
Of ordinary intercourse, our minds
265   Are nourished and invisibly repair'd,
A virtue by which pleasure is enhanced
That penetrates, enables us to mount
When high, more high, and lifts us up when fallen.
This efficacious spirit chiefly lurks
270   Among those passages of life in which
We have had deepest feeling that the mind
Is lord and master, and that outward sense
Is but the obedient servant of her will.
Such moments worthy of all gratitude,
275   Are scatter'd everywhere, taking their date
From our first childhood; in our childhood even
Perhaps are most conspicuous. Life with me,
As far as memory can look back, is full
Of this beneficent influence. At a time
280   When scarcely (I was then not six years old)
My hand could hold a bridle, with proud hopes
I mounted, and we rode towards the hills:
We were a pair of Horsemen; honest James
Was with me, my encourager and guide.
285   We had not travell'd long, ere some mischance
Disjoin'd me from my Comrade, and, through fear
Dismounting, down the rough and stony Moor
I led my Horse, and stumbling on, at length
Came to a bottom, where in former times
290   A Murderer had been hung in iron chains.
The Gibbet-mast was moulder'd down, the bones
And iron case were gone; but on the turf
Hard by, soon after that fell deed was wrought
Some unknown hand had carved the Murderer's name.
295   The monumental writing was engraven
In times long past, and still, from year to year,
By superstition of the neighbourhood,
The grass is clear'd away; and to this hour
The letters are all fresh and visible.
300   Faltering, and ignorant where I was, at length
I chanced to espy those characters inscribed
On the green sod; forthwith I left the spot
And, reascending the bare Common, saw
A naked Pool that lay beneath the hills,
305   The beacon on the summit, and more near,
A Girl who bore a Pitcher on her head
And seem'd with difficult steps to force her way
Against the blowing wind. It was, in truth,
An ordinary sight; but I should need
310   Colours and words that are unknown to man

To paint the visionary dreariness
Which, while I look'd all round for my lost Guide,
Did at that time invest the naked Pool,
The Beacon on the lonely Eminence,
315 The Woman, and her garments vex'd and toss'd
By the strong wind. When, in a blessed season
With those two dear Ones, to my heart so dear,
When in the blessed time of early love,
Long afterwards, I roam'd about
320 In daily presence of this very scene,
Upon the naked pool and dreary crags,
And on the melancholy Beacon, fell
The spirit of pleasure and youth's golden gleam;
And think ye not with radiance more divine
325 From these remembrances, and from the power
They left behind? So feeling comes in aid
Of feeling, and diversity of strength
Attends us, if but once we have been strong.
Oh! mystery of Man, from what a depth
330 Proceed thy honours! I am lost, but see
In simple childhood something of the base
On which thy greatness stands, but this I feel,
That from thyself it is that thou must give,
Else never canst receive. The days gone by
335 Come back upon me from the dawn almost
Of life: the hiding-places of my power
Seem open; I approach, and then they close;
I see by glimpses now; when age comes on,
May scarcely see at all, and I would give,
340 While yet we may, as far as words can give,
A substance and a life to what I feel:
I would enshrine the spirit of the past
For future restoration. Yet another
Of these, to me, affecting incidents
345 With which we will conclude.
                                        One Christmas-time,
The day before the Holidays began,
Feverish, and tired, and restless, I went forth
Into the fields, impatient for the sight
Of those two Horses which should bear us home;
350 My Brothers and myself. There was a crag,
An Eminence, which from the meeting-point
Of two highways ascending, overlook'd
At least a long half-mile of those two roads,
By each of which the expected Steeds might come,
355 The choice uncertain. Thither I repair'd
Up to the highest summit; 'twas a day
Stormy, and rough, and wild, and on the grass

I sate, half-shelter'd by a naked wall;
Upon my right hand was a single sheep,
360   A whistling hawthorn on my left, and there,
With those Companions at my side, I watch'd,
Straining my eyes intensely, as the mist
Gave intermitting prospect of the wood
And plain beneath. Ere I to School return'd
365   That dreary time, ere I had been ten days
A dweller in my Father's House, he died,
And I and my two Brothers, Orphans then,
Followed his Body to the Grave. The event
With all the sorrow which it brought appear'd
370   A chastisement; and when I call'd to mind
That day so lately pass'd , when from the crag
I look'd in such anxiety of hope,
With trite reflections of morality,
Yet in the deepest passion, I bow'd low
375   To God, who thus corrected my desires;
And afterwards, the wind and sleety rain
And all the business of the elements,
The single sheep, and the one blasted tree,
And the bleak music of that old stone wall,
380   The noise of wood and water, and the mist
Which on the line of each of those two Roads
Advanced in such indisputable shapes,
All these were spectacles and sounds to which
I often would repair and thence would drink,
385   As at a fountain; and I do not doubt
That in this later time, when storm and rain
Beat on my roof at midnight, or by day
When I am in the woods, unknown to me
The workings of my spirit thence are brought.

TEXT.   The extract given here is Book xi, lines 258–389 of the 1805 text, corresponding to Book xii, lines 208–332 in 1850. Note that the 1850 version is usually reprinted in standard editions of Wordsworth's poems, but the 1805 version is available in Oxford Standard Authors, edited by E. de Selincourt. Those wishing to study the development of the text should consult *Wordsworth's Prelude*, edited by E. de Selincourt and H. Darbishire, which has the two versions printed on facing pages, and lists all variants in the notes.

In general, Wordsworth's changes were often simple adjustments aimed at tidying up the poem—he removed lines 343–4 in our extract; but he also altered the language in the direction of the exaggerated poetic diction which he had campaigned against in earlier days—there are no examples in our extract, except perhaps 'the female' for 'the Woman' in line 315. More seriously, Wordsworth changed the ideas of the poem to conform with his later religious and political opinions, though this did not affect our extract.

Although the 1805 version shows all the indications of fast and unrevised writing its total impression of freshness and honesty has led most readers to prefer it.

LENGTH OF EXTRACT. The reader may justly ask why this extract is so long. Selections from Wordsworth usually contain short narrative passages from the early books of *The Prelude*; the 'philosophy' is omitted. This practice can be justified on the grounds that many narrative pieces, including the second half of our extract, were written separately in Germany in 1798–9; and so the philosophy can be regarded as a later intrusion. I am against the custom of pillaging a long work for its 'beauties' and letting the rest sink or swim. In a long poem we expect to find breathing-spaces interspersed between the more important sections of the poem; in *The Prelude* the real matter is the philosophy, and the narrative passages, as can be clearly seen here, are *illustrations* of it. Our extract shows the interweaving of philosophy and narrative characteristic of the poem.

SUMMARY

258–268 This passage has been chosen because it is central to our understanding of *The Prelude*. Wordsworth tells us that our memories are selective: certain 'spots of time' are able to restore us when we are 'depress'd'—compare the recollections of the Wye Valley in *Tintern Abbey*.

269–273 This restoration comes from moments when our minds, presumably also our imaginative powers, are in control of 'outward sense', presumably our normal perceptions.

274–279 These moments are particularly to be found in early childhood.

280–308 Wordsworth illustrates this with an example. When he was five years old he lost his guide when out riding; frightened by the 'horrid imaginations' conjured up by the inscription in the turf, he saw a pool, a beacon, and a woman.

309–316 These impressions may seem 'common', but were invested with 'visionary dreariness'.

317–324 Many years later, in the 'time of early love', he wandered in the same area, which was now invested with 'youth's golden gleam' (see *Elegiac Stanzas*, p. 152).

325–328 This gleam was strengthened by the early associations. So one 'feeling' reinforces another.

329–334 At this point the poet 'takes off' and in a moment of vision tells us that Man's 'greatness' is derived from early childhood experiences—provided that we have contributed something from ourselves to the bare impressions.

334–337 His own experiences crowd upon him, even from earliest infancy; he recognizes them as the sources of his own creative powers; it is as if doors were 'open'.

337–339   But when he tries to 'approach', he is frustrated. Now, in 1805, he can only see 'glimpses', and fears that in old age nothing will be left. (Compare the *Immortality Ode*).

340–343   It is therefore imperative to record these experiences in words *now*, to recreate them 'in substance and in life', so that they can restore him in the future.

343–364   He therefore tells us how he waited impatiently for transport home, the day before his Christmas holidays. He sheltered by a wall, and observed a hawthorn and a sheep.

365–375   Shortly afterwards his father died: he felt that he had been punished for expecting too much.

376–385   Yet (because of the association of ideas), the experience of that day and all its elements, sheep, tree, wall and mist, has remained with him; he has benefited from it.

386–389   Even today, he is sure that subconsciously the experience continues to affect him, especially when storm, rain or trees trigger off the train of associations.

COMMENT ON SUBJECT-MATTER.   Although it is commonplace today to stress the importance of the experiences of early childhood in forming the personality, Wordsworth did not have the benefit of recent theories of psychology. The idea was not of course original to Wordsworth, but his expression of it is unusually convincing; and he is ahead of his time in his recognition of the 'subconscious mind'—this phrase had not yet come into the language, and Wordsworth's 'workings of the spirit'—he has many other phrases—are not always seen to refer to this.

In the light of this passage we can interpret one of Wordsworth's gnomic sayings—'The Child is Father of the Man'—and can understand what the attractive childhood episodes are doing in Books i and ii; they are now seen to be similar 'spots of time . . . enshrined . . . for future restoration'.

Philosophically, we might comment on the extraordinary qualities of Wordsworth's perceptions. He seems at times to be reassuring himself of his grip upon a world of his own devising. In a note dictated to Isabella Fenwick about the *Immortality Ode*, Wordsworth said that in childhood

I was often unable to think of external things as having external existence, and I communed with all that I saw as something not apart from, but inherent in, my own immaterial nature. Many times while going to school have I grasped at a wall or tree to recall myself from this abyss of idealism to the reality. At that time I was afraid of such processes. In later periods of life I have deplored, as we have all reason to do, a subjugation of an opposite character, and have rejoiced over the remembrances.

The disappearance of 'the visionary gleam . . . the glory and the dream' is regretted in the *Immortality Ode*, and its truth is questioned in *Elegiac Stanzas*, our next poem.

BLANK VERSE. Wordsworth composed aloud while walking, 'his jaws working the whoal time', to quote a peasant's recollections. The womenfolk noted down completed sections of the poem, and probably supplied the punctuation—we often feel that there is no reason why one sentence stops and another begins. The method of composition helps to explain the feel of the blank verse; it should be read aloud, in a quiet meditative manner, as if we were listening to a man trying hard to clarify his own thoughts about a difficult topic and at the same time explaining it to somebody else.

CONCLUSION. Great works are usually difficult; they are often rather long. We are not used to long poems these days, and it is unfair to attack Wordsworth, as many critics do, simply because he makes use of a poetic form which has gone out of fashion. In *The Image of Childhood* Peter Coveney points out that after Wordsworth's day poetry 'suffered continuous enfeeblement. The sphere of poetry became more and more peripheral, and it has remained so ever since. . . . It is sobering to reflect that a case could be made out for the judgment that the last extensive exercise of the English poetic sensibility was Wordsworth's *Prelude.*'

'The set is broken' 1805

The normal routine of settled peace and domestic happiness which now made up Wordsworth's life could never have lasted for ever; it was like a challenge to the gods. On 5 February 1805 *The Earl of Abergavenny*, a merchant ship bound for India, was wrecked in Weymouth Bay. A contemporary newspaper account stated that 'as the Abergavenny was laden with an immense quantity of porcelain ware and 27,000 ounces of silver she sank with unusual speed'. Wordsworth's brother John, who had put his capital into this trading venture and was in personal command, went down with his ship. The impact of this news upon the whole Wordsworth set was shattering; many of his biographers feel that the experience was the pivot on which Wordsworth swung from youthful to middle-aged attitudes, from liberal to Tory opinions, from atheism to orthodox Christianity. But of course these tendencies can be traced back to earlier stages in his development; and the *Ode to Duty*—'Me this unchartered freedom tires'—was written the year before. But the death of John not only confirmed Wordsworth's adherence to these opinions; it undermined his former self-sufficiency and cast doubts upon the validity of poetry. 'I feel that there is something cut out of my life which cannot be restored', he wrote in a letter of March 1805; and in the *Elegiac Stanzas*, our next poem, written in 1806, he declared:

> I have submitted to a new controul:
> A power is gone, which nothing can restore:
> A deep distress hath humaniz'd my Soul.

The question is whether the 'power' referred to was the power to write poetry; for though the *Poems In Two Volumes* (1807) are of high quality they mark for most people the end of Wordsworth's poetic life.

Elegiac Stanzas

Suggested by a Picture of Peele Castle in a Storm
painted
by Sir George Beaumont

I was thy Neighbour once, thou rugged Pile!
Four summer weeks I dwelt in sight of thee:
I saw thee every day; and all the while
Thy Form was sleeping on a glassy sea.

So pure the sky, so quiet was the air!
So like, so very like, was day to day!
Whene'er I look'd, thy Image still was there;
It trembled, but it never pass'd away.

How perfect was the calm! it seem'd no sleep;
10   No mood, which season takes away, or brings:
I could have fancied that the mighty Deep
Was even the gentlest of all gentle Things.

Ah! THEN, if mine had been the Painter's hand,
To express what then I saw; and add the gleam,
The light that never was, on sea or land,
The consecration, and the Poet's dream;

I would have planted thee, thou hoary Pile!
Amid a world how different from this!
Beside a sea that could not cease to smile;
20   On tranquil land, beneath a sky of bliss:

Thou shouldst have seem'd a treasure-house, a mine
Of peaceful years; a chronicle of heaven:—
Of all the sunbeams that did ever shine
The very sweetest had to thee been given.

A Picture had it been of lasting ease,
Elysian quiet, without toil or strife;
No motion but the moving tide, a breeze,
Or merely silent Nature's breathing life.

Peele Castle in a Storm, by Sir George Beaumont

Such, in the fond delusion of my heart,
30   Such Picture would I at that time have made:
And seen the soul of truth in every part;
A faith, a trust, that could not be betray'd.

So once it would have been,—'tis so no more;
I have submitted to a new controul:
A power is gone, which nothing can restore;
A deep distress hath humaniz'd my Soul.

Not for a moment could I now behold
A smiling sea and be what I have been:
The feeling of my loss will ne'er be old;
40   This, which I know, I speak with mind serene.

Then, Beaumont, Friend! who would have been the Friend,
If he had lived, of Him whom I deplore,
This Work of thine I blame not, but commend;
This sea is anger, and that dismal shore.

Oh 'tis a passionate Work!—yet wise and well:
Well chosen is the spirit that is here;
That Hulk which labours in the deadly swell,
This rueful sky, this pageantry of fear!

And this huge Castle, standing here sublime,
I love to see the look with which it braves,
50   Cased in the unfeeling armour of old time,
The light'ning, the fierce wind, and trampling waves.

Farewell, farewell the Heart that lives alone,
Hous'd in a dream, at distance from the Kind!
Such happiness, wherever it be known,
Is to be pitied; for 'tis surely blind.

But welcome fortitude, and patient chear,
And frequent sights of what is to be born!
Such sights, or worse, as are before me here.—
60   Not without hope we suffer and we mourn.

TEXT. Taken from *Poems in Two Volumes* (1807). At one stage the text was altered in an attempt to make lines 15 and 16 clear; these lines are ambiguous as they stand, and can be taken as approving of 'the light that never was, etc.' This would wreck the sense of the entire poem: Wordsworth tried to make it clear that 'the gleam' refers to an illusion which the poet has now seen to be wrong. The original text of the poem was later restored. We may take the ambiguity to imply that Wordsworth was unwilling to admit that the visionary gleam was *entirely* self-deception, and was trying to have it both ways. If this were so, we could argue that the poem only represents a *temporary* loss of faith, instead of the turning-point in Wordsworth's career.

SUBJECT MATTER. Sir George Beaumont's painting depicts Peele Castle in a storm (See illustration). In the foreground a ship is battling with heavy seas. Wordsworth had stayed near the castle in 1794.

In the first half of the poem (lines 1–32) Wordsworth tells us that he once visited the castle in a season of calm weather. The castle seemed asleep, and the sea was tranquil (line 12). If he had been a painter at that time, he would not have produced a picture like Beaumont's storm scene ('different from this'—this picture, line 18); he would have reproduced the tranquillity and the smiling sea, and added 'the light that never was'—the Poet's illusions. Wordsworth's painting would have been 'a mine of peaceful years, etc.' (lines 21–32); that is, it would have represented his youthful ideas about life, which he really thought were true, though he now sees that they were deluded (line 29).

Now come the *turn* of the poem. The second half represents the emotions of 1806. ''Tis so no more', that is, he can no longer consider himself the same person—he has become, at last, a human being (line 36), not a dreaming poet, and he cannot go back to the earlier state. He is stoical (line 40), and sees that Beaumont's conception of the castle in the storm is the *true* image of human life; further, he welcomes what it tells him (lines 43, 45 and 50). So he rejects his former selfish hiving-off from the rest of the human race (lines 53–6); from now on even worse sights than Beaumont's painting will be welcome, for they will reinforce his resolve to endure in patience to the end (lines 57–9). Note that 'born' (line 58) = 'borne'. He is encouraged to go on with the process of living (line 60) and perhaps hints at compensation for suffering in an after-life.

COMMENT. This is a complete reversal of Wordsworth's former teaching—that the Child is Father of the Man, and that in this world 'we find our happiness' (*Prelude* 1805, x, 728). I cannot see that this represents a temporary disillusionment: see the discussion of the religious aspects of the poem in Chapter 3 (p. 88). The expression 'cased in the unfeeling armour of old time' exactly represents the impression Wordsworth made on certain observers at a later date (see Chapter 1, p. 38).

CRITICISM. How eighteenth-century this poem is! The slow, deliberate verse movement; the invocation of such abstractions as 'fortitude and patient chear'; the careful avoidance of metaphorical expressions; the weight of moral earnestness; the balancing of word against word, of phrase against phrase, of the first half against the second half of the poem—in listing these characteristics we move back fifty years. For this is the poetry of statement, of clear prose exposition of what is known to be true—'This, which I know, I speak with mind serene' (line 40).

Besides eighteenth-century excellencies, there are just those faults which the author of the *Preface to Lyrical Ballads* attacked. Some of the diction—'thou rugged Pile!' (line 1) is certainly not 'the language of men', and there is a cumbrous elegance about the 'wit' of

> Then, Beaumont, Friend! who would have been the Friend,
> If he had lived, of him whom I deplore,   (lines 41–2)

which is far removed from the simplicity which Wordsworth is thought to exemplify.

Nevertheless, this seems to me the greatest short poem ever written by Wordsworth, comparable to Dr Johnson's magnificent exposure of *The Vanity of Human Wishes*. One cannot prove a personal judgment of this kind, and I do not expect immediate assent to it. But listen to Wordsworth on the definition of poetry, again from the *Preface to Lyrical Ballads*:

> Aristotle, I have been told, has said that Poetry is the most
> philosophic of all writing: it is so: its object is truth, not individual
> and local, but general and operative; not standing upon external
> testimony, but carried alive into the heart by passion. . . .

It is poems like this which prove that Wordsworth knew what he was talking about.

Middle age, after 1807

Wordsworth produced quantities of verse in the next forty-three years: I stress the exact number of years because it amounts to over half his lifetime, and certainly to two-thirds of his poetic existence. It has often been pointed out that even if he had written nothing before this stage of his career he would still be regarded as an important poet.

In recent years *The White Doe of Rylstone* (published 1815, but written 1807–8) has provoked critical discussion by John Jones and J. F. Danby among others. But the work which really made Wordsworth's reputation, *The Excursion* (1814), is usually dismissed as almost unreadable; it offers Wordsworth's mature opinions 'on Man, on Nature, and Society', and one must grant that, as *The Prelude* was not published in 1814, it appeared to be his most considerable poem. Nevertheless, the following sentence from a letter of 1814 defending *The Excursion* reveals how far we have travelled since 1798.

> Do you not perceive that my conversations almost all take place
> out of doors, and all with grand objects of Nature surrounding
> the speakers for the express purpose of their being alluded to
> in illustration of the subjects treated of?

One would never have expected that the author of *Tintern Abbey* would be reduced to this sort of stage-management! In the same letter he refers to 'a passionate expression uttered incautiously in the Poem upon the Wye' (see p. 85) and adds significantly: 'Unless I am greatly mistaken, there is nothing of this kind in The Excursion.'

Even Wordsworth's friends and admirers sensed that something had gone wrong. Charles Lamb could not believe in the Pedlar who narrates most of Book i, and Keats was suspicious of 'poetry that has a palpable design on us'. By 1819, if Shelley is to be taken as a reliable guide, Wordsworth's stock had gone down and down: 'He was at first sublime, pathetic, impressive, profound; then dull; then prosy and dull; and now dull—oh so very dull! it is an ultra-legitimate dulness' (*Dedication to Peter Bell the Third*). It is necessary, therefore, to turn to a sonnet written on a personal theme for evidence of poetic survival.

Surprised by Joy

Surprised by joy—impatient as the Wind
I turned to share the transport—Oh! with whom
But Thee, deep buried in the silent tomb,
That spot which no vicissitude can find?
5   Love faithful love, recalled thee to my mind—
But how could I forget thee? Through what power,
Even for the least division of an hour,
Have I been so beguiled as to be blind
To my most grievous loss!—That thought's return
10   Was the worst pang that sorrow ever bore,
Save one, one only, when I stood forlorn,
Knowing my heart's best treasure was no more;
That neither present time, nor years unborn
Could to my sight that heavenly face restore.

TEXT.   From *Poetical Works*, iii, p. 16. The sonnet was written between 1812 and 1815.

SUBJECT.   Wordsworth tells us that the poem refers to his daughter Catherine, who died in 1812. Another child, Thomas, died in the same year. He was so deeply moved by this double loss that he was still able to describe his children's last illnesses over thirty-five years later (Aubrey De Vere, *Essays*, vol. ii). De Quincey's morbid account of 'the death of little Kate Wordsworth' is to be found in the second volume of his *Works* edited by Masson (*Reminiscences* vol. ii, pp. 440–5).

EXPLANATORY NOTES.   'Transport' (line 2) means 'rapturous emotion'; 'vicissitude' (line 4) has a long poetic history going back to Milton—it means 'alternation', or 'change of circumstances'. The question mark at the end of line 4 refers back to 'with whom?' 'No vicissitude can find' is therefore a statement of fact, implying a pagan, not a Christian attitude.

CRITICISM.   It is the movement of the verse which makes this sonnet come alive, as has been brilliantly demonstrated by Professor Leavis

(*Scrutiny* vol. xiii, pp. 119–34, especially pp. 125 ff). We may need to read the poem several times to appreciate the way in which an effect of spontaneity is achieved within an extremely rigid verse form. The poet appears at first to be unable to utter his thoughts clearly; he circles wildly, stumbling from one half-finished sentence into another, and breaking up the lines awkwardly (1, 2, 6, 9). Yet this is exactly the way in which people do speak, especially 'in a state of excitement', as any tape-recorder can prove. The 'poetic', almost sentimental, 'Love, faithful love, recalled thee to my mind' is abruptly cut off by 'the true voice of feeling'—'But how could I forget thee?' But after the first $8\frac{1}{2}$ lines these crosswinds of emotion are harmonized, and the poem concludes with a dignified and controlled recognition of the fact of death.

Victorian precursor

In the 1820s and 1830s a strong moralizing voice takes firm control of the poetry. In spite of the increasing stiffness in the handling of the verse, Wordsworth continued to experiment with varied stanza forms, and also, I feel, with language: but the aureate diction frequently conceals the tritest sentiments. If we do pay attention to his thought, we feel we are listening to a public orator of unimpeachably orthodox Christian principles, a Poet Laureate in training—he did not in fact attain this honour until the reign of Queen Victoria in 1843.

Many of his verses, for example *Ecclesiastical Sketches, Sonnets upon the Punishment of Death* (in favour of capital punishment), several sonnets on *Railways* (both for—in general; and against—in the Lake District), and one on *Illustrated Books and Newspapers* (against!) might well find their present day equivalent in irate letters to national or local newspapers, or in an 'Any Questions' discussion. But more typical poems point forward to the quiet effusions of Victorian clergymen and hymn writers. Since the Victorians in general thought of Wordsworth as a Nature poet and in particular as a writer of flower pieces, I have chosen *The Primrose of the Rock* as a representative example. The confidence of this poem in Christian doctrine is unchallengeable. I do not think it is complacent or smug; one feels it has been worked for. The style of the poem is in many ways seventeenth-century, though there are plenty of resemblances to later hymns; but it could be described as an emblem-poem in the seventeenth-century tradition. One could perhaps compare *The Oak*, by the Rev. John Keble:

> Come take a woodland walk with me,
> And mark the rugged old Oak Tree. . .

to see how Wordsworth can still avoid lapsing into utter platitude and sentimentality.

The Primrose of the Rock

A Rock there is whose homely front
  The passing traveller slights;
Yet there the glow-worms hang their lamps,
  Like stars, at various heights;
5 And one coy Primrose to that Rock
  The vernal breeze invites.

What hideous warfare hath been waged,
  What kingdoms overthrown,
Since first I spied that Primrose-tuft
10 And marked it for my own;
A lasting link in Nature's chain
  From highest heaven let down!

The flowers, still faithful to the stems,
  Their fellowship renew;
15 The stems are faithful to the root,
  That worketh out of view;
And to rock that root adheres
  In every fibre true.

Close clings to earth the living rock,
20 Though threatening still to fall;
The earth is constant to her sphere;
  And God upholds them all:
So blooms this lonely Plant, nor dreads
  Her annual funeral.

. . .

25 Here closed the meditative strain;
  But air breathed soft that day,
The hoary mountain-heights were cheered,
  The sunny vale looked gay;
And to the Primrose of the Rock
30 I gave this after-lay.

I sang—Let myriads of bright flowers,
  Like Thee, in field and grove
Revive unenvied;—mightier far,
  Than tremblings that reprove
35 Our vernal tendencies to hope,
  Is God's redeeming love;

That love which changed—for wan disease,
  For sorrow that had bent
O'er hopeless dust, for withered age—
40 Their moral element,
And turned the thistles of a curse
  To types beneficent.

159

Sin-blighted though we are, we too,
The reasoning Sons of Men,
45   From one oblivious winter called
Shall rise, and breathe again;
And in eternal summer lose
Our threescore years and ten.

To humbleness of heart descends
50   This prescience from on high,
The faith that elevates the just,
Before and when they die;
And makes each soul a separate heaven,
A court for Deity.

TEXT.   From *Poetical Works* ii, p. 303. The poem was probably written in 1831, but may be earlier.

SUBJECT.   Wordsworth has observed a primrose perched on top of a rock; in the second stanza he remembers that he first saw it many years ago (actually 1802. See Dorothy Wordsworth's *Journals* 24 April 1802). He also used the flower as the starting point for *The Tuft of Primroses—Poetical Works*, v, p. 348 ff, written in 1807–8. He thinks of it as a link in 'the great chain of Being', a medieval idea which survived into the eighteenth century (see A. O. Lovejoy's book of the same title). Therefore the flower is ultimately linked to the earth itself, which is thought of as part of a 'sphere'—this refers to the Ptolemaic system, already out of date in the seventeenth century. The earth is upheld by the providence of God; so the plant revives each year.

In the second part of the poem the springtime revival of the plant need not cause envy of an old man. It is a symbol of God's love which—stanza 7—can triumph over disease, sorrow and age and reverse Original Sin (lines 41–2). This leads to the thought of the Resurrection of the Dead—stanza 8—and shows that God visits the 'humble in heart' with individual consolation and reassurance.

STYLE.   Lines like 41–2, 'turned the thistles of a curse/To types beneficent', are quite remarkable and are an example of what I mean by 'experimental'. One might compare the language of Thomas Hardy. The usual gibes about 'Romantic imprecision' have no weight here, but then this is hardly a Romantic poem. I do not see that a poet who can write like this in old age, again like Thomas Hardy, deserves to be sneered at and abused with phrases like 'fossilized' and 'quite dead'.

Is the later poetry so bad?

It would be unfair to leave the discussion of the later Wordsworth without a rejoinder to what is usually said. During his final years he extensively revised, rewrote and rearranged his poems, especially *The Prelude*, and although the changes he made are not always improvements, they add up to the formation of the definitive text of the poems, so that many lines and phrases which we think of as unmistakably Wordsworth date from these latter years.

He went on going through the motions of being a poet until the very end, and inevitably, because he kept in practice, hit upon some successes—'gleams like the flashing of a shield'occur in unexpected places. One should certainly look at the following poems:

Composed Upon an Evening of Extraordinary Splendour and Beauty—where Wordsworth faces his own decline—

<blockquote>
the light
Full early lost, and fruitlessly deplored.
</blockquote>

Extempore Effusion upon the Death of James Hogg—a great dirge for his own generation of Romantic poets.

The River Duddon—a series of sonnets. The 'After-Thought' (xxxiv) is famous, but try to read more than this.

Processions—a very strange poem about religious ceremonies, the last stanza of which seems to describe the Imagination as a

<blockquote>
licentious craving in the mind
To act the God among external things . . .
</blockquote>

In reading this last poem we may glimpse a solution to the problem of Wordsworth's decline—the Imagination had become a power so terrible that he could not risk indulging it, and yet it would not release him from its grip. As he said in the Preface to the 1815 edition of his poems:

The Imagination is conscious of an indestructible Dominion;—
The Soul may fall away from it, not being able to sustain its grandeur; but, if once felt and acknowledged, by no act of any other faculty of the mind can it be relaxed, impaired or diminished.

Whatever this may mean, it is a brave utterance; the man who believed this would never admit defeat.

Part Three

Reference Section

Wordsworth and his circle

There is a spiritual community binding together the living and the dead, the good, the brave, and the wise, of all ages. We would not be rejected from this community.

WORDSWORTH, On the Convention of Cintra

ARNOLD, MATTHEW (1822–1888) Son of Dr Thomas Arnold *q.v.* Spent many school holidays at Fox How; walked, skated, boated under Wordsworth's eye. Educated at Rugby and Oxford. Fellow of Oriel, 1845. Inspector of Schools, 1851. Poet and critic. For his views on Wordsworth see in particular *Memorial Verses* and *The Youth of Nature*; there is also an essay on Wordsworth in *Essays in Criticism II*. Further than this, one could argue that many of Arnold's poems are saturated with Wordsworthian echoes. Nevertheless, Arnold devalued Wordsworth's achievement; he saw Wordsworth as primarily a 'healing' influence to those fallen upon an 'iron time', and he was not interested in the intellectual content of Wordsworth's poetry. This is illustrated by the selection of Wordsworth's poems which Arnold edited for the Golden Treasury series in 1879, a selection which had a very pervasive influence on the general reader's view of Wordsworth's achievement.

ARNOLD, THOMAS (1795–1842) Headmaster of Rugby School. Read *Lyrical Ballads* in 1811, and acquired a 'lofty, imaginative, spiritual' view of Wordsworth. Fellow of Oriel from 1815, where he joined the Noetics, a discussion club where Wordsworth was much admired. Called on Wordsworth in 1824. After appointment as Headmaster of Rugby (1828) he built a holiday house in the Lake District, Fox How, which Wordsworth helped to design. After 1834 most school vacations were spent there. Dr Arnold and Wordsworth became great friends, although they differed in religion and politics. (Dr Arnold was a great Liberal reformer and modernizer—one should ignore distorted twentieth-century views which derive from Lytton Strachey.) Dr Arnold had nine children, and they were encouraged to join in the usual Lake District activities, so that Wordsworth complained that 'he could not see enough of his neighbour, the Doctor, on a mountain walk, because Arnold was always so surrounded with children and pupils, "like little dogs", running round and after him' (Mrs Humphry Ward, *A Writer's Recollections*).

BAUDOUIN, CAROLINE Married name of Wordsworth's French daughter. See VALLON.

BEAUMONT, SIR GEORGE (1753–1827) Patron of the arts. Landscape painter, and illustrator of Wordsworth's poems. He had known Dr

Johnson and Sir Joshua Reynolds, so that his enthusiasm for the work of Wordsworth, Scott, Coleridge etc. shows a remarkable leap of taste. In painting he was not so progressive, and was not really able to understand John Constable, though he encouraged the younger man. 'Sir George recommended the colour of an old Cremona fiddle for the prevailing tone of everything, and this Constable answered by laying an old fiddle on the green lawn before the house' (Leslie, *Life of John Constable*). Beaumont was the nearest thing to a patron in Wordsworth's career; he bought the poet a small estate, and invited him to stay at his house at Coleorton, Leicestershire. He died in 1827, and left Wordsworth £100 a year for life; he is chiefly remembered for his efforts towards the foundation of the National Gallery.

BEAUPUY, MICHEL ARMAND (1755–96) French military officer, who converted Wordsworth to the ideals of the Revolution. (*Prelude* 1805, ix) Born at Mussidan, Périgord, of an aristocratic family, his mother and four brothers were sympathetic to the cause of the people. Although he entered the army at sixteen he was clearly an intellectual, and impressed Wordsworth by reason and argument. At Blois he was the lone 'patriot' in a Royalist regiment. Wordsworth says in *The Prelude* that Beaupuy died fighting in the Vendéan Civil War (1793), but in fact he recovered from his wounds, became a general, and died fighting the Austrians at the battle of the Elz, 19 November 1796. The influence of Beaupuy on Wordsworth is usually underestimated; de Selincourt considered it second only to that of Coleridge.

BELL, ANDREW (1753–1832) Educated at St Andrews. Sailed for India in 1787. Superintendent of Madras Male Orphan Asylum, 1789, where he introduced a system of monitorial or pupil-teacher instruction. (One teacher instructed a few pupils, who in turn passed on the information to their own classes. The chain could be infinitely extended, it was argued, and thousands taught at little cost.) He returned to England in 1796, and next year published *An Experiment in Education made at the Asylum of Madras*. The system was adopted at many schools, including the Charterhouse and Christ's Hospital. When Dr Bell visited Keswick in 1811, he interested Wordsworth in his ideas; Wordsworth taught in the Grasmere village school for some months according to the new system, which he considered 'with the exception of the abolition of the Slave Trade, the most happy event of our times'. Bell was appointed Superintendent of the National Society for Promoting the Education of the Poor in the Principles of the Established Church, which indicates the interest of the establishment—and Wordsworth—in using education to prevent revolution. In fact the system was not particularly successful. Later Dr Bell became prebendary of Westminster and is buried in Westminster Abbey. He must not be confused with the inventor of the telephone. I have seen one comment in print which so embroidered the confusion that Wordsworth emerged as an early version of Big Brother, telephoning instruction to a mass audience!

BLAKE, WILLIAM (1757–1827) Poet, painter and engraver. Although Blake is now considered to be the most important poet of the Romantic period, his work was not well known in his own lifetime. There is no record of any meeting between Blake and Wordsworth, but Coleridge and Lamb may have communicated their enthusiasm to friends. We have little evidence as to Wordsworth's feelings about Blake's work, apart from an anecdote by Samuel Palmer, who tells us that Wordsworth borrowed a copy of *Songs of Innocence* from a friend— 'He read and read and took it home to read and read again'— and a note by Crabb Robinson, who says that Wordsworth thought that Blake's poems 'had the elements of poetry a thousand times more than either Byron or Scott'. Crabb Robinson also visited Blake and recorded that 'his delight in Wordsworth's poetry was intense'. But Blake had many reservations about Wordsworth's work taken as a whole—'Some of Ws poems he maintained were from the Holy Ghost, others from the Devil'. Other detailed comments are to be found on pp. 821–4 of the Nonesuch *Blake*. Against the poem *Influence of Natural Objects* (actually the skating scene from the then unpublished *Prelude*) Blake wrote: 'Natural Objects always did and now do weaken, deaden, and obliterate Imagination in Me. Wordsworth must know that what he Writes Valuable is Not to be found in Nature.'

Blake did not share the general Romantic anxiety about the decline of the imagination in middle and old age. He went on to the end. During his last illness he worked at the Illustrations to Dante while propped up in bed. He called himself 'an old man, feeble and tottering, but not in spirit and life, not in the real man, the imagination, which liveth for ever'. He died singing, and was buried in a common grave in Bunhill Fields.

BRISSOT, JACQUES PIERRE, DE WARVILLE (1754–93) Journalist and revolutionary. He had been imprisoned in the Bastille before the French Revolution, and was in the mob which stormed the Bastille on 14 July 1789. In the Convention, although he spoke out for 'peoples against kings', he became the leader of the moderate Girondin party, who were also called Brissotins. He was guillotined in Paris, on 31 October 1793.

BURNS, ROBERT (1759–96) Poet. Wordsworth first read Burns' poems in 1787. He had few difficulties over dialect, since Cumberland is the next county to Dumfries. On his Scottish tour of 1803 Wordsworth visited the grave of Robert Burns, and afterwards produced three poems commemorating it—*Memorials of a Tour in Scotland*, ii, iii, iv. Burns showed Wordsworth

> How verse may build a princely throne
> On humble truth.

In poem iii Wordsworth is moved to praise which is exceptionally forceful in expression, considering that it was probably written as late as 1839:

Through busiest street and loneliest glen
Are felt the flashes of his pen;
He rules 'mid winter snows, and when
    Bees fill their hives;
Deep in the general heart of men
    His power survives.

     . . .

Sweet Mercy! To the gates of Heaven
This minstrel lead, his sins forgiven;
The rueful conflict, the heart riven
    With vain endeavour,
And memory of Earth's bitter leaven,
    Effaced for ever.

But why to Him confine the prayer,
When kindred thoughts and yearnings bear
On the frail heart the purest share
    With all that live?—
The best of what we do and are,
    Just God, forgive!

In 1816 Wordsworth published a defence of Burns, since it was necessary to correct the mistaken idea that the poet had died of drink. But Wordsworth did not attempt to hide the realities of Burns's life; the *Letter to a Friend of Burns* is a useful corrective to the idea that Wordsworth was incapable of appreciating 'the felicities of love and wine'. He praises Burns for trusting to the 'primary instincts' and gloried in *Tam o' Shanter*, defending it against the 'impenetrable dunce or narrow-minded puritan' who was too inhibited to appreciate Burns's poetry. But he thought that 'Scots wha hae' was 'wretched stuff'.

BYRON, GEORGE GORDON, 6th Baron (1788–1824) Poet. Attacked Wordsworth, largely from ignorance, in *English Bards and Scotch Reviewers* (1809), but soon made capital out of blatant imitation of Wordsworth's reverence for Nature. This is especially noticeable in *Childe Harold* iii, of which Wordsworth said that his ideas had been 'spoiled in the transmission'. In general, the two were opposites and their remarks about each other were usually uncomplimentary; although politics entered into it, Byron thought that the Lake School had weakened the great tradition of English poetry; in 1820 he described Wordsworth as 'essentially a bad writer', and continued to recommend the Augustans, especially Pope, as literary models. Wordsworth was most annoyed by 'the noble poet's public poetical attacks' in *Don Juan*. Byron's fame obscured that of Wordsworth for many years, and it was not until the 1830s that the young intellectuals turned away from Byron to Wordsworth.

CALVERT, RAISLEY (1773–1795) Benefactor of Wordsworth. William Calvert, Raisley's elder brother, had known Wordsworth at school, and supported him financially during the summer of 1793. From June 1794 to January 1795 Wordsworth nursed Raisley Calvert, who was dying of pulmonary tuberculosis. In his will he left Wordsworth £900.

CARLYLE, THOMAS (1795–1881) Historian. He came from Dumfriesshire, across the Solway Firth from Cumberland. Author of *Sartor Resartus, The French Revolution, Past and Present* etc. His influence was enormous; through him Romantic ideas 'came to power' in men's minds. After 'fearful wrestlings with the foul and vile and soul-murdering Mud-Gods of my Epoch' he offered a new vision of life, a religion stripped of its 'Hebrew old-clothes'. He met Wordsworth, probably in 1840, and recorded in his *Reminiscences* that Wordsworth had witnessed the execution of Gorsas. Wordsworth did not like Carlyle's interpretation of the French Revolution and said so in a sonnet *In Allusion to Various Recent Histories and Notices of the French Revolution*.

CHRISTIAN, FLETCHER (fl. 1789) Led the mutiny on the *Bounty*, 28 April 1789. The connections between the Wordsworth and Christian families arose from the fact that they had been neighbours at Cockermouth. In 1796 Wordsworth wrote to a newspaper to expose certain spurious letters which were said to have been written by Christian. In *The Wake of the Bounty* (1953) C. S. Wilkinson tried to prove that Fletcher Christian returned to England and met Wordsworth.

CLARE, JOHN (1793–1864) Poet. Son of a cottager, who became the victim of enclosure. Grew up at Helpstone, Northants., working as a herd-boy and under-gardener. Published *Poems of Rural Life* (1820) and was taken up by London society as a 'peasant-poet'. Other volumes followed, but Clare was soon 'dropped' back into poverty. Certified insane (1837) but continued to write in the asylum.

Those who still feel that Wordsworth is a 'nature-poet' should read, for example, Clare's *Autumn* or *Summer Images*. Clare's observation is more detailed than Wordsworth's, and he can describe natural phenomena without making symbolic use of them. Clare also provides ample evidence of the change in the landscape brought about by enclosure; the thickets and commons were taken away, 'All levelled like a desert by the never-weary plough' and only then did the peasants realize what they had lost. In Clare the poetic consciousness wanders through the waste places, trying to recreate what has been destroyed.

CLARKSON, THOMAS (1760–1846) Lifelong campaigner against slavery; not only did he try to influence British opinion, but also attempted to persuade the French government to abolish slavery (1789–90) and urged his opinions on the Tsar (1816). Thomas and his wife Catherine were great friends of the Wordsworths; until 1804 they lived at Pooley Bridge, Ullswater. For Wordsworth's tribute to his friend see the sonnet *To Thomas Clarkson, On the Final Passing of the Bill for the Abolition of the Slave Trade. March 1807.* He lived to see abolition of slavery in the West Indies, 1837.

COBBETT, WILLIAM (1762–1835) Political journalist. Born at Farnham, Surrey, the son of a small farmer. Received his education 'by rolling down a slope'. Lived in Canada, France and America as a soldier, then turned journalist and set up in London in 1800 as a Tory propagandist. Soon changed to the Radical side, publishing his opinions in *Cobbett's Weekly Political Register.* M.P. for Oldham (1832). His *Rural Rides* (1830) give an opinionated but vivid picture of agricultural conditions in southern England.

COLERIDGE, HARTLEY (1796–1849) Eldest son of S. T. Coleridge. Many prophecies were made for his future. See Wordsworth's poem *To H.C. Six Years Old.* Hartley is also 'the Child' in stanzas vii and viii of the *Immortality Ode.* After S. T. Coleridge separated from his wife, Hartley attended school at Ambleside, and paid a weekly visit to the Wordsworths at Grasmere. This soon grew into a foster-father attitude on Wordsworth's part, as Coleridge lived in London and was unable to help his son in any tangible way. It was Wordsworth who arranged for Hartley's entry to Merton College, Oxford. Hartley obtained a fellowship at Oriel College, but was dismissed for intemperance. Thereafter he lived by sporadic journalism and school-teaching in the area of Ambleside. The Wordsworths occasionally settled his debts. One of Tennyson's two good stories about Hartley (recorded by Hallam Tennyson in his *Life of Lord Tennyson*) is as follows: 'Hartley started on a walking tour with some friends.—They suddenly missed him, and could not find him anywhere, and did not see him again for six weeks, when he emerged from some inn.'

Hartley made many shrewd comments about Wordsworth; he also wrote several sonnets which show suitable reverence for the older poet; but unofficially he was capable of witty parody, such as this 'Lucy poem' on *The White Doe of Rylstone's* sales:

> He lived amidst th' untrodden ways
>   To Rydal Lake that lead:—
> A bard whom there were none to praise
>   And very few to read.
>
> Behind a cloud his mystic sense,
>   Deep-hidden, who can spy?
> Bright as the night, when not a star
>   Is shining in the sky.
>
> Unread his works—his 'Milk-white Doe'
>   With dust is dark and dim;
> It's still in Longman's shop, and Oh!
>   The difference to him!

In later years Hartley lived at Nab Cottage, near Grasmere—he tried to get his spelling, 'The Knbbe', accepted. When he died, in January 1849, Wordsworth arranged to have him buried next to the plot chosen for his own grave (see Grasmere Churchyard, p. 194).

COLERIDGE, SAMUEL TAYLOR. See pp. 101–108.

CONSTABLE, JOHN (1776–1837) Landscape painter. Born at East Bergholt, Suffolk. Said later of the Essex/Suffolk border: 'Those scenes made me a painter.' Helped by Sir George Beaumont *q.v.* In 1806 made a tour in the Lake District; sketches from this time were the basis of pictures which he exhibited in 1807, 1808 and 1809. But, as his biographer, C. R. Leslie, says: 'The solitude of mountains oppressed his spirits . . . He required villages, churches, farmhouses, and cottages.' Because Constable's work is now so acceptable, it is difficult to realize that he was in his own day outstandingly original, and was not therefore recognized in England. But his work caused a sensation when exhibited in Paris in 1824.

Wordsworth met Constable on several occasions, but it is not possible to build any significance upon this. Several critics have tried to claim that Constable in painting is an equivalent to Wordsworth in poetry, but it seems that neither was aware of it. Constable linked *Weymouth Bay* with John Wordsworth's death: '"This sea in anger and that dismal shore."—I think of Wordsworth, for on that spot perished his brother in the wreck of the *Abergavenny*.' (See the oil-sketch used as dust-jacket.) The links between Wordsworth and Constable are discussed in an article by Dr J. R. Watson—'Wordsworth and Constable' *Review of English Studies*, November 1962 pp. 361–4.

COOKSON, REV. WILLIAM (fl. 1800) Uncle of William Wordsworth. Fellow of St John's College, Cambridge. Introduced W. W. to that College. After 1788 looked after Dorothy W. at Forncett, Norfolk. Tried to persuade Wordsworth to take holy orders. Quarrelled with Wordsworth after return from France in 1793, presumably over W's proposal to marry a Roman Catholic (Annette). Reconciled by 1802, and later praised the Christian sentiments in *The Excursion*.

COOPER, THOMAS (1805–92) Started his working life as a shoemaker; self-educated; *c.* 1835 became a journalist. Joined the Chartist movement in 1840, and strongly advocated the use of physical force. In 1842 he demanded a universal strike 'because it meant fighting' and was upbraided by Feargus O'Connor. From 1843–5 he was imprisoned on charges of sedition and conspiracy. In 1845 he published a political poem, *The Purgatory of Suicides*. Visited Wordsworth in 1846, and was surprised to be so kindly treated by one of opposite political opinions. Read his *Autobiography* (1876).

COTTLE, JOSEPH (1770–1853) A Bristol bookseller. After meeting Coleridge and Southey in 1794 he published Coleridge's *Poems* and Southey's *Joan of Arc* (1796). In 1798 he published *Lyrical Ballads*, and on giving up his publishing activities the next year handed over the copyright to Longman. Since Longman valued this new asset at *nothing*, Cottle asked for the copyright to be returned to him and gave it to Wordsworth. In 1837 Cottle published his *Recollections* of the poets he had known.

CRABBE, GEORGE (1754–1832) Poet. He came from Aldeburgh in Suffolk. His poems were regarded by Wordsworth as 'mere matters-of-fact', and this, combined with other derogatory nineteenth-century comments, led to neglect of his work for many years. He is now regarded far more highly, and this is not only for his analyses of human motives and realism of description; he is in fact a poet of considerable verbal resource. To tackle Crabbe without guidance, however, may be disastrous; one should begin with *The Borough* (Peter Grimes is in Letter xxii) and *Tales in Verse*. (*A Selection from George Crabbe*, edited by John Lucas, is available in the Longmans English Series.)

Wordsworth used to visit Crabbe in London and their walks together are commemorated in *Extempore Effusion upon the death of James Hogg*:

> Our haughty life is crowned with darkness,
> Like London with its own black wreath,
> On which with thee, O Crabbe! forth-looking,
> I gazed from Hampstead's breezy heath.
>
> As if but yesterday departed,
> Thou too art gone before; but why,
> O'er ripe fruit, seasonably gathered,
> Should frail survivors heave a sigh?

DAVY, SIR HUMPHRY (1778–1829) Scientist, inventor of the miner's safety lamp (1815). Came from the West country, and had written a poem, *The Sons of Genius*, in 1795. Coleridge met him in Bristol in 1800 and persuaded him to take on the proof-correcting of the second volume of *Lyrical Ballads*. (He had not met Wordsworth.) He climbed Helvellyn with Wordsworth and Sir Walter Scott in 1805. The friendship of poets and chemist was based on genuine sympathies. Davy had experienced sublime feelings at Tintern—

When I cast my eyes on the remains of mortality—when I considered, that in that deserted spot, where the song of the nightingale and the whispering of the wings of the bat were the only signs of life, thousands of thoughts, an immense mass of pleasurable ideas, had rolled through the minds of a hundred intelligent beings,—I was lost in a deep and intense social feeling. I began to think, to reason, what is existence?

He had also appreciated the beautiful appearance of potassium and sodium, which he had discovered; his son wrote:

When he saw the minute globules of potassium burst through

the crust of potash and take fire as they entered the atmosphere, he could not contain his joy—he actually bounded about the room in ecstatic delight.

Chemistry, with its sudden and magical changes, was *the* Romantic science, especially when experiments were productive of electrical effects (think of the chemical equipment in Shelley's rooms at Oxford). Coleridge attended Davy's lectures to 'increase his stock of metaphors'.

DE QUINCEY, THOMAS (1785–1859) Journalist; author of *Confessions of an English Opium Eater*. A very early admirer of Wordsworth, but at first too shy to approach him. Met Coleridge, Southey and Wordsworth in 1807. Became the tenant of Dove Cottage after the Wordsworths (from 1809). But the friendship soon deteriorated after De Quincey spoilt the garden; the Wordsworths also disapproved of his marriage to a Westmorland peasant girl, apparently on class grounds. Through Wordsworth's influence he obtained the editorship of the *Westmorland Gazette* (1819–20). In the 1830s De Quincey published anecdotes of the Wordsworths and S. T. Coleridge. In their final form, *Reminiscences of the Lake Poets*, there is a good deal of useful material, but one must treat De Quincey with caution; he exaggerates, and is frequently inaccurate over detail; but in spite of this he vividly recreates *the effect of having met Wordsworth*, noticing personal matters that others were unable to see.

FABER, FATHER FREDERICK WILLIAM (1814–63) Oxford Movement clergyman; stayed at Ambleside in 1837 and conducted services in the church; he continued to visit the Lake District every summer for some years, and Wordsworth visited Faber at Elton, Huntingdonshire, where he was rector. Faber wrote facile poetry, which does not seem to have impressed Wordsworth overmuch. This example shows how Wordsworth's ideas could easily be sentimentalized:

> I met a little child in Rydal Vale,
> With a huge bunch of daffodils; a posy
> Large as the child herself, who was but frail,
> And hot with climbing; and in all the rills,
> With both hands clasped, she dipped her daffodils . . .
>
> My sainted Mother! was I once like this,
> A creature overflowed with simple bliss?

Faber was involved in the revival of the rush-bearing ceremony (see *Ecclesiastical Sonnets* xxxii). In 1845 Faber became a Roman Catholic; he established the London Oratory in 1849, and became its superior.

FENWICK, ISABELLA (1783–1856) Friend of Wordsworth in his later years. In the winter of 1842–3 she took down at Wordsworth's dictation a series of notes about his poems which are reprinted in most big editions. She is the subject of two sonnets which Wordsworth wrote in 1840, which is a fair reward for an unpaid secretary.

FOX, CHARLES JAMES (1749–1806) Whig politician. He supported many causes which young Wordsworth would also have agreed with, such as the American rebellion, the French Revolution and parliamentary reform. In 1798 he was dismissed from the Privy Council for toasting 'Our sovereign, the people'. While Wordsworth swung over to the side of the war party after 1798, he continued to respect Fox, who wished to make peace with France. In 1801 Wordsworth sent him *Lyrical Ballads*, together with a letter (see p. 58). Fox's reply is interesting; he did not like *Michael* and *The Brothers*—poems suggested by Wordsworth for special study—but preferred *Goody Blake and Harry Gill*, *We Are Seven*, *The Mad Mother* and *The Idiot Boy*. This judgment shows how difficult it is to generalize about the reception of *Lyrical Ballads*, for Fox was a typical eighteenth-century aristocrat. Wordsworth met Fox at a party in London in 1806. According to an account quoted by Mrs Moorman, the conversation was as follows:

Fox, rising from the card-table: 'I am glad to see Mr Wordsworth, though we differ as much in our views of politics as we do in our views of poetry.'

Wordsworth: 'But in poetry you must admit that I am the Whig and you the Tory.'

A few days before his death Fox moved the abolition of the Slave Trade; Wordsworth's *Lines*, written when *the dissolution of Mr Fox was hourly expected*, are one of the greatest tributes ever addressed by an English poet to a British politician.

GILL, JOSEPH (fl. 1794) Caretaker at Racedown. Kept a diary with several references to the Wordsworths. There is probably more than coincidence in the fact that the name was used in the Lyrical Ballad of *Goody Blake and Harry Gill*, for the poor people of Dorsetshire had a habit of stealing fences for fuel.

GLADSTONE, WILLIAM EWART (1809–98) Liberal prime minister. Devoted to Wordsworth's poetry from an early age, and shows some critical penetration in his remarks. When a young M.P., in 1836, Wordsworth solicited his interest in the Bill to extend the term of copyright. They met frequently in London at this time; Gladstone's diaries contain records of their conversation, including evidence of Wordsworth's admiration for Shelley's poetry. In 1842 Gladstone obtained a Civil List pension for Wordsworth from Sir Robert Peel; in 1844 Wordsworth wrote to Gladstone, who was then at the Board of Trade and concerned with railway administration, about the proposed extension of the railway from Kendal to Windermere, enclosing a sonnet.

GODWIN, WILLIAM (1756–1836) Philosopher and novelist. Originally a dissenting minister until converted to atheism. Published *Political Justice* (1793) and *Caleb Williams* (1794). Married Mary Wollstonecraft, author of *Vindication of the Rights of Woman*, in 1797. Their daughter became Shelley's second wife. Wordsworth met Godwin in 1795 during his stay in London, and visited him several times that year. Thereafter Wordsworth usually called on Godwin when he visited London and did not break off the friendship when he ceased to agree with Godwin's ideas. Godwin visited Wordsworth at Rydal Mount in 1816, and was distressed by Wordsworth's extreme Right-wing views.

HAYDON, BENJAMIN ROBERT (1786–1846) Painter. At first his historical paintings were successful, but he soon ran into financial trouble. (One difficulty was to find purchasers with room for his enormous canvases.) Friend of Keats and Wordsworth, who were used as models for the spectators in *Christ's Entry into Jerusalem*. He named one of his sons Frederick Wordsworth. Committed suicide after the failure of an exhibition of his paintings.

Haydon's *Autobiography* and *Journals* should be read. He was much involved in the proposal to bring the Elgin marbles to England, and interested Keats in these sculptures. The account of the Christmas party in 1817 attended by Wordsworth, Keats and Lamb must not be missed. Haydon's attempts to portray Wordsworth bring out the heroic side of his nature, and the life mask which he took makes an impressive frontispiece to Sir Herbert Read's *Wordsworth*—this in turn inspired a good poem by Sidney Keyes.

Wordsworth wrote two sonnets to Haydon, one about his picture of Napoleon, and one which contains the lines:

> Through longlived pressure of obscure distress
> Still to be strenuous for the bright reward
> And in the soul admit of no decay

which would make a fair epitaph for Benjamin Robert Haydon.

HAZLITT, WILLIAM (1778–1830) Critic. Visited Coleridge in June 1798. After a discussion with Hazlitt Wordsworth wrote *Expostulation and Reply* and *The Tables Turned*. Stayed at Keswick in 1803 and painted portraits of Wordsworth and Coleridge. After this time Hazlitt, who was a Godwinian and an admirer of Napoleon, began to publish public criticism of Wordsworth's politics and poetry. The final break came in 1815, when Wordsworth refused to see Hazlitt during a visit to London, and some of Hazlitt's later remarks on Wordsworth are merely spiteful. Nevertheless, Hazlitt makes so many good points about Wordsworth that one should read at least the essay on Wordsworth in *The Spirit of the Age*.

HOGG, JAMES (1770–1835) Known as the Ettrick Shepherd. Poet. Wordsworth met Hogg in Scotland in 1814. Offended by a derogatory remark of Wordsworth's Hogg produced parodies of his poetry. Nevertheless, it was the news of Hogg's death which made Wordsworth write the dirge on his friends Coleridge, Crabbe, Lamb etc. (*Extempore Effusion upon the Death of James Hogg*, 1835).

HUTCHINSON, MARY *see* WORDSWORTH, MARY

HUTCHINSON, SARA (1775–1835) Wordsworth's sister-in-law. Although it seems to have been expected that she would marry Wordsworth's brother John, she is chiefly remembered as Coleridge's 'other Sara' to whom the poem *Dejection* is addressed. After Wordsworth's marriage she was usually to be found in the Wordsworth household, and looked after Coleridge when he was staying at Grasmere. Her death is commemorated in Sonnet xxix of *Miscellaneous Sonnets*.

JEFFREY, FRANCIS, LORD JEFFREY (1773–1850) Critic. Whig lawyer and journalist, who edited the *Edinburgh Review* from 1803 to 1829. At this time the personality of the editor of a magazine was all important, and Jeffrey was able to impose his own taste in poetry on the reading public as a whole, since the circulation of the *Edinburgh Review* was so widespread. More people read its reviews of Wordsworth's poetry than the poetry itself. Jeffrey's tastes were Augustan, and he effectively held back the wide appreciation of Wordsworth's work for a generation. See, for example, his review of *The Excursion*, which begins: 'This will never do.'

JONES, ROBERT (fl. 1790) Clergyman. Educated at Ruthin Grammar School. Cambridge friend of Wordsworth, whom he accompanied on tour to Switzerland in 1790. He obtained a fellowship at St John's, but returned to Denbighshire, where Wordsworth visited him at Llangynhafal in 1791 and 1793. On one of these visits, probably 1791, Wordsworth and Jones climbed Snowdon (see the last book of *The Prelude*). Wordsworth revisited North Wales in 1824, and together with Jones toured the Snowdon district. Jones is addressed in the dedication of *Descriptive Sketches* and in the sonnet beginning: 'Jones! as from Calais southward you and I. . . .'

KEATS, JOHN (1795–1821) Poet. Met Wordsworth in London in 1817—see descriptions in his *Letters*. Keats called at Rydal Mount on his way to Scotland in 1818, but Wordsworth was out, busy with Tory politics. Keats's opinions of Wordsworth are scattered throughout his letters, but one of the important passages has been quoted in this book (see p. 84) He greatly admired Wordsworth's poetry, particularly the Fourth Book of *The Excursion*, which, it is claimed, is echoed in the *Ode to a Nightingale*. Wordsworth does not seem to have been much impressed by Keats's early poetry, and is reported to have called a passage from *Endymion* 'a pretty piece of Paganism'. The anecdote has been somewhat garbled in transmission, however, and judging from Wordsworth's other uses of the word 'pretty' the judgment expressed may have been favourable rather than derogatory.

KEBLE, JOHN (1792–1866) Originator of the Oxford Movement. Poet. Became enthusiastic about Wordsworth's poetry while a student at Oxford in 1806. Wordsworth wrote to Keble about the admission of his son John to Oxford, and in 1839 Keble, as Professor of Poetry, spoke at the ceremony when Wordsworth received an honorary degree.

LAMB, CHARLES (1775–1834) Essayist. Met Wordsworth through Coleridge in 1797. See Lamb's letters for many amusing references to
Wordsworth and his poems. Lamb was also able to help Wordsworth
after John Wordsworth's death in 1805, since he was an employee of
the East India Company and had access to their sources of information. He also produced a sympathetic review of *The Excursion*. Wordsworth dedicated *The Waggoner* to him, was highly amused by *The Essays
of Elia*, and wrote a long epitaph upon him (*Written after the death
of Charles Lamb*, 1835). Lamb's powers as a comic writer have frequently
led people to underestimate his capabilities as a critic, (see, for
example, his selection from the Elizabethan and Jacobean dramatists
and his essay upon Hogarth.) Wordsworth recognized Lamb's good
judgment, sent him poetry to criticize, and should have listened to his
opinions more often. Lamb was surely right to wish for the retention of
the washing-tub in *The Blind Highland Boy*.

LOSH, JAMES (1763–1833) Barrister from Carlisle. Kept a diary in which
meetings with Wordsworth are recorded. He remained a liberal and
asked Wordsworth about the change in his opinions. The letter which
Wordsworth sent to Losh in 1821 gives an interesting and full account
of the history of Wordsworth's political evolution.

MARTINEAU, HARRIET. (1802–76) Writer. One of the most remarkable
women of her age, combining (to quote Caroline Fox), 'the smoker,
the moralist, the political economist, the gossip, and the woman'. In
1844, after recovery from a serious illness, she proclaimed the healing
powers of mesmerism, and shortly afterwards settled in Ambleside to
be near friends of similar views. Considering that her opinions were
liberal in the extreme, it is strange that a friendship should have
sprung up between her and the aged poet. But we soon find Wordsworth assisting her in the planning and building of her house, calling
her decision to build:

'The wisest step in her life; for . . .' and we supposed he was
going to speak of the respectability, comfort, and charm of such
a retreat for an elderly woman; but not so. 'It is the wisest step
in her life; for the value of the property will be doubled in ten
years.'

She supported the introduction of railways to the Lake District:
'The morals of rural districts are usually such as cannot well be made
worse by any change', and resolved to 'clean up' Ambleside, which
contained not a single bath. She also set up a model farm on her
property—Wordsworth was of some assistance in looking after her
cow—and started a Building Society and a temperance movement,
maintaining that Wordsworth could not see the vice that went on
under his nose.

Miss Martineau's evidence is important in one respect: 'In regard
to politics . . . and even to religion, he grew more and more liberal in

G

his later years', and her picture of the old man out walking 'in his cloak, his Scotch bonnet, and green goggles, attended by perhaps half a score of cottagers' children—the youngest pulling at his cloak, or holding by his trousers, while he cut ash switches out of the hedge for them' is worth pages of the usual accounts of 'the venerable Sage'.

MILL, JOHN STUART (1806–73) Philosopher. The intensive education provided by his father (James Mill) neglected the emotions. In 1826 he entered a state of blank dejection, from which he was saved by reading Wordsworth—

'What made Wordsworth's poems a medicine for my state of mind was that they expressed, not mere outward beauty, but states of feeling, and of thought coloured by feeling, under the excitement of beauty. They seemed to be the very culture of the feelings, which I was in quest of'.

See Mill's *Autobiography*, chapter V, for a full account of Wordsworth's 'healing power'.

MONTAGU, BASIL, the elder (1770–1851) Barrister and legal writer. Natural son of John Montagu, Earl of Sandwich. Contemporary of Wordsworth at Cambridge. His wife died in 1793, and Wordsworth and Dorothy agreed to look after 'little Basil' in 1795. He borrowed money from Wordsworth which was eventually repaid. In 1810 he precipitated the quarrel between Wordsworth and Coleridge by repeating a confidence. He eventually became famous as an expert on bankruptcy and also edited Bacon.

MONTAGU, BASIL, the younger (1791–1830) Wordsworth and Dorothy looked after him at Racedown and Alfoxden. This arrangement brought them in £50 a year, a considerable addition to their slender income—when the elder Montagu was able to pay it. Little Basil had one great fault: 'He lies like a little devil', and is the hero of the poem *Anecdote for Fathers, showing how the Art of Lying may be taught*. In later life Basil continued to lie, saying that the Wordsworths had ill-treated him. He became mentally ill, having failed to pursue any career.

POOLE, THOMAS (1765–1837) Tanner of Nether Stowey. Friend of Coleridge, whom he assisted financially. Helped Wordsworth to obtain the tenancy of Alfoxden. A democrat, who impressed Wordsworth by his kindness to his neighbours.

QUILLINAN, DORA, formerly Dora Wordsworth (1804–47) The only daughter of Wordsworth to survive infancy. She was always delicate, and probably suffered from tuberculosis. Her death in 1847 effectively terminated her father's interest in staying alive, for he had been devoted to her, and had been very reluctant to allow her to marry.

QUILLINAN, EDWARD (1791–1851) Poet. Settled at Ambleside in 1821 after a military career. His first wife died in 1822. As he was an Irishman and a Roman Catholic, his courtship of Wordsworth's daughter was not likely to proceed without difficulty, and the marriage did not take place till 1841. His most important work was his translation of Camoens's *Lusiad*.

ROBINSON, HENRY CRABB (1776–1867) Diarist. Attorney at Colchester and in London. Travelled in Germany and met Goethe and Schiller (1800–2); studied at Jena University until 1805. Then foreign correspondent for *The Times*. His diary makes fascinating if exhausting reading, for he knew all the important writers of his time. He met Wordsworth in London in 1808 and thereafter corresponded with him, frequently visiting him in the Lake District and accompanying him on his tours. He held liberal views and although he disagreed with Wordsworth's politics the fact that the friendship continued argues more than mere persistence on Crabb Robinson's part. 'The Crabb' did not in any case use his famous friends merely as diary material; he was a keen defender of Coleridge, and left us accounts of Blake which are indispensable.

ROGERS, SAMUEL (1763–1855) Banker and poet. Published the popular *Pleasures of Memory* in 1792; the poem said little, but offended nobody; smooth heroic couplets carried on the tradition of Pope and Goldsmith; and nineteen editions of the poem were brought out before 1816. In many ways it typified the 'inane' poetry which Wordsworth rebelled against.

Rogers met the Wordsworths on tour in Scotland in 1803, after calling at Dove Cottage. Like Crabb Robinson, he knew everybody, and introduced Wordsworth to Charles James Fox in 1806. The friendship continued to the end of Wordsworth's life. Rogers lent him his court dress in 1845 when he was expected as Poet Laureate to attend a ball given by the Queen. On Wordsworth's death he refused the laureateship, which passed to Tennyson, who also, incidentally, made use of the same court dress.

SCOTT, SIR WALTER (1771–1832) Poet and novelist. Began by collecting folk ballads. Published *Border Minstrelsy* (1802–3) and *Lay of the Last Minstrel* (1805). The Wordsworths went to see him at Lasswade in 1803, and the Scotts visited Grasmere in 1805. The acquaintance was kept up, though Wordsworth was not very keen on Scott's poetry, or the novels which he produced from 1814 onwards. Wordsworth visited Scott at Abbotsford shortly before his death, and produced a sonnet, *On the departure of Sir Walter Scott from Abbotsford, for Naples*, which shows some understanding of Scott's greatness.

SEDGWICK, ADAM (1785–1873) Geologist. Woodwardian Professor of Geology at Cambridge, 1818. Wordsworth met him in 1822, when he was making a geological map of the Lake District. Sedgwick added an appendix to Wordsworth's *Guide to the Lakes* in 1842.

SHELLEY, PERCY BYSSHE (1792–1822) Poet. After his marriage to Harriet Westbrook he arrived at Keswick in the winter of 1811, and called on Southey, also hoping to meet Wordsworth. But it is probable that he would have been as disillusioned with Wordsworth as he was with the one-time Pantisocrat. See the sonnet *To Wordsworth* and *Peter Bell the Third* for Shelley's later opinion of Wordsworth.

SOUTHEY, ROBERT (1774–1843) Poet. Friend of Coleridge. Originally Left-wing, his change of heart has always seemed more opportunist than that of Wordsworth and Coleridge. He settled at Greta Hall, Keswick, jointly with the Coleridges, and soon found that he was responsible for Coleridge's family as well as his own. Became Poet Laureate in 1813, and was attacked by Byron for flattering the dead King George III in *The Vision of Judgement*. As neighbours of a sort, Wordsworth and Southey had to cooperate, particularly over such problems as Coleridge's children, but it cannot be said that Wordsworth ever liked him, frequently referring to him as 'cold and bookish'.

Southey is an unfairly neglected member of the Lake Poets; he was poetically a great influence on Shelley, and his social thinking, which is against the political economists, may be described as pre-Ruskinian.

TALFOURD, SIR THOMAS NOON (1795–1854) Judge and author. Early admirer of Wordsworth, defending him in 1817 and 1819 in literary debates when the poet was most unpopular. Made 'Serjeant' in 1833; M.P. 1835. Spoke for Wordsworth in Parliament during the debates on the Copyright Bill. He wrote plays and a biography of Charles Lamb.

TAYLOR, WILLIAM (1754–86) Headmaster of Hawkshead Grammar School from 1781 to 1786. See Book x of *The Prelude*, and, presumably, the 'Matthew' poems.

THELWALL, JOHN (1764–1834) English revolutionary 'agitator', supported the French. Arrested in 1794 and sent to the Tower of London. Acquitted, but not released for some time, for the government had suspended the Habeas Corpus Act. Visited Coleridge and Wordsworth at Alfoxden; retired from politics to Liswyn Farm, Brecknockshire, where the Wordsworths and Coleridge saw him in August 1798. Later became a lecturer upon elocution and set up an institution in London for the cure of speech defects.

TYSON, ANN (1713–96) Wordsworth's landlady at Hawkshead. Wife of a joiner. See Wordsworth's appreciation of her in *The Prelude*. The Tyson account book, with entries concerning the Wordsworth boys, still survives.

VALLON, ANNETTE (1766–1841) Daughter of a surgeon of Blois; met Wordsworth in 1791; their child, Caroline, was born in 1792. No episode in Wordsworth's life has called forth more anxiety and speculation from his biographers, though Wordsworth himself was reasonable and straightforward about the matter. When he returned to England he was separated from Annette by the war, but one wonders, in any case, whether his guardian uncles would have allowed him to marry a Roman Catholic. A disguised account of the episode was inserted in the *Prelude* 1805, Book ix, and later published as *Vaudracour and Julia*, and this again has struck critics as either too honest or too concealed. Wordsworth met Annette again at Calais in 1802 and arranged a financial settlement. Annette had become a leading member of the Royalist counter-revolutionaries. Later Dorothy tried to attend Caroline's wedding, but was prevented by Napoleon's escape from Elba; in 1820 and 1837 the Wordsworths visited Annette in Paris.

The Annette affair was omitted from the official biography published by Wordsworth's nephew, and was not brought to light until the twentieth century. It then became the psychological key to some, if not all, of Wordsworth's life and poetry, making Wordsworth a very simple case history indeed.

VALLON. CAROLINE (b. 1792) Wordsworth's daughter. He first saw her at Calais in 1802 when she was nine. Nearly every evening they walked by the sea-shore—see the sonnet *It is a beauteous evening, calm and free*. She married Jean Baptiste Martin Baudouin in 1816; there are, apparently, numerous descendants.

WILKINSON, THOMAS (fl. 1803) Quaker, of Yanwath, near Penrith. Simple farmer, poet and journal-writer. *The Solitary Reaper* is taken from an account in his journal of the Highlands. See the poem *To the Spade of a Friend (An Agriculturist)*.

WORDSWORTH, ANN née Cookson (1748–78) Mother of William Wordsworth. Idealized in memory—see *Prelude*, 1850, v. 246–93.

WORDSWORTH, CATHERINE (1808–12) Wordsworth's younger daughter. See *Surprised by Joy* (p. 157).

WORDSWORTH, CHRISTOPHER (1774–1846) Brother of William Wordsworth. Successful churchman. Became Master of Trinity College, Cambridge, and twice vice-chancellor of Cambridge University.

WORDSWORTH, CHRISTOPHER (1807–85) Nephew of William Wordsworth, son of Christopher above. Fellow of Trinity College. The poet's first biographer. He discovered the site of Dodona, and eventually became Bishop of Lincoln.

WORDSWORTH, DORA, see QUILLINAN.

WORDSWORTH, DOROTHY, see p. 97.

WORDSWORTH, JOHN (1741–83) Father of William Wordsworth. Lawyer in the service of the Lowther family.

WORDSWORTH, JOHN (1772–1805) Wordsworth's sailor brother. A 'silent poet'. His father called him 'Ibex, the shyest of all the beasts'. There is a book about him called *Wordsworth's Mariner Brother* by Frank Prentice Rand (The Newell Press, 1966).

WORDSWORTH, JOHN (1803–75) Eldest son of William Wordsworth. Clergyman.

WORDSWORTH, MARY, née Hutchinson. (1770–1859) Wife of William Wordsworth. An enigma. Her few recorded utterances are baffling. De Quincey said that 'though liberally endowed with sunshiny temper and sweetness of disposition, [she] was perhaps a person weak intellectually beyond the ordinary standards of female weakness'. But this is mostly spite.

Wordsworth had known her from childhood. She seems to have been prepared to put up with anything, and was in fact the rock upon which the whole Wordsworth tribe depended. She kept journals, contributed two lines to *I wandered lonely as a cloud*:

> They flash upon that inward eye
> Which is the bliss of solitude,

and named *The Prelude*.

WORDSWORTH, THOMAS (1806–12) Second son of William Wordsworth.

WORDSWORTH, WILLIAM (Willy) (1810–83) Third son of William Wordsworth. Succeeded his father as Distributor of Stamps.

A Wordsworth Gazetteer

We read fine things but never feel them to the full until we have
gone the same steps as the author.

JOHN KEATS

Unwilling to lose Mr Wordsworth's company, I accepted his
proposition that we should walk together until I was fatigued.
At the end of half a mile my strength began to fail.

DR CHANNING

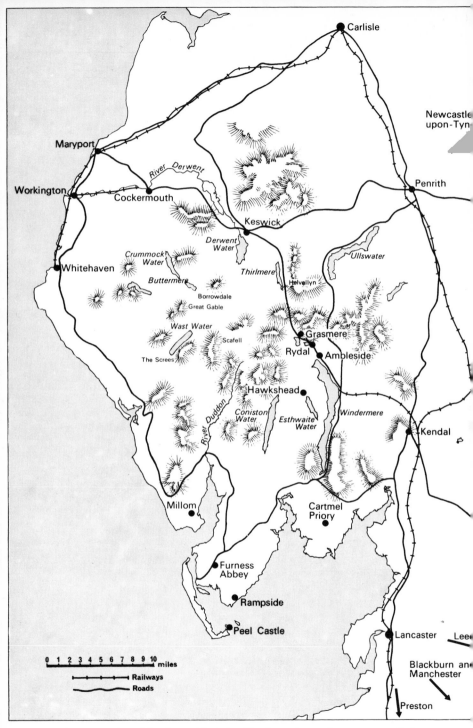

A map to show Wordsworth's Lake District redrawn from a map of 1845.

Introductory Note: THE LAKE DISTRICT

> Parempi omalla maalla
> Vetonenki virsun alta,
> Kuin on maalla vierahalla
> Kultamaljasta metonen.

(It is better to drink ditchwater in one's own country, than mead from golden cups in the land of strangers.)

FINNISH FOLK-SONG

Since most of the places mentioned here are in the Lake District, it would seem necessary at this point to describe the area in a general way. Overseas readers often fail to realize apparently obvious facts, and it is no longer possible to assume that British students will have been on a walking holiday in the Lake District, though this would have been part of the upbringing of a middle-class Victorian child.

In the north-western corner of England the Cumbrian group of mountains are spread across the counties of Cumberland, Westmorland and Lancashire. They are the highest mountains in England, though not, of course, in Great Britain; they are certainly not high by world, or even European standards—the highest, Scafell Pike, is 3210 feet. But they do *look* like mountains; instead of being masked by foothills they seem to rise suddenly and very steeply.

Among these mountains, or 'fells', are fifteen lakes, arranged 'like the spokes of a wheel'; Wordsworth's cottage at Grasmere is roughly in the centre. The local names for the lakes are 'mere' or 'water'; for example, we find Thirlmere, Buttermere, Coniston Water and Crummock Water. The largest and longest lake is Windermere, $10\frac{1}{2}$ miles long by $1\frac{1}{2}$ miles wide; it is also the largest lake in England. The surface of this lake is 130 feet above sea-level; the greatest depth is 210 feet. Again, this is nothing outstanding in comparison with other countries, for everything in England is on a moderate scale. On somebody from the London region or the Midlands, however, the contrast of scenery makes a dramatic and exhilarating impact; here at last is a place where man is not obviously in control of the entire environment. This may be an illusion, but generations of travellers from the South have felt that the scenery is romantic and wild.

The whole district is only about thirty miles square, but it contains such a variety of landscape that it seems inexhaustible, even to the conventional tourist who never leaves the main roads. This variety is partly owing to the geological foundation; some of the rocks are very old—Lower Palaeozoic—and have undergone much weathering; the area has also known volcanic activity and in the central section igneous rock rises to the surface. Some areas are littered with volcanic

The screes above Wastwater

debris, or with boulders dislodged and carried along by glaciers in the Ice Ages; it was, of course, the glaciers which carved out the U-shaped valleys and were ultimately responsible for the lakes themselves. (Wordsworth lived during the great age of geological discoveries, and though his attitude to geology was ambivalent, he succeeds in conveying to us the 'ancientness' of the rocks and the elemental quality of the landscape.)

The other reason for variety of scenery is the climate, which some people find intolerable. Let Wordsworth speak in its defence:

It may now be proper to say a few words respecting climate and 'skiey influences', in which this region, as far as the character of its landscapes is affected by them, may, upon the whole, be considered fortunate. The country is, indeed, subject to much bad weather, and it has been ascertained that twice as much rain falls here as in many parts of the island; but the number of black drizzling days, that blot out the face of things, is by no means *proportionately* great. Nor is a continuance of thick, flagging, damp air so common as in the West of England and Ireland. The rain here comes down heartily, and is frequently succeeded by clear, bright weather, when every brook is vocal, and every torrent sonorous;* brooks and torrents, which are never muddy, even in the heaviest floods, except, after a drought, they happen to be defiled for a short time by waters that have swept along dusty roads, or have broken out into ploughed fields. Days of unsettled weather, with partial showers, are very frequent; but the showers, darkening or brightening, as they fly from hill to hill, are not less grateful to the eye than finely interwoven passages of gay or sad music are touching to the ear. Vapours exhaling from the lakes and meadows after sunrise, in a hot season, or in moist weather, brooding upon the heights, or descending towards the valleys with inaudible motion, give a visionary character to everything around them.

All this is from Wordsworth's own *Guide* which is still in print; one should consult this when planning a tour (Wordsworth is not above quoting his own verse on appropriate occasions); one should also make as much use as possible of Victorian rather than modern guidebooks in order to see the landscape imaginatively. Harriet Martineau's *Guide* is amusing and readable. Among recent books, Norman Nicholson's *The Lake District* and *The Lakers: the First Tourists*, written by a Cumberland poet, provide excellent literary and historical background.

For walking on the fells at the present day one should put one's trust in A. Wainright's seven Guides (*The Northern Fells*, *The Eastern Fells*, etc.) which will always get you down safely if caught in a mist. It is worth noticing how much ground Wordsworth and Coleridge

* See the poem *Loud is the Vale* where this phenomenon is used.

were able to cover in three weeks in 1799—see Coleridge's *Notebooks*, i, 510–553. After reading or retracing this itinerary one will never again think of S.T.C. as 'torpid'.

In this Gazetteer the Lake District entries are under Cumberland, Westmorland or Lancashire. Many more could be cited than are listed here, but I wished to call attention to Wordsworth associations *outside* the Lake District. In fact Wordsworth lived in the area until he was seventeen, and from the age of twenty-nine until his death; there were also visits home in the interval, but on the other side one must note the extensive travels which he made. He lived for a year in France (1791–2) and eight months in Germany (1798–9); a born wanderer, he also made journeys to Europe in 1790, 1802, 1820, 1823, 1828 and 1837. Allowing for the war years and difficulties of transport, this is not a bad score for a man whom some critics dismiss as 'provincial'.

Cambridgeshire

CAMBRIDGE. See St John's College, Wordsworth's own college, where he was in residence from 1787–91 in rooms on the south side of First Court. Also portrait by Pickersgill.

Trinity College was where Wordsworth's brother was Master. He stayed at the Master's lodge in 1820, and in 1830, having ridden all the way from Lancaster. The statue of Newton by Roubiliac is in the antechapel.

King's College Chapel is commemorated in *Tax not the royal saint with vain expense . . . (Ecclesiastical Sonnets)*

Christ's College first saw Wordsworth drunk in Milton's rooms.

Jesus College was Coleridge's college.

Cumberland

BRIGHAM: Wordsworth's eldest son, John, became Rector of Brigham.

COCKERMOUTH, situated on the fringe of the Lake District, is Wordsworth's birthplace. He lived there till he was seven, and came home for holidays until 1783 when his father died and the children were dispersed.

Wordsworth House in Main Street is the house where Wordsworth was born. Built in 1745, it is a large double-fronted residence, suitable for the law-agent of Sir James Lowther; the house was, in fact, one of the perquisites of Wordsworth's father's employment. In *The Buildings of England: Cumberland and Westmorland* Sir Niklaus Pevsner says: 'It is quite a swagger house for such a town: standing on its own, nine windows wide and with moulded window-frames and a porch with Tuscan columns. It is mid- C18, but the porch is of course later.' Inside, the original staircase, fireplace and panelling are still preserved. The garden runs down to the River Derwent, where the young Wordsworth used to play (*Prelude* 1805, i, 271–285). The house now belongs to the National Trust, and visitors are taken on guided tours; it is open from April onwards on Mondays, Wednesdays and Saturdays, 10.30–12.30, 2–4.30. Admission 1*s*, children 6*d*.

Cockermouth Castle was also a favourite youthful haunt. See *Poetical Works*, iv, p. 23, *Address from the Spirit of Cockermouth Castle.* Other *Itinerary poems of 1833* refer to sites in Cumberland and to rivers not mentioned in this gazetteer.

The RIVER DERWENT, however, had a symbolic meaning for Wordsworth, for it was intertwined with memories of his mother and the influence of natural objects. It flows through Borrowdale, merges into lake Derwentwater, and then on to Cockermouth. Coleridge named his third son after it. Wordsworth recalls its meaning for him in a fragment:

> Yet once again do I behold the forms
> Of these huge mountains, and yet once again,
> Standing beneath these elms, I hear thy voice,
> Beloved Derwent, that peculiar voice
> Heard in the stillness of the evening air,
> Half-heard and half-created.
>
> *Poetical Works*, v, p. 340

The RIVER DUDDON provides the title for a remarkable series of sonnets, which trace a journey from the source to the mouth. A poem about the course of a river had originally been Coleridge's idea in the 1790s.

KESWICK: Wordsworth lived at Windy Brow in 1794 and 1795. Coleridge lived at Greta Hall from 1800–3; the Southeys shared the house with Coleridge's family from 1803–43. (Greta Hall is now part of Keswick School.)

In Crosthwaite Church see the memorial to Robert Southey with its long inscription by Wordsworth. In the churchyard look for Southey's tomb, restored by the Brazilian Government, 1961.

PENRITH was the home of Wordsworth's maternal grandparents. Wordsworth and his brothers often stayed there for the holidays. (The draper's shop where the Cooksons lived has been altered—it is called Arnison's. See Moorman, i, p. 4.)

Penrith Beacon is the scene of *Prelude* 1805, xi, 279–323 (See p. 145–148)

THIRLMERE. When Manchester Corporation raised the level of the lake, they destroyed a rock carved with the initials of Wordsworths, Hutchinsons and Coleridge. Some portions have been saved, but are difficult to find. I was directed to the fifth telegraph pole north of the Victorian pumping-station, but have to admit defeat.

WHITEHAVEN. Wordsworth's guardian uncle Richard lived in this busy port. The boys usually spent their Christmas vacations there. Something needs to be stressed here, because Wordsworth is not usually associated with urban backgrounds. The Industrial Revolution came early to Whitehaven; in 1715 the first James Lowther employed Thomas Newcomen to erect a steam engine to pump water out of the coal mines. By 1755 the mines had reached a depth of 800 feet; they were below the level of the sea, and were so extensive that four Newcomen engines were necessary to prevent flooding. These had begun to attract tourists before the opening-up of the Lake District—see Dr John Dalton's *Descriptive Poem adressed to two ladies on their return from viewing the mines near Whitehaven* (1755)

> Pumps moved by rods from ponderous beams
> Arrest the unsuspecting streams,
> Which soon a sluggish pool would lie;
> Then spout them foaming to the sky.

The later effects of industrialization were also visible at the Whitehaven mines; about the year 1810 the workers there were described as

mere machinery, of no worth or importance beyond their horsepower. The strength of a man is required in excavating the workings, women can drive the horses, and children can open the doors; and a child or a woman is sacrificed, where a man is not required, as a matter of economy, that makes not the smallest account of human life in its calculations.

Derbyshire

DOVEDALE. Wordsworth visited Dovedale on June 8th 1788, and wrote a description which is reprinted in Moorman, i, 105. See also *Prelude* 1850, vi, 190–3. The heroine of the 'Lucy' poems

> dwelt among the untrodden ways
> Beside the springs of Dove. . . .

but there are other rivers called by this name; Dovedale in Westmorland actually looks like the scene of the poems.

Dorset

RACEDOWN LODGE, where Wordsworth and Dorothy lived from October 1795 till June 1797, was lent to them by the Pinney family. The house is isolated, and is near the road from Crewkerne to Lyme Regis, north of a hill called Pilsdon Pen. It is eight miles from the sea at Lyme.

WEYMOUTH BAY. Scene of the wreck of *The Earl of Abergavenny* and death of John Wordsworth. Subject of sketches and paintings by John Constable.

WYKE, near Weymouth. John Wordsworth is buried in the churchyard. There is no gravestone.

Herefordshire

BISHOPSTONE. The sonnet beginning 'While poring Antiquarians' refers to a Roman pavement discovered here (*Miscellaneous Sonnets XX*).

BRINSOP. Wordsworth stayed here with his wife's family, the Hutchinsons, at Brinsop Court. He helped to lay out the Rectory Garden.

GOODRICH CASTLE. Visited in 1793, 1798 and 1841. The scene of *We Are Seven*.

KINGTON possesses a tree known as Wordsworth's tree.

Kent

DOVER. Several sonnets about Dover were written by Wordsworth, stressing in general its peaceful contrast to France. Parodied by Keats: 'Dover—who could write upon it?' But Wordsworth's idea of Dover as a frontier between two worlds was inherited by Matthew Arnold in *Dover Beach*.

Lancashire

CARTMEL PRIORY. In the churchyard is the tomb of William Taylor, with an inscription from Gray's *Elegy*. Wordsworth visited the grave in 1794.

ESTHWAITE is the small lake near to Hawkshead mentioned frequently in *The Prelude*. Wordsworth was in the habit of walking round the lake before school began.

FURNESS ABBEY. The abbey and the sands near it are described in Book ii of *The Prelude* and again form the scene of the 'Robespierre is dead' sequence at the end of Book x. See also *Miscellaneous Sonnets* xlvii and xlviii.

HAWKSHEAD. The pleasant atmosphere of the little town should be savoured first. Wordsworth was at the Grammar School from 1779 to 1787; it is no longer in use; as one might expect, a desk with the bard's name on it is now a relic. The controversy over Ann Tyson's cottage is discussed by Mrs Moorman; it is not in the town, but at Colthouse, a hamlet to the east (Moorman, i, 84–5). Since Beatrix Potter (Mrs Heelis) was mainly responsible for this discovery, it would be a pleasant act of piety to walk up to Sawrey and visit her house.

PEEL CASTLE, which Wordsworth commemorated in *Elegiac Stanzas* (p. 152) is near Rampside, where he stayed in 1794, at the house now known as Clarkes Arms Hotel. The castle is variously spelt—Piel, Peile etc.

Leicestershire

COLEORTON. Home of Sir George Beaumont, the Hall now belongs to the National Coal Board. Wordsworth stayed at Coleorton Hall Farm during 1806 and 1807, and visited the neighbourhood on several occasions.

London

Wordsworth said in a letter of 1794: 'I begin to wish much to be in town. Cataracts and mountains are good occasional society, but they will not do for constant companions.' In fact Wordsworth was not an infrequent visitor to London, considering the problem of communications by road at that time. His 1791 visit forms the subject of Book vii of *The Prelude*, and subsequent visits took place in 1793, 1795, 1796, 1797 and 1798. For later journeys, see Moorman.

Wordsworth and Dorothy passed through London on their way to Calais in 1802. On 31 July, says Dorothy in her Journal:

We mounted the Dover coach at Charing Cross. It was a beautiful morning. The city, St Paul's, with the river and a multitude of little boats, made a most beautiful sight as we crossed Westminster Bridge. The houses were not overhung by their cloud of smoke, and they were spread out endlessly, yet the sun shone so brightly, with such a fierce light, that there was even something like the purity of one of nature's own grand spectacles.

(The sonnet *Composed upon Westminster Bridge* is actually dated September 3rd.) The present bridge is not, of course, Wordsworth's bridge, but a replacement.

Monmouthshire

TINTERN ABBEY. A Cistercian foundation, sited in a remote valley. Wordsworth first visited the Abbey in 1793, when he was in quest of picturesque scenery. The visit recorded in the poem took place in July 1798. Wordsworth also included the Abbey in a last round-up of old associations in 1841. The Abbey was a popular tourist attraction after the publication of Gilpin's *Observations on the River Wye* (1770). Wordsworth's poem is really about the Wye Valley rather than the Abbey itself. At the present time the Abbey is no longer in a Romantic state, as the plant-life has been removed and the vagrants who once inhabited it evicted. Gilpin records that a whole hamlet had grown up within the ruin: 'One woman showed us the monks' library, a place overgrown with nettles and briars, with the remains of a shattered cloister. It was where she lived, her own mansion.' See the water colour by J. M. W. Turner (1794) on p. 66.

Somerset

ALFOXDEN, near Holford, also spelt Alfoxton. The background to *Lyrical Ballads*, Wordsworth and Dorothy stayed there from 14 July 1797 for approximately a year at a rent of £23 (see p. 103). Close to the Quantock Hills, the house is now a hotel.

NETHER STOWEY. The National Trust maintains Coleridge's Cottage, where Wordsworth stayed in 1797.

Westmorland

AMBLESIDE was the nearest small town to the Wordsworths when they settled at Grasmere. It soon became a fashionable centre, and in the 1840s Harriet Martineau reports: 'It was all very gay and charming. . . . There is a perpetual change going on in such neighbourhoods. . . . Retired merchants and professional men fall in love with the region, buy or build a house, are in a transport with what they have done, and, after a time, go away. . . .' Harriet Martineau's house is *the Knoll*; ask at *South Knoll* for permission to see her sun-dial.

At the parish church, St Mary's, see the Wordsworth Chapel, with windows in memory of the poet and his family. The original Bible was presented by Mrs Wordsworth and there are two chairs from Rydal Mount. Notice also the mural by Gordon Ransom, depicting the Rushbearing Festival. Near the church, notice the Wordsworth Library, 1863.

The Arnold family lived at *Fox How*; the exterior of the house is largely unaltered, apart from the porch. Notice the chimneys; we know Wordsworth had a strong influence on the design of the house, and planted trees in the garden. (You must ask for permission to see this house, as it is a private residence.)

See also *Miscellaneous Sonnets* xliii.

GRASMERE. Dove Cottage is situated at TOWN END. Originally a pub, the cottage was rented by the Wordsworths from 1799–1808; De Quincey lived there afterwards. The cottage has been as far as possible restored to its nineteenth century condition, though the furniture is not the same as when Wordsworth lived there—some of it is described as 'of his period' and other items have been brought in from Rydal Mount. (As a purist, I would rather have no furniture than this mixture.) The chunk of Tintern Abbey, which some vandal has looted and placed on the mantelpiece of the first room which the visitor enters, gives quite the wrong impression; there is a very full collection of material and portraits here, which should be lingered over. Try therefore to avoid going with a whole coachload.

The surrounding environment is very pleasant, if one can ignore the main road and the toadstoolly antique-shops along it. All this is invisible from the garden behind the cottage, which must be enjoyed at leisure. Town End also contains the Wordsworth Museum, with such relics as the poet's skates, gun, and eye-shade; the books and manuscripts can only be consulted after permission has been obtained from the trustees. There is also a book and postcard shop. All in all, these buildings form a tasteful and sensible memorial to Wordsworth; the attendants are courteous and informative, and a great deal of work has been put in to make the place interesting without descending to the showmanship which has wrecked Stratford-upon-Avon. (The buildings are open daily, except Sundays, morning and afternoon; one must pay an entry fee.)

In the main-part of Grasmere village notice the church, dedicated to St Oswald. It is medieval, but, as Sir Niklaus Pevsner says, 'the exterior is so thickly encrusted with pebble-dash that no dating is possible'. Inside there is a memorial to Wordsworth by Thomas Woolner. The churchyard contains the graves of all the important Wordsworths except John. Hartley Coleridge is buried nearby.

Wordsworth lived at Allan Bank (1808–11) and at the Rectory (1811–13). When Allan Bank was built in 1805 Wordsworth wrote to a friend: 'When you next enter the sweet paradise of Grasmere you will see staring you in the face . . . a temple of abomination, in which are to be enshrined Mr and Mrs Crump.' Nevertheless, Wordsworth rented the house, which also sheltered Coleridge, his two sons, and De Quincey, until the smoky chimneys proved intolerable. The house has been extensively altered; it now belongs to the National Trust, but is not open to visitors. It contains Wordsworth's bookcase.

Before leaving Grasmere remember to sample the Grasmere gingerbread; the gingerbread shop was the school-house where Wordsworth 'taught Madras' in 1811.

HELVELLYN. So far no mountains have been singled out for attention, since Wordsworth was not thought of locally as a 'mountain man'. One should, however, ascend Helvellyn, which he climbed many times, remembering, if fatigued, that Wordsworth went up when over seventy. Haydon painted him as if standing on the top of it (see p. 40).

RYDAL. Rydal Mount is not open to visitors at present, but will probably be opened in mid-1970. A far more 'genteel' residence than Dove Cottage, it nevertheless had no bath, and Wordsworth installed a primitive shower which frightened the local peasantry. He also saw that the garden contained only native trees, and deliberately kept part of it 'wild'. In a note to *Poor Robin*, Wordsworth reported: ' "What a nice well that would be," said a labouring man to me one day, "if all that rubbish was cleared off." ' The "rubbish" was some of the most beautiful mosses, and lichens, and ferns and other wild growths, as could possibly be seen.'

See also Rydal Church, with Wordsworth's pew in front of the pulpit. Behind the church is Dora's Field (the Rash) which belonged to Wordsworth (Now National Trust). It contains daffodils—originally planted by the poet, a boulder with an inscription, and a gate from which one can see the garden of Rydal Mount and its terraces.

ULLSWATER was probably the scene of the famous incident of 'stealing the boat'. (See illustration on p. 20.) It is also associated with *I wandered lonely as a cloud*.

Wiltshire

Wordsworth crossed SALISBURY PLAIN in 1793 and visited STONEHENGE. (See *Guilt and Sorrow*.)

Yorkshire

FALTHWAITE was the original home of the Wordsworth family.

The Hutchinsons lived at SOCKBURN-ON-TEES, and later at GALLOW HILL. Wordsworth and Mary Hutchinson were married at BROMPTON Church, near Scarborough, in 1802.

HARTLEAP WELL is five miles from Richmond on the old road to Layburn (see poem p. 130). The monuments referred to by Wordsworth were already in decay during his lifetime, but seem to have been removed by 1895, according to Harry Speight's *Romantic Richmondshire*. The well has now been covered over with concrete and the water is led off in a pipe—see illustration. If one follows through the interpretation of the poem which I have suggested the present century is guilty of more hideous desecration of the natural order than Sir Walter with his cup of stone.

On the same journey of 1799 which *Hartleap Well* commemorates Wordsworth also visited the waterfalls at ASKRIGG and HARDRAW.

There is a Wordsworth's Walk at SKIPTON, but I have been unable to establish the connection with the poet.

Scotland

Wordsworth first visited Scotland in 1801. He made a six-week tour in 1803; further visits took place in 1814, 1831 and 1833. Dorothy Wordsworth recorded the 1803 visit in her *Journals*, together with a later visit which she made with Joanna Hutchinson in 1822. (De Selincourt's edition contains a map.) The poems produced on these

Hartleap Well today

visits are conveniently grouped in the collected editions of Wordsworth's poetry, and many of them refer to local sites and traditions. But as the placenames are so well indicated by titles of poems, it seems unnecessary to give a detailed list here.

Wales

For the ascent of SNOWDON, see the last book of *The Prelude*. Near RUTHIN, Denbighshire, is Llangynhafal, where Robert Jones lived at the house by the church, i.e. Plas-yn-Llan. In 1793 Wordsworth followed the Wye up to BUILTH; in 1824 he visited the 'ladies of LLANGOLLEN', a Welsh castle and the DEVIL'S BRIDGE (See *Miscellaneous Sonnets* viii–x).

Ireland

Wordsworth made a comprehensive tour in 1829, but produced little evidence of this in poetry (see Moorman ii, 436–41).

France

Wordsworth usually started at CALAIS, which is referred to in several sonnets; he also stayed there in 1802 when visiting Annette and Caroline. (See Dorothy Wordsworth's 1802 *Journal*.) In 1791 he stayed at ORLEANS in the Rue Royale; his daughter was baptised in the church of Ste Crois. Annette's home was at BLOIS. He visited PARIS in 1791, 1792, possibly in 1793, stayed for four weeks in 1820 in the Rue Charlot, and passed through Paris on his Italian visit in 1837.

Germany

In 1790 Wordsworth and Jones floated down the Rhine in a small boat from Basle to COLOGNE. In 1798 Wordsworth, Dorothy and Coleridge visited Klopstock at HAMBURG (see Dorothy's *Journals*. Wordsworth's account of the visit is incorporated in Satyrane's Letters at the end of Coleridge's *Biographia Literaria*). They stayed for two weeks in an inn called 'Der Wilde Mann'. In BRUNSWICK their inn was called 'The King of England' or 'The English Arms' (Dorothy could not translate clearly). Their lodgings at GOSLAR were at 86 Breite Strasse —there is a plaque on the building. Coleridge stayed at RATZEBURG and GÖTTINGEN.

The Wordsworths visited the Rhineland in 1820 and 1828, on the latter occasion with Coleridge.

Switzerland

For the 1790 visit see *Descriptive Sketches*, *Prelude* vi and Wordsworth's letters; for the 1820 visit see Dorothy's *Journal*.
'Crossing the Alps' in Book vi of *The Prelude* is a description of the SIMPLON PASS.

Italy

Only the extreme north was seen in 1790 and 1820, though the latter occasion included a visit to MILAN. Wordsworth toured Italy with Crabb Robinson, going no further south than ROME, where they stayed in the Piazza di Spagna. See *Memorials of a Tour in Italy* (1837).

Spain

Wordsworth never visited Spain, but he was deeply concerned over Spanish independence, to which he transferred his revolutionary idealism in the years *c.* 1810. See *Poems dedicated to National Independence and Liberty* xxiii–xxxii, and, of course, the tract *On the Convention of Cintra*.

Romanticism

... there must be a resemblance, which does not depend upon their own will, between all the writers of any particular age. They cannot escape from subjection to a common influence which arises out of an infinite combination of circumstances belonging to the times in which they live; though each is in a degree the author of the very influence by which his being is thus pervaded.

SHELLEY, Preface to *The Revolt of Islam*

[Wordsworth's poetry] is one of the innovations of the time. It partakes of and is carried along with the revolutionary movement of our age.... Had Wordsworth lived in any other period of the world he would never have been heard of.

WILLLIAM HAZLITT, *The Spirit of the Age*

The most important cultural phenomenon of the age can only be summarized here. Politics and the arts, philosophy and social life are all affected, against a *European* rather than an English background.

1. INFLUENCE OF THE FRENCH REVOLUTION
(*a*) Romanticism can be seen as a *parallel* eruption—revolt against paternal authority, kings, empires and God the Father.
(*b*) after 1800 Romanticism more frequently appears to be a disillusioned *reaction*—an anti-liberal retreat from reason and progress into mystery, the Middle Ages and Catholic revival.
(*c*) both positions may be complicated by differing attitudes to Napoleon—either seen as a great deliverer, recasting the ancient kingdoms, or as yet another tyrant.

2. NATIONALIST ASPIRATIONS
(*a*) discovery of the *folk* ties in with political self-determination for the *People*.
(*b*) in literature a revival of interest in folk-song, legends and ballads (Gray, Bishop Percy, German poets).
(*c*) through the historical novels of Sir Walter Scott suppressed or half-forgotten nations rise to political and literary consciousness and demand independence.
(*d*) the poets side with this movement (Byron in Greece, general Romantic love of Italy, Pushkin and the Decembrists).

3. REJECTION OF SOCIAL CONVENTION
(*a*) aristocratic society was corrupt and to avoid contamination one should live with the folk.

(b) in fact a good many of the younger poets and artists were middle-class, and lived with similar associates in sets or cliques, in which collaboration was encouraged.

(c) for the *individual* the ideal existence was solitude.

4. LITERARY THEORY AND CULTURE

(a) *inspiration* (symbolized by 'wind' or 'breeze') was all-important.

(b) the poet trusted in the creative imagination and the validity of his own emotional experience—an idea must be *felt* to be true.

(c) music, being non-verbal, was the most Romantic of all the arts.

(d) 'When composition begins, inspiration is already on the decline' (Shelley, *Defence of Poetry*).

(e) therefore the resulting poem might be obscure or fragmentary (Coleridge, *Kubla Khan*).

(f) if inspiration failed one might need to resort to dreams or drugs (Coleridge, De Quincey), the irrational and the supernatural (Fuseli, Mary Shelley) to tap the 'deep well' of the unconscious mind, and release a stream of symbols and images.

The reader may care to decide for himself how far Wordsworth is to be described as Romantic.

Acknowledgements

Since this book is largely a compilation, I freely acknowledge my indebtedness to the many scholars on whose work I have drawn. I recall with gratitude the efforts of my teachers—Edward Malins, David Jesson-Dibley, Hugo Dyson and Philip Collins—to make me aware of many aspects of Wordsworth's achievement which would otherwise have escaped my notice.

I should like to thank Patricia Hodgart and Ian Gordon for reading the manuscript, R. A. Church for his advice on matters of economic history, F. J. Chambers for help with the bibliography, and Iris Hutchinson and Virginia Valdambrini for assistance with typing.

The author and publisher are grateful to the following for permission to reproduce photographs: G. T. Abraham Ltd., pages 96 and 99; G. V. Berry, pages 112 and 186; The British Museum, page 66; Dove Cottage Museum, Grasmere, page 107; Jennifer Elliot, page 196; A. F. Kersting, page 25; Leicester Museums, page 153; Mansell Collection, pages 33 and 116; Musée de l'armée Paris, page 34; National Portrait Gallery, pages 40, 59 and 102; Ian Reynolds, page 83; Routledge and Kegan Paul Ltd., page 44; Tom Sharpe, page 20; The painting of Weymouth Bay by John Constable reproduced on the cover is by courtesy of the Victoria and Albert Museum.

Further Reading

... in the firm expectation, that when London shall be an habitation of bitterns; when St Paul's and Westminster Abbey shall stand, shapeless and nameless ruins, in the midst of an unpeopled marsh; when the piers of Waterloo Bridge shall become the nuclei of islets of reeds and osiers, and cast the jagged shadows of their broken arches on the solitary stream, some transatlantic commentator will be weighing in the scales of some new and now unimagined system of criticism, the respective merits of the Bells and the Fudges, and their historians

SHELLEY, Dedication to *Peter Bell the Third*

Editions of Wordsworth's Poetry

The Poetical Works of William Wordsworth, ed. E. de Selincourt and H. Darbishire (5 vols. Oxford University Press, 1940–9) is the standard edition. It is arranged according to Wordsworth's own system of classification, so that the poems are grouped by subject matter and Hartleian psychological categories. It includes poems from manuscripts which are not in the usual one-volume editions, but it does not reprint *The Prelude* (see below). Its notes are useful and often accumulate earlier annotation, e.g. Miss Fenwick's, in extended or summary form.

There are many single-volume collected editions, of which that edited by T. Hutchinson (Oxford Standard Authors, 1904, with later revision by E. de Selincourt, O.U.P., 1936) is most convenient. It contains *The Prelude*, 1850, and preserves Wordsworth's classification.

An edition of the poems in chronological order would be useful. The volumes in Everyman's Library fulfil this in part, and there are several selections which break away from traditional arrangements of the poems.

Separate editions of *Lyrical Ballads* exist, of which the most recent are the 1798 volume by W. J. B. Owen (O.U.P. 1967) and 1800–5 volumes by R. L. Brett and A. R. Jones (Methuen, 1963). *Poems* (1807) have been edited by H. Darbishire (O.U.P. 1952). The big edition of *Wordsworth's Prelude*, ed. E. de Selincourt and revised by H. Darbishire (O.U.P. 1959), had the 1805 and 1850 texts on facing pages. The 1805 text is also available separately in Oxford Standard Authors.

NOTE ON THE TEXTUAL PROBLEM

At one time it was thought sufficient to reprint the last edition of an author's works which he had himself supervised. The Oxford edition does this, and consigns earlier variants to the notes, though in the case of *The Prelude* the first complete text is available. Wordsworth's poems are usually reproduced in the polished versions which the elderly poet thought less offensive than his former and presumably cruder efforts. But this means that it is extremely difficult to discover from a standard text why Wordsworth was ever thought of as a revolutionary poet. It is a revelation to look at a first edition of *Lyrical Ballads*, for example. Some editors have reproduced earlier variants in selections or critical studies, but there is no consistent or shared policy about this at present. Personally, I would like to see the earliest printed versions in normal use, with the later variants in the notes; in some cases even the manuscript readings should be restored.

Editions of Wordsworth's other writings

There is no modern edition of the prose works available at present. The *Preface to Lyrical Ballads*, the *Essay Supplementary to the Preface*, and later prefatory and postscript material are available at the end of the one-volume Oxford edition. The *Guide to the Lakes* is still in print, and still seems to sell in the Lake District. The Reynard library edition of *Wordsworth: Selections*, compiled by W. M. Merchant (Hart-Davis, 1955) contains extracts of other works, such as the tract *Onde the Convention of Cintra*.

The *Letters of William and Dorothy Wordsworth* were edited by de Selincourt (6 vols. O.U.P., 1935–9). The *Early Letters* have recently been revised by C. L. Shaver (O.U.P., 1966). A selection is available in the World's Classics.

Dorothy Wordsworth's Journals

Macmillan publish a full two-volume edition by E. de Selincourt with maps and illustrations. Selections are available in the World's Classics and in *Home At Grasmere* ed. Colette Clark (Penguin Books, 1960).

Biographies

William Wordsworth by Mary Moorman (2 vols. O.U.P., 1957–65, now available in paperback) is the most comprehensive and up-to-date life. It makes reference to earlier lives unnecessary, though Mrs Moorman's preface contains an evaluative account of the works which preceded hers. Nevertheless it is not a book which one would recommend to a student approaching Wordsworth for the first time: it is far too long to read through easily, and is best kept as a work of reference. The best introductory work is still H. M. Margoliouth's *Wordsworth and Coleridge 1795–1834* (O.U.P. , 1953).

Chronology

Everything known about the early life of Wordsworth is to be found in M. L. Reed's *Wordsworth Chronology of the early years 1770–1779* (Harvard University Press, 1967).

Education

There is a good deal of background information in Wordsworth's

Cambridge Education by Ben Ross Schneider Jnr (Cambridge University Press, 1957).

Politics

See F. M. Todd, *Politics and the Poet* (Methuen, 1957). This is a lucid account of Wordsworth's political development. R. J. White's *Political Tracts of Wordsworth, Coleridge and Shelley* (C.U.P., 1953) is also useful.

Portraits

All known portraits are listed and reproduced in F. M. Blanshard's *Portraits of Wordsworth* (Cornell University Press, 1959).

The changing of the landscape

For those who are daunted by specialist studies of social and economic history, books like *The Making of the English Landscape* by W. G. Hoskins (Hodder & Stoughton, 1955) are indispensable. A good deal of background can be gleaned from biographies of the great engineers (Telford, Brunel etc.). The difficulty is that so many books assume automatically that industrialization always wrecked the countryside. A study of *The Industrial Archaeology of the Lake Counties*, by J. D. Marshall and M. Davies-Shiel, was published by David and Charles in 1969. For Wordsworth's own views on landscape gardening and painting, see *Wordsworth and the Art of Landscape* by Russell Noyes (Indiana University Press, 1968).

Philosophy and Religion

R. D. Haven's *The Mind of a Poet* (Johns Hopkins University Press, 1941) is still standard, and contains a good chapter on religion. For studies of thinkers who influenced Wordsworth see Basil Willey, *The Seventeenth Century Background* (chapters on Locke and Wordsworth), *The Eighteenth Century Background* (chapters on Hartley, Godwin and Wordsworth), *Nineteenth Century Studies* (Coleridge) (all published by Chatto & Windus, and also available in Peregrine Books). A quite different approach to Wordsworth as a *philosophical poet* is John Jones's *The Egotistical Sublime* (Chatto & Windus, 1954).

Romanticism

A comprehensive study of European Romanticism is to be found in H. G. Schenk, *The Mind of the European Romantics* (Constable, 1966). M. H. Abrams, *The Mirror and the Lamp* (O.U.P., 1953) is a discussion of literary theory. On the general question of English Romanticism see the last chapter of Ian Jack's *Oxford History of English Literature*, vol. 10, *1815–1832* (O.U.P., 1963), and Chapter viii of F. W. Bateson's *A Guide to English Literature* (Longmans, 1967).

Society

The change in the temper of society during this period is difficult to follow at first; for a study of how Regency licence was replaced by Victorian prudery, see Muriel Jaeger, *Before Victoria* (Chatto & Windus, 1956; Penguin Books, 1967).

Readers and Critics 1793–1968

A full discussion is impossible. The first generation of readers and reviewers is covered in John Wain's *Contemporary Reviews of Romantic Poetry* (Harrap, 1953) and in *Romantic Perspectives* by Patricia Hodgart and Theodore Redpath (Harrap, 1964). Parody is one of the most perceptive forms of criticism, and there were many hostile parodies of Wordsworth. One should at least look at Shelley's *Peter Bell the Third*.

Wordsworth became popular in the 1830s, but as the century progressed he was more and more regarded as the Nature-poet. See 'Wordsworth's Fame', an essay by Humphry House in *All in Due Time* (Hart-Davis, 1955). The generation represented by Matthew Arnold, Arthur Hugh Clough, George Eliot and John Stuart Mill were all strongly influenced by Wordsworth's *power*—a key word in criticism at the time. *The Autobiography of Mark Rutherford* by William Hale White (1881) is a classic study of Wordsworth's effect upon an enclosed mind, a conversion experience of a quasi-religious nature. Wordsworth became an accepted figure in the literary history of England, but more for his message than for his poetry.

The discovery of the Annette affair provided exactly the ammunition which the anti-Victorians of the 1920s needed. Wordsworth was largely ignored by the new schools of criticism, and it was Keats or Blake who stepped into his place as the great Romantic poet. But Wordsworth scholarship made great advances in the first fifty years of this century, even if published criticism seemed largely a prolongation of Victorian attitudes.

The watershed in Wordsworth criticism is the mid-1950s. John Jones's *The Egotistical Sublime* (Chatto & Windus, 1954) was an entirely original book, a rare occurrence in criticism. This coincided with F. W. Bateson's *Wordsworth: a reinterpretation* (Longmans, 1954). A later new approach was J. F. Danby's *The Simple Wordsworth* (Routledge, 1960), which is particularly good on close analysis of some of the *Lyrical Ballads*. The high peak of recent work is Geoffrey Hartman's *Wordsworth's Poetry 1787–1814* (Yale University Press, 1964) and though some of the book is difficult, the bibliographies at the back cover previous discussion of Wordsworth in a comprehensive yet readable way. There are many other studies of Wordsworth now in print, but I restrict myself to recommending these four in the hope that students, by perhaps reading only one of them, will pierce through the miasma of inherited preconceptions about Wordsworth which still enshrouds so many classrooms and lecture theatres. We are in the middle of a great revival of interest in the nineteenth century, yet one feels that its greatest poet is only beginning to be understood.

General Index

Since William Wordsworth occurs *passim*, there is no entry under his name, but see alphabetical entries e.g. *accent, appearance* etc, where W. = Wordsworth. References to illustrations are in italics. Works appear under the name of their author; for the works of William Wordsworth, see separate Index.

Index to Wordsworth's Poetry and Prose

208